Virginia Woolf and
Christian Culture

Best wishes

Jane dop

Virginia Woolf and Christian Culture

Jane de Gay

EDINBURGH
University Press

Edinburgh University Press is one of the leading university presses in the UK. We publish academic books and journals in our selected subject areas across the humanities and social sciences, combining cutting-edge scholarship with high editorial and production values to produce academic works of lasting importance. For more information visit our website: edinburghuniversitypress.com

Edinburgh University Press Ltd
The Tun – Holyrood Road,
12(2f) Jackson's Entry,
Edinburgh EH8 8PJ

First published in hardback by Edinburgh University Press 2018

Typeset in 11/13 Adobe Sabon by
IDSUK (DataConnection) Ltd, and
printed and bound in Great Britain
by CPI Group (UK) Ltd, Croydon,
CR0 4YY.

A CIP record for this book is available from the British Library

ISBN 978 1 4744 1563 7 (hardback)
ISBN 978 1 4744 5488 9 (paperback)
ISBN 978 1 4744 1564 4 (webready PDF)
ISBN 978 1 4744 1565 1 (epub)

Contents

Acknowledgements   vii

Abbreviations   ix

Introduction   1

1. Family Background: Clapham and After   19

2. Contemporary Conversations   52

3. Reverend Gentlemen and Prophetesses   88

4. Sacred Spaces: Churches and Cathedrals   114

5. Domestic Sacred Spaces   143

6. The Purple Triangle and Blue Madonnas: The Virgin Mary   165

7. How Should One Read the Bible?   186

Conclusion: A New Religion?   219

Bibliography   226

Index   237

Acknowledgements

This book is the product of many years' work, and many people have inspired and encouraged me on the way.

I have benefited from research trips to the Leonard and Virginia Woolf Library at Washington State University, Pullman, with kind thanks to Trevor Bond and Julia King, as well as to Rev. Mary Beth Rivetti for making me feel at home in Pullman; and to the Rare Book Room at Smith College, Massachusetts, with special thanks to Karen Kukil. The Gladstone Library in Hawarden, North Wales, awarded me a Scholarship in 2015 to research in their archives and gave me a room of my own for a writing retreat. They have also made me very welcome on subsequent trips. The Virginia Woolf Society of Great Britain invited me to give the Birthday Lecture in 2009 and my talk, 'Virginia Woolf and the Clergy' (which was subsequently published as a pamphlet), was the starting point for Chapter 3. Jackie Jones has been an encouraging Commissioning Editor and Sarah M. Hall a meticulous and patient copy editor.

This book has benefited from the scholarly generosity of many Woolf scholars and from many rich conversations, especially through the International Virginia Woolf Society and at the annual Virginia Woolf Conference. However, I would like to acknowledge especially the support, encouragement and intellectual engagement of Suzanne Raitt, Eleanor McNees, Alexandra Harris, Dinah Birch, Madelyn Detloff, Anne Fernald, Christine Froula, Elsa Högberg, Marion Dell, Beth Rigel Daugherty and Diane Gillespie. I would like to thank my friends and colleagues at Leeds Trinity University, especially Rosemary Mitchell and Juliette Taylor-Batty, as well as Jon Simons and the Writing Group. Tom Breckin and Anne Reus have shared my enthusiasm for Woolf and it has been a great joy working with them.

This book has grown out of my two vocations, as Priest and Professor. It has emerged from a critical dialogue between me and Virginia Woolf, who resented both roles. And I was prepared for that dialogue by my father, Edmund de Gay, architect and freethinker, who constantly challenged me on both vocations, and by my mother Joan de Gay, a woman of quiet faith and common sense, who would have been deeply proud of both. I also owe a debt to Michael Argyle, who set this project in motion a quarter of a century ago by asking me in a discussion group at the University Church of St Mary the Virgin, Oxford: 'So, what did Virginia Woolf believe in?'

Wayne Stote has supported me every step of the way and this book is dedicated with love and thanks to him.

Abbreviations

3G	*Three Guineas*
BA	*Between the Acts*
CE	*Collected Essays* (4 vols)
CSF	*Collected Shorter Fiction*
D	*Diary* (5 vols)
E	*Essays* (6 vols)
FG	*Friendship's Gallery*
JR	*Jacob's Room*
L	*Letters* (6 vols)
LS	*The London Scene*
MB	*Moments of Being*
MD	*Mrs Dalloway*
ND	*Night and Day*
O	*Orlando*
PA	*A Passionate Apprentice*
Room	*A Room of One's Own*
TL	*To the Lighthouse*
VO	*The Voyage Out*
W	*The Waves*
Y	*The Years*

Introduction

For many readers, Virginia Woolf and Christianity would appear to have very little to do with one another. Virginia Stephen was brought up as an agnostic, by not one, but two agnostic parents, both of whom had very carefully and conscientiously renounced Christianity. Their courtship had involved a lengthy correspondence on the limitations of religion and they had both written studies of agnosticism: Leslie Stephen's *An Agnostic's Apology* was a seminal work on the subject, while Julia Stephen's unpublished 'Agnostic Women' was a cautious but nonetheless brave foray into the field. Woolf would seem to have taken the agnosticism of her upbringing a stage further by declaring in 'A Sketch of the Past' that 'certainly and emphatically there is no God' (*MB* 72). Other selected statements from her work are often cited as evidence of a thoroughgoing anti-religious stance: she regarded Christina Rossetti's poetry as being impoverished by faith (*D1* 178–9), pronounced T. S. Eliot 'dead to us all' on becoming an Anglo-Catholic (*L3* 457), and responded to Ethel Smyth's *Mass in D* with the comment that 'I hate religion!' (*L5* 282). In *Three Guineas,* she condemns the Church of England as one of the bastions of the patriarchal establishment that persisted in excluding women, and she argues that women should eschew such institutions by joining the 'Outsider's Society', starting with the simple passive-resistant act of staying away from church.

Furthermore, Woolf lived and worked in an era that has often been characterised by declining religious belief when the nineteenth-century crisis of faith brought about by rationalist discourses, Darwinism and sceptical biblical scholarship had given way to an indifference towards religion among intellectuals: the so-called secularisation thesis. Church attendance is said to have dropped and public support for Christianity is thought to have declined sharply as a result of criticism of the role of the church in the First World War. Modernist writers and artists side-lined Christianity as they became increasingly aware of cultural and religious relativism. Influential anthropological studies such as Jessie Weston's *From Ritual to Romance* (1920) and James Frazer's *The Golden Bough* (1890–1915), alongside the work of Woolf's mentor Jane Harrison on pre-Christian religions, had raised awareness that Christianity was by no means the only belief system available, and certainly not the earliest, and writers began to wake up to the creative potential of Eastern religions such as Buddhism and Hinduism. Additionally, since Virginia Woolf was married to a Jew, albeit one who had distanced himself from the faith of his fathers, Christianity was not the only religion known to her and it would appear to be a less significant one at that.

Why, therefore, write a book on Woolf and Christian culture? To be clear at the outset, this book does not seek to claim that Woolf had secret leanings towards Christianity or that she lamented her distance from it; the book will not attempt to claim Woolf's work for Christianity but neither will it suggest that her work is impoverished by anti-religious views. Rather, this study aims to show that Woolf's debates with Christianity form a more powerful undercurrent in her work than has been acknowledged and that this was because she had detailed knowledge and understanding of the faith. The book will show that Woolf's critique of the church as an institution was integral to her attack on patriarchy: she was aware of how the church as a male-dominated institution played a key role in shaping the political landscape, and how the ideologies of religion supported the patriarchal status quo by prescribing feminine role models and behaviour. Moreover, it will show that Woolf's feminist analysis of society was informed by an understanding of how Christian beliefs and institutions had helped shape society as she saw it and that her critical observation of religion was intense, even obsessive at times.

All of this is in turn attributable to the fact that Woolf's engagement with Christianity was far more complex and subtle than my opening examples suggest and that Christian culture was more significant as a context for her work than it appears to be from a twenty-first-century perspective. Woolf was writing in an age when Christianity, although contested, was by no means regarded as passé. Woolf argued with it because it was both an integral part of the literary, artistic and architectural heritage of England, and a live social and political force to be reckoned with. Woolf's awareness of these complementary dynamics can be seen in a journal entry on a visit to Wells Cathedral in 1908:

> But if Christianity is ever tolerable, it is tolerable in these old sanctu-
> aries; partly because age has robbed it of its power, & you can fondle
> a senile old creature, when you must strike with all your force at [a]
> young & lusty parson. (*PA* 376)

Woolf's argument with present-day religion is described figuratively as a tussle with the 'young & lusty parson': her forceful language here suggesting that the parson is a sexual predator to be repulsed. However, the statement also shows a fondness for history and a strong sense of place that lead her to declare Christianity almost tolerable, a temptation that conflicts with an awareness that the apparently elderly and docile animal that was Christian heritage had not lost its bite. Woolf's understanding of the ideological influence of Christianity on architecture – likewise art, culture and literature – therefore formed a counterpoint to her battle with Christianity as a political force.

Furthermore, one doesn't have to scratch very deeply beneath the surface to see that Woolf's parents, though agnostic, nonetheless provided an upbringing in which the vestiges of Christianity remained by means of its moral and social principles. When Leslie Stephen renounced his Holy Orders, thereby giving up his Cambridge career, he vowed to 'live and die like a gentleman':[1] in other words, keeping middle-class principles that owed much to muscular Christianity and ideologies of feminine behaviour. While Woolf continued her parents' quarrels with Christianity, she also set about breaking with their adherence to established conceptions of society and morals by taking a feminist approach to the debate.

Moreover, rather than having no religious background, as is often assumed, there were deep and persisting religious influences in Woolf's wider family, for she was descended from two prominent Evangelical Clapham Sect families – the Stephens and the Venns – that included clergy, theologians, hymn writers and spiritual writers. Woolf's aunt Caroline Emelia Stephen was a devout Quaker and her cousin Dorothea Stephen was a missionary. Woolf's maternal grandmother Maria Jackson had been 'deeply religious' (*MB* 90) and her maternal aunt Julia Margaret Cameron was a devout Christian who had made an art of photography with religious themes. The influence of Caroline Emelia Stephen is particularly important, as this book will show, and it has rightly attracted considerable scholarly interest.[2] However, as we will see in Chapter 1, Woolf interrogated the values of a 'large connection' (*MB* 65) when she critiqued religion, challenging a family religious script that had been set out in copious published writings.

Christian culture: competing trends

Christianity was also a more significant context for modernism than has been acknowledged until recently. The 'secularisation thesis' prevalent among critics for many years is set out at its bluntest by Adrian Hastings, who characterises the intellectual climate of the 1920s as one of 'confident agnosticism' and names Woolf among several writers holding to the 'seldom breached' 'post-Darwinian consensus' that there is 'no God' and that religion was 'the delusion of a primitive past'.[3] However, scholars now recognise that religious interests and beliefs had not disappeared so completely or so abruptly. As Pericles Lewis has demonstrated, 'Victorian earnestness' did not give to 'modern irony'[4] but in fact interest in religion was increasing in the early twentieth century. Examining the representation of religious experience in an international selection of writers (Woolf, Henry James, Proust, Joyce and Kafka), he demonstrates that the 'modern novel is strikingly concerned with the spiritual rather than the material aspects of life'.[5]

Lewis underpins his study by drawing on Max Weber's thesis that the twentieth century saw a process of 're-enchantment' as a reaction against rationalism and secularism. Weber's insights are useful for setting out a general background for Lewis's wide-ranging study, but Weber's work also has a more specific relevance for Woolf. First, Weber's *Protestant Ethic and the Spirit of Capitalism* (developed between 1904–5 and 1920), provides a context for the continuing influence of Evangelical tradition of her wider family. Weber traces how motives that were originally religious in purpose, along with the 'ethical ideas of duty based on them', became formative influences on behaviour.[6] He demonstrates the importance of vocation to the Protestant tradition and the anxieties this stirred: he notes how it took a particularly punitive form through the influence of John Calvin's emphasis on predestination, whereby only certain people were saved and displayed their salvation through works, but even these could lose their status through not putting their labour to the work of God; indeed, work became a way of counteracting feelings of religious anxiety brought about by this doctrine.[7] As Weber shows, this ethic developed through different Protestant denominations, particularly Quakerism (a movement that Woolf knew well through her aunt, as well as friends Violet Dickinson and Roger and Margery Fry). The Clapham Sect can also be located into Weber's scheme, as an Evangelical movement that arose within the Anglican Church in the late eighteenth century and had an impact on a middle-class ethic. As Weber notes, the values of dedication to hard work and purpose thrived even as religious ideas about calling, Providence and God's purpose declined. Weber therefore provides an account of the mechanism by which religious motives passed into everyday life and informed the modern worldview in key ways. It therefore provides an explanation of the work ethic that Woolf inherited, including a desire to produce work that was 'worth while' (*CE2* 105).

Second, Weber is useful to a study of Woolf for acknowledging the range of different attitudes towards religion that sprung up in the early twentieth century. In 'Science as a Vocation' (1918), Weber notes that although modern science had produced a particular drive towards rationalism, intellectualism and secularisation that had left the world 'disenchanted', there was also a growing dissatisfaction with science as a discipline because it seeks to explain life rather than considering its values: he quotes Tolstoy's maxim that 'Science is meaningless because it gives no answer to our question, the only question important for us: "what shall we do and how shall we live?"'[8] Woolf was likewise deeply engaged with questions of the value and purpose of life.

Weber notes that younger people were now wanting to explore these values and were craving religion to seek 'redemption from the intellectualization of science'. He notes that they were doing this by turning to a variety of different cultures, collecting religious artefacts from throughout the world in a 'sort of domestic chapel', and writing books about mystical experience. This helps to describe the element of cultural relativism within modernism, represented by T. S. Eliot's invocation of the words of Buddha and the Hindu Vedas in *The Waste Land* (1922) and by the African statuette in D. H. Lawrence's *Women in Love* (1920), and by Woolf's interest in pre-classical matriarchal myths and the religion of ancient Egypt.[9]

While this strand of Weber's argument provides support for Lewis's argument that religion became privatised in the modernist era, Weber notes another trend represented by the intellectual returning to the conventional churches: 'The arms of the old churches are opened widely and compassionately for him . . . If he can really do it [make his intellectual sacrifice] we shall not rebuke him.' The important implication for our study is that the old churches were still open and flourishing: T. S. Eliot, John Middleton Murry and C. S. Lewis were among the intellectuals who would embrace the traditional churches, and who then produced writings that sought to give faith academic credibility, while also bringing religion into political debates. Weber's essay thus enables us to appreciate the variety of different attitudes towards religion in the early twentieth century: rationalist rejection of religious ideas, privatised religion, cultural relativism and devout church membership. Recognising these competing trends enables us to see the religious context of the era as rather more complex than the trend of 're-enchantment' that Pericles Lewis draws from Weber.

This insight will inform my study of how Woolf relates to the religious contexts of the early twentieth century in Chapter 2. The chapter will look closely at Woolf's awareness of contemporary religious movements and debates, including her close study of the involvement of the Church of England in politics and her engagement with religious debates among Hogarth Press authors (Leonard Woolf was fascinated by religions of all sorts including Christianity, and the Hogarth Press published works on religious topics). As well as noting her affinities with sceptics like E. M. Forster and her interests in the scholarship of Jane Harrison, then, it will also look at how she responded to the faith of her close friends, including Violet Dickinson and Ethel Smyth, who had grown up with strong Christian influences, and other friends and associates such as Vita Sackville-West, T. S. Eliot, and J. M. Murry, who had become persuaded by Christianity. However, since Woolf also engaged with networks outside the confines of Bloomsbury (as Anna Snaith has shown, not least in her edition of the *Three Guineas* letters in which Woolf corresponded with people from a variety of classes and faith positions), the chapter will consider Woolf's interactions with the religiosity of groups such as the local community at Rodmell.

Within a complex religious demographic, Woolf's response to religion was in itself complex and variable, not least because she was caught in a tussle between different influences: she was deeply provoked by the Evangelical ideals of members of her extended family, she was persuaded by the scepticism of her parents, and she engaged in religious debates with her contemporaries. As a result, unlike Eliot, Woolf did not identify with any particular tradition but instead interacted with competing traditions from a detached standpoint (this is a reason why this book's title is 'Christian Culture' rather than 'Christian Tradition').

Virginia Woolf's responses and attitudes towards Christian culture, which have been relatively neglected, are therefore more significant than might at first appear. As the next three sections of this introduction will show, these are relevant to three dimensions of her work: the political and ethical, the cultural and literary, and the spiritual. The aspects are important, and this book will explore them all as well as demonstrating interconnections between them. The book will range widely across Woolf's work, including her novels, essays, stories, letters, diaries and memoirs, but five texts are especially relevant and will feature prominently in the discussion: *Mrs Dalloway* (1925); *To the Lighthouse* (1927); *The Waves* (1931); *Three Guineas* (1938); and 'A Sketch of the Past' (1939–40). Each one is particularly rich: they will be used across the chapters, read and re-read from different angles; their relevance to the debate will be sketched in the following sections.

Religion, politics and ethics: *Three Guineas*

Three Guineas will be a touchstone for discussion of Woolf's explorations of religion from the political point of view. Religion is on one level a social organisation: one account of its etymology (favoured by Augustine) comes from *religare* 'binding together', or 'that which ties believers to God'.[10] The flip side of this is that it also becomes a marker of exclusion and discrimination, and the keynote of *Three Guineas* is an argument that organised religion, and the Church of England specifically, has enforced the exclusion of women. As Christine Froula has argued, using scapegoat psychology, Woolf's essay analyses how bonds between men have been secured by the violent exclusion of women.[11]

Three Guineas is a key text for demonstrating Woolf's knowledge and understanding of Christian institutions, for it features Woolf's most detailed writings on organised religion. Religious works are prominent among the contemporary and historical texts she uses to demonstrate the role of patriarchal institutions in excluding women from public life: these include the Bible, clergy memoirs, writings by prominent churchmen, and contemporary news reports and official documents. Woolf makes strong and clear arguments against the church and its clergy: members of a profession that remained firmly closed to women throughout her lifetime. She also shows how exclusion of women from the public sphere had an impact on the role of women in the private home, and how the ideology of separate spheres was cemented by religious discourse. As Froula has noted, *Three Guineas* 'like the gospels tells the story from the victims' perspective in order to advance from tyranny to freedom, from xenophobia and nationalism to the "desire to give to England first what she desires of peace and freedom for the whole world.'"[12] Woolf traces a complex set of arguments, both in the body of the essay and through the footnotes, and different layers of her discussion will be unpacked over several chapters of this book. Woolf's responses to the Clapham Sect will be discussed in Chapter 1; her interest in the role of religion in contemporary politics will be explored in Chapter 2; and her engagement with the debate over women priests will be examined in Chapter 3, which will also look at how Woolf frequently invokes the Bible as part of her rhetorical strategy in this essay.

Christianity in cultural and literary life

While the Church had a continuing role in public life, and religious views still influenced the ideology of the home, Christianity also remained part and parcel of everyday life and Britain remained nominally Christian throughout Woolf's lifetime. Clergy did not only conduct ceremonies dressed in robes that asserted patriarchal domination, but they also wrote to *The Times* to report the first hawthorn flower of spring. Churches and cathedrals functioned symbolically as bastions of the establishment, but they were also open for tourism and private prayer. The Bible was not only a collection of myths reinforcing the ideology of patriarchy and the subjection of women, but it was common currency – everyday speech was peppered with biblical allusions, and religious terminology like 'heaven be praised' and 'God knows' were common phrases even for Woolf.

This book therefore examines the ways in which Woolf engaged with, critiqued and responded Christian influences on culture. The central four chapters will discuss how Woolf deals with particular expressions of Christian culture: Chapter 3 reveals Woolf's fascination with the clergy, showing that she had a deeply informed but critical understanding of the clerical role, in its pastoral, liturgical, sacramental and social aspects, as well as its political dimension. Chapters 4 and 5 interrogate how Woolf conceptualised sacred space, particularly as it relates to gender: in designated places of worship and in the home, respectively. Chapter 6 explores Woolf's responses to the iconography of the Virgin Mary, particularly as she is represented in art, arguing that such references form part of a deep-seated investigation of cultural presumptions about womanhood within her novels.

Woolfian spirituality

It is widely accepted that Woolf was interested in spiritual questions. This has been recognised by critics from the earliest reviews onwards, some of whom even claimed her as a religious writer: *The New Republic* praised *To the Lighthouse* as a 'thing to thank God for' (a comment that was used as the headline for an advertisement in *The Dial*); and W. H. Auden wrote that 'what she felt and expressed with the most intense passion was a mystic, religious vision of life.'[13] However, most critics who have described Woolf's attitude as religious have done so in a qualified sense. The earliest such statement was made by a near-contemporary, R. L. Chambers, who argued in 1947 that 'one of the many troubles of our troubled age is that many truly religious people have no religion to profess', naming Woolf as one of these because there is nothing of 'religion proper' in her work. His view that Woolf was a religious person without a religion has been echoed by Jean Love and Douglas Howard, and by Emily Griesinger, who suggests that Woolf explored the 'possibility of private religion with no theological strings attached'. Quentin Bell suggested that 'using the word in a very wide sense we may find a "religious" element in her novels; she tended to be, as she herself put it, "mystical"; but she entertained no comfortable beliefs.' Mark Hussey very cautiously argues that '[b]eginning with Woolf's ideas of self and identity, we are led eventually to realise that her concept of the essential nature of human being was religious *in character*', and Alyda Faber comes to a carefully worded conclusion that 'a religious sense of subjectivity, without God or Gods, except as necessary fictions, allows Woolf to express her sense of herself as a writer making precarious and necessary efforts to love other humans'.[14]

What all of these comments point towards is the sense that Woolf was interested in exploring questions that have interested people of faith, without adhering to any tradition or belief system personally. Discussion of Woolf as a 'religious' writer has sometimes been hampered by the slipperiness of the terms 'religion' and 'religious experience', and by the failure of many critics to define or unpack these terms.[15] If we return to the etymology of 'religion' as 'binding', we can see that Woolf was not a religious writer in the sense of being part of a church or organised belief system but she did have a set of beliefs that involved other sorts of connection, as she explored what unites us with other people, with the world around us, and with a deeper reality. Julia Briggs concludes that Woolf believed in 'some kind of communal spirit',[16] and Alex Zwerdling noted that Woolf 'did experience an emotion that Freud called "the oceanic feeling" – a sense of oneness with her kind and with nature.'[17] Pericles Lewis argues that a 'great deal' of her work 'engages in a search for new models of sacred community and experience that could potentially accommodate the "process[es] of change" typical of modernity'.[18] Woolf's concern to accommodate and value female experience was even more pressing than a need to respond to modernity, however, for in a crucial move in *Three Guineas,* she argues that women need to 'free the religious spirit from its present servitude' by creating a 'new religion'. Woolf therefore envisaged a new form of joining together, but one that escaped the exclusivity of institutionalised religion: this would include, as Froula suggests, the uniting of men and women against Fascism.[19]

Woolf articulates her ideas about communality with a frequency that suggests a preoccupation that goes beyond the views of individual characters. It is found in all three of our key novels, but it has its fullest expression in Clarissa Dalloway's feeling that we live through one another:

> Did it matter then, she asked herself, walking towards Bond Street, did it matter that she must inevitably cease completely; all this must go on without her; did she resent it; or did it not become consoling to believe that death ended absolutely? But that somehow in the streets of London, on the ebb and flow of things, here, there, she survived, Peter survived, lived in each other, she being part, she was positive, of the trees at home; of the house there, ugly, rambling all to bits and pieces as it was; part of people she had never met; being laid out like a mist between the people she knew best, who lifted her on their branches as she had seen the trees lift the mist, but it spread ever so far, her life, herself. (*MD* 8)

Reminded of her own mortality by feeling an irregular heartbeat (something Woolf herself was experiencing at the time),[20] Clarissa moves swiftly from contemplating extinction to the more positive alternative that she will survive in people and places that she has known, and also in 'people she had never met'. The novel becomes an outworking of this 'transcendental theory' (*MD* 136) when Clarissa is touched by the news of the suicide of Septimus Warren Smith and empathises with him even though they have never met. As Froula notes, 'As theorized by Clarissa and practised in *Mrs Dalloway's* intersubjective character-drawing, odd affinities lift elegiac consolation out of the register of the sentimental to counter the "death of the soul".'[21]

In *To the Lighthouse,* Mrs Ramsay pursues a theory of survival in and through other things, as she becomes one with the beam of the lighthouse: 'inanimate things; trees, streams, flowers; felt they expressed one; felt they became one; felt they knew one, in a sense were one' (*TL* 87). Woolf explores this even more extensively in *The Waves* which, she noted, was to be about 'lives together'. The novel persistently suggests connections between the six characters, most notably in the final scene where Bernard reflects on how there is 'no division' between him and his friends:

> Here on my brow is the blow I got when Percival fell. Here on the nape of my neck is the kiss Jinny gave Louis. My eyes fill with Susan's tears. I see far away, quivering like a gold thread, the pillar Rhoda saw, and feel the rush of the wind of her flight when she leapt. (*W* 231)

In addition to a belief that we live in and through one another, and to a certain extent in tension with this belief, Woolf also had an understanding of the individual soul as the essential part of a person beyond appearances which may have the capacity to survive death. Hussey notes that Woolf was deeply concerned with the nature of the self and that although 'an ardent atheist, Woolf gradually came to hold what can best be described as a faith, the essential element of which was belief in a "soul".'[22] In fact, Woolf was comfortable speaking about the soul throughout her life. Her early writings show her using it as part of a religious register with which to speak to believing friends, such as when she asks Violet Dickinson in 1903 to 'say your prayers every night – if only for sake of Sparroys soul – which doesn't get many prayers to wash it' (*L1* 71). However, she later uses the notion of 'soul' to understand herself as a person and as a writer: commenting in 1919 on her self-presentation in her diary, she notes that 'it looks as if I had a soul after all; these are revelations, self analyses' (*D1* 315). In 1926, she comments on the difficulty in writing about the soul, but that 'the soul slips in' when she tries to write about other things (*D3* 62). Woolf frequently used the word 'soul' for the creative self: when writing *The Waves,* Woolf noted that 'these premonitions of a book – states of soul in creating – are very queer & little apprehended' (*D3* 253). In her final diary entry, Woolf amalgamates the idea of the soul with that of living in and through another person: 'Nessa is at Brighton, & I am imagining how it wd be if we could infuse souls' (*D5* 359).

Woolf also believed in a transcendent reality, which she frequently approached using the word 'mystic'. A diary entry that Woolf made in February 1926 suggests that she was on a spiritual quest for something beyond the self and everyday experience: 'I have some restless searcher in me. Why is there not a discovery in life? Something one can lay hands on & say, "This is it"?' (*D3* 62). She elaborated on these questions in her diary entries at the earliest inception of *The Waves*, where she reflects on the 'mystical side' of solitude: 'it is not oneself but something in the universe that one is left with . . . One sees a fin passing far out' (*D3* 113). *The Waves* was to be a 'mystical eyeless book' (*D3* 203) and 'an endeavour at something mystic, spiritual; the thing that exists when we aren't there' (*D3* 114). On completing the novel, Woolf felt that she had succeeded in 'netting the fin' (*D4* 10).

As an extension of this, Woolf had a concept of revelation. This word appears with some frequency in her writing, but it is used most significantly in her concept of 'moments of being', as put forward in 'A Sketch of the Past', where she suggests that her openness to revelations is fundamental to her vocation as a writer. Woolf describes unexceptional everyday life as nondescript – or a state of 'non-being'. Exceptional moments intrude through this cotton-wool in the form of shocks, which signify 'being', or fully lived experience. She describes three shocks, all from her childhood: fighting with her brother Thoby (bringing a terrifying awareness of human beings' capacity to hurt one another); overhearing the story of a suicide (an equally awful awareness of the human being's capacity for self-harm); and seeing a flower, its leaves and the surrounding earth as a pleasing integral whole (leading to a sense of understanding). Woolf notes that this receptivity to 'shocks' is what has made her a writer, but, crucially, she sees herself as receiving something that has come from outside the self: it is an 'intuition . . . so instinctive that it seems given to me, not made by me.' As Alyda Faber notes, Woolf 'ascribes a kind of holiness, or ensoulment, to that within and beyond herself which she cannot control.'[23] The 'moments of being' provide insight to a deeper truth about the world, for Woolf sees them as entailing 'a revelation of some order', a 'pattern behind the cotton wool' and that pattern is that of a work of art to which we all belong. And in writing about these, she says, she is able to overcome the pain of the shocks by putting the severed pieces together.

Alongside these beliefs, however, Woolf also had a persistent concern that she never resolved: the question of life after death. While her wider family background had exposed her to a mindset in which salvation and damnation in the hereafter were crucially important, she had also grown up with her parents' scepticism about an afterlife. So, while Woolf's ideas of a spiritual community, the soul, transcendence and revelation all work towards a hope that one does not 'cease completely' with death (*MD* 8), she continued to give expression to, and lament, the harsh realities of death and loss. Woolf famously saw her novels as elegies: 'I have an idea that I will invent a new name for my books to supplant "novel". A new ___ by Virginia Woolf. But what? Elegy?' (*D3* 34). Making this suggestion in June 1925, she was putting a label to a preoccupation that was already evident in her novels, and which would continue to be a concern, for the death of at least one individual and the mourning of those left behind is a persistent theme in her work.

The problem was both personal to Woolf and an expression of wider societal trauma. It is well-attested that Woolf was deeply affected by multiple bereavements in her youth and that she commemorates family members in her fictional characters: recalling her parents, Thoby and her half-sister Stella Duckworth in *To the Lighthouse* in Mr and Mrs Ramsay, Andrew and Prue; also commemorating Thoby in eponymous protagonist of *Jacob's Room* and Percival in *The Waves*. Woolf recalls details from her mother's death in several of her novels, such as the unpleasant smell of lilies in the hallway in *The Voyage Out* and *The Years* and the memory of her father brushing past her as he stumbled from the room in *To the Lighthouse* and *The Years*. Woolf's elegiac project in her novels involved the emotional and psychological exercise of adjusting her relationship with her loved ones and seeking to come to terms with their deaths: she speculated that in writing *To the Lighthouse*, 'I expressed some very long felt and deeply felt emotion. And in expressing it I explained it and then laid it out to rest' (*MB* 81). The fact that Woolf continued to write about her loved ones long after *To the Lighthouse*, however, suggests that she never laid them, or the emotions, to rest. As Sybil Oldfield has suggested, Woolf's persistent attempts to write about her loved ones was a way of using her writing as an antidote to the scepticism of her upbringing: 'Virginia Woolf's deepest need of all was to give to her beloved dead, her necessary ones, the immortality otherwise impossible to hope for in an indifferent, unjust, God-less universe.'[24]

Woolf commemorates wider societal losses in *Jacob's Room* and *To the Lighthouse*, where the lost sons Jacob and Andrew are killed in the war, rather than dying of illness like Thoby Stephen, so that they represent the generation of war dead. *Mrs Dalloway* is in part an elegy for 'thousands of poor chaps, with all their lives before them, shovelled together, already half-forgotten' (*MD* 103), and Septimus Warren Smith represents the far-reaching losses of the First World War. The individual deaths in *To the Lighthouse* are set against a backdrop of the First World War, while *Between the Acts* contemplates the prospect of another war and the threat of extinction.

The tension between mourning an individual and an awareness of death on a vast scale is an important one in Woolf's work, as it sets up a desire to value the individual against an anxiety that human lives and deaths are insignificant when viewed in the wider perspective ('I am . . . like the shadow passing over the downs' (*D3* 188)). Integral to this elegising process is the aesthetic challenge of finding a means of writing about someone who is no longer there. This is brought out reflexively in Lily Briscoe's attempt to paint Mrs Ramsay, and Bernard's efforts to sum up the life of his circle of friends, but it is implicit within much of Woolf's writing, and a recurrent theme in Woolf's novels is the question of what has become of those who have already died and what will become of us after death.

Woolf and Christianity: an uneasy relationship

Woolf's persistent wrestling with the problem of death highlights a particular tension in her relationship with Christianity, and, although she used theological vocabulary to articulate her ideas – the soul, mystic, transcendence, revelation – it is difficult to read these systematically. For example, her theory of 'lives together' though consistently expressed across her work, remains almost deliberately undefined. Furthermore, while she used words such as 'God', 'the Almighty', 'the Creator', regularly, her discussion of moments of being crucially ends with the statement that 'certainly and emphatically there is no God.' Critics exploring Woolf's relationship with Christianity have found her use of Christian language and symbolism confusing: Christopher Knight in a seminal article on the topic declares it 'extraordinary',[25] and Lewis suggests that Woolf's attitude is one of 'incomprehension' and 'puzzlement' tempered with 'sympathy'.[26] Rather than trying to accommodate Woolf's thinking into a Christian theology, then, it is important to remain attentive both to conflicts and to points of sympathy. Woolf's position towards Christianity is liminal: it is certainly not a profession of faith, but it is not an outright rejection either. What this book aims to do, therefore, is to explore how Woolf developed her views in dialogue with people she knew and through her readings of Christian culture around her.

Scholarship on Woolf and mysticism is helpful here precisely because this movement has had an ambiguous relationship with mainstream Christianity. For a long time Woolf critics, such as Julie Kane, assumed that mysticism was an entirely Eastern movement and used it to align Woolf with religions such as Buddhism.[27] However, mysticism has been an important part of Christian history, and Stephanie Paulsell and Val Gough have made useful close readings between Woolf and historical Christian mystics to identify mystical dispositions within Woolf's thought. Paulsell has contrasted Woolf with the medieval writer Marguerite D'Ouigh to show that, although both were interested in mystical ideas, Woolf's focus was on 'reality' not God, on this world not the hereafter.[28] Val Gough compares Woolf with literary mystics who have produced 'innovatory, highly literary discourses which functioned to leave the door open for meaning in an attempt to avoid reifying God'. Gough's analysis is helpful for showing how Woolf sought to devise a form of writing for expressing mystical experience that went beyond 'religious dogma': that is, one that avoided the ready-made phrases and analogies for speaking of the divine, thereby also avoiding ready-made conceptions of the divine. As Gough notes, such discourses 'trace the path to radical alterity': the reaching-out beyond the self, be it sympathy with other human beings or a more radical attempt to think beyond the human.[29]

Critics have also recently recognised that Woolf engaged with particular contemporary expressions of mysticism. Woolf found sympathy with Caroline Emelia Stephen's mysticism, as Heininge has pointed out.[30] Caroline Emelia's formulation of belief is close to Woolf's: 'agnosticism with mystery at the heart of it seems another description of the "rational mysticism" which is my favourite expression of my own ground.'[31] In *The Years*, Woolf has Sara Pargiter (often seen as a representation of her aunt) use a liturgical text – the Athanasian Creed – to sum up a resistance to pinning down an idea of God: 'the father incomprehensible; the son incomprehensible' (Y 207). Woolf was later particularly exercised by Vita Sackville-West's increasing interest in mysticism. Woolf's dialogue with these two women will therefore be of particular interest to this study.

A recognition of Woolf's liminal position towards Christianity raises important objections to the tendency in recent criticism to categorise Woolf as an atheist, such as Michael Lackey's description of Woolf and Forster as 'unconditional honest atheists, who dispense with God, a God's eye perspective, and a realm of ultimate Meaning and Value.'[32] Labelling Woolf as an atheist ignores the fact that she used the word in a derogatory way to describe a dogmatism she resented. As Lewis notes, Woolf's atheists are not sympathetic characters, the most prominent being Charles Tansley in *To the Lighthouse*: a 'disagreeable', 'odious' and 'miserable man'.[33] We hear nothing of his religious views (and, in fact, there is an incongruous mention of him 'preaching brotherly love' at a meeting in London), but his besetting sin is pessimism, dashing James Ramsay's hopes of going to the lighthouse and intimidating Lily Briscoe with his pronouncement what 'women can't paint'. His atheism is therefore negativity and dogmatism: something Lily sums up as 'meagre fixity' (*TL* 10, 12, 265, 115).

It is therefore inaccurate to align Woolf with late twentieth-century formulations of confident atheism such as those of Richard Dawkins or A. C. Grayling. Rather, Woolf's delineation of sceptical positions is far more nuanced, such as Clarissa's 'atheist's religion' of doing good for the sake of goodness, or Peter Walsh's state of being 'perhaps an atheist' but nonetheless prone to revelations. Both of these characters suggest that even if there is no god, this does not rule out either ethical behaviour or spiritual experience. Alexandra Harris's subtle paradox describing Woolf's stance as 'devout atheism' is useful here, for Woolf did not see scepticism and devotion as mutually exclusive.[34]

Indeed, on closer inspection, Woolf's work exhibits an even-handed approach to faith and to characters' beliefs. As Knight points out, invoking William James, Woolf was interested in the 'variety of religious experience',[35] so that her novels taken on a 'dialogic character', with anti-religious voices being balanced by more devoted ones. This accords with Woolf's view that the novel exists 'to express character – not to preach doctrines' (*CE*1 324). Woolf displays greater sympathy with Christian characters than one might expect. Knight offers the examples of Neville's atheism being countered by Louis's faith in *The Waves,* and Bart's scepticism being balanced by Lucy's beliefs in *Between the Acts.* To these examples we can add the way in which Woolf balances the qualified atheism of Clarissa and Peter with Miss Kilman's piety, treating her with genuine sympathy when she struggles to pray at Westminster Abbey, and also with Septimus who asserts that 'there is a God'. As Kristina Groover notes, by 'juxtaposing . . . religious metaphors with Miss Kilman's dogma', *Mrs Dalloway* 'seems not to dismiss religious considerations outright, but to adopt a posture of exploration and inquiry that is a hallmark of Woolf's writing'; Griesinger agrees that this novel shows Woolf's 'respect and genuine curiosity about Christian beliefs, truths and values.'[36] Woolf also imagines a prayer life for Minnie Marsh in 'An Unwritten Novel', probing as she does with Doris Kilman, why someone might need prayer and religion (*CSF* 154–5). Characters are often placed in specific denominational contexts, too: we are told that Clarissa grew up in an Evangelical household that had a tradition of family prayers before her faith was shattered by the death of her sister. This attention to detail suggests that Woolf's depiction of her characters' faith is more subtle than a simple pitting of viewpoints against one another. It is therefore more accurate to see Woolf's work as polyphonic rather than simply dialogic.

Once we appreciate this complexity of Woolf's position, it becomes possible to identify threads of Christian ideas and concepts as intertexts within the intricate skein of her work. We will explore the significance of Woolf's engagement with Christian symbolism, practices, metaphors and ideas throughout this book, but Chapter 7 will look particularly at how Woolf engaged with the Bible as an intertext to assert the value of life and to interrogate the Christian doctrine of salvation, particularly as it is seen in the Passion narrative.

The conclusion will bring the book's findings to bear on the wish Woolf expressed in *Three Guineas* that women should formulate 'a new religion based it might well be upon the New Testament' (*3G* 189). Seeking to bring together the political, cultural and spiritual strands of Woolf's engagement with Christianity, it shows how Woolf critiqued and adapted Christian concepts from a feminist perspective and in doing so worked towards a 'literature of commitment' that valued women and all humanity and sought connections with a wider reality as part of the elegiac strain within her work.

Notes

1. Annan, *Leslie Stephen*, p. 2.
2. See especially Heininge, *Reflections;* also Marcus, *Languages of Patriarchy*, pp. 75–96; Lewis, 'Caroline Emelia Stephen and Virginia Woolf'; and Griesinger, 'Religious Belief in a Secular Age'.
3. Hastings, *A History of English Christianity*, p. 223.
4. Lewis, 'Churchgoing in the Modern Novel', p. 673.
5. Ibid., p. 671.
6. Weber, *The Protestant Ethic*, pp. xxxv, 49.
7. Weber criticises the 'extreme inhumanity of this doctrine' (ibid., p. 60) and the 'deep spiritual isolation' (63) and 'intense suffering' (66) that it caused.
8. Weber, 'Science as a Vocation', n.p.

9. For Woolf's use of matriarchal myths see, for example, Barrett, 'Matriarchal Myth' and Lilienfeld, '"The Deceptiveness of Beauty"'. For religions of Ancient Egypt, see Bradshaw, 'Beneath *The Waves*'.

10. *Oxford English Dictionary*, <http://www.oed.com/view/Entry/161944> (last accessed 13 December 2017), section on Etymology.

11. Froula, 'St. Virginia's Epistle', p. 32.

12. Ibid.

13. The advertisement can be seen on Woolf Online, <http://www.woolfonline.com> (last accessed 13 December 2017), filed under *To the Lighthouse* – Contexts; Auden, 'A Consciousness of Reality'. See also https://www.newyorker.com/magazine/1954/03/06/a-consciousness-of-reality (last accessed 18 December 2017)

14. Chambers, *The Novels of Virginia Woolf*, pp. 5–6; Love, *Worlds in Consciousness*, p. 71; Howard, 'Virginia Woolf', p. 629; Bell, *Virginia Woolf*, vol. 2, p. 136; Griesinger, 'Religious Belief in a Secular Age', p. 444; Hussey, *The Singing of the Real World*, p. xv; Faber, '"The Shock of Love"', p. 63.

15. See, for example, Tsang, 'Desecularizing Modernism', p. 195.

16. Briggs, *Inner Life*, p. 354.

17. Zwerdling, *Virginia Woolf and the Real World*, p. 279. See also Scott, 'Ecofeminism, Holism'.

18. Lewis, *Religious Experience and the Modernist Novel*, pp. 142–3.

19. Froula, 'St. Virginia's Epistle', p. 47.

20. *D2*, 17 Feb 1922. Briggs notes the potential influence of Woolf's health scares on this novel (*Inner Life*, p. 156).

21. Froula, '*Mrs Dalloway's* Postwar Elegy', p. 137.

22. Hussey, *Singing of the Real World*, p. xv.

23. Faber, '"Shock of Love"', p. 60.

24. Oldfield, *Child of Two Atheists*, pp. 8, 11.

25. Knight, 'The God of Love is Full of Tricks', p. 42.

26. Lewis, *Religious Experience and the Modernist Novel*, pp. 143–4.

27. Kane, 'Varieties of Mystical Experience.'

28. Paulsell, 'Writing and Mystical Experience'.

29. Gough, '"That Razor Edge of Balance"', p. 59.

30. Heininge, *Reflections*.

31. C. E. Stephen, *Vision of Faith*, p. cxi.

32. Lackey, *Modernist God State*.

33. Lewis, *Religious Experience and the Modernist Novel*, p. 147.

34. Harris, *Virginia Woolf*, p. 96.

35. Knight, 'The God of Love is Full of Tricks', p. 27.

36. Groover, 'Enacting the Sacred in *Mrs Dalloway*', pp. 11–13; Griesinger, 'Religious Belief in a Secular Age', p. 443.

Chapter 1

Family Background: Clapham and After

Although Virginia Stephen was brought up in an agnostic household, this did not mean that she grew up in an environment from which religious discussion, literature, language and mores had been eradicated. Indeed, an agnostic household without religious discussion would be a contradiction in terms: Leslie Stephen's writings on agnosticism demonstrate a continual preoccupation with disproving the existence of a god he no longer believed in. Yet though Gabrielle McIntire sums up a popular conception of the Stephen home when she describes it as a place where 'God was spoken about primarily through an intellectualized, post-Darwinian agnostic lens of skepticism and doubt . . . rationally but not reverentially',[1] this was not the case because many of the Stephens' friends and visitors were believers. These included Oliver Wendell Holmes, the prominent American lawyer and hymn writer who was Woolf's 'dear godpapa' (*L1* 2) (the Stephens gave their children sponsors even though they did not have them baptised). Virginia and Vanessa had friends from clergy families, including the Milman sisters, granddaughters of the dean of St Paul's (*PA* 60; *D1* 25 & n). Not least among their friends was Violet Dickinson, a Quaker friend of Stella who became an even closer companion for Virginia. Many members of the extended family were religious: George Duckworth took a highly conventional view of religion, as he did of everything, and cousins Dorothea and Rosamond Stephen were Evangelicals who persistently tried to convert the Stephen siblings.

The Stephen home was therefore not an exclusion zone from religion, but rather a place where conflicting religious positions were played out. While Leslie Stephen was dying of cancer, Virginia wrote to Violet that 'the Almighty keeps you supplied' with sick people to visit, going on to explain that the

> religious allusion on the last page drifted in, or was pounded in, by a fat religious cousin [Dorothea], very red in the face, who is arguing Christianity with Thoby. She is trying to prove that certain sections of her soul are alive and afloat while ours are 'atrophied'. (*L1* 85)

This grimly comic scenario of an agnostic daughter of a dying agnostic being comforted by a Quaker, while her equally agnostic brother is being threatened with damnation by a fervent Evangelical, shows the range of religious perspectives that came into play. Woolf's account of the episode also shows her humorously touching upon key theological questions: the existence and nature of God (whom she suggests is one who makes people ill), the nature of the soul, salvation, and the final judgment. These questions had exercised her family for generations and she would continue to explore them, often far more seriously, in her later work.

Evangelical heritage

In order to gain a fuller picture of the Christian cultural nexus in which Woolf grew up, including persisting concerns with theological questions and social and moral attitudes, we need to explore the religious history of the Stephen family. Religious observance, as opposed to nominal Christianity, was deeply ingrained within Woolf's family background and heritage, for many of her ancestors were devout Christians and several had influenced religious trends over the previous two centuries. The Stephen family originated from Scottish Calvinists[2] and by the nineteenth century they were staunch and hugely influential Evangelical Anglicans, including leading members of the Clapham Sect. There were clergy in the Stephen family, including William Stephen (half-brother of Woolf's grandfather), as well as Leslie Stephen briefly, but ordination was even more of a tradition within Leslie Stephen's mother's family, the Venns, whom he described as 'the very blue blood of the [Evangelical] party' who 'traced their descent through a long line of clergymen to the time of Elizabeth'.[3] The most recent and notable of these were his great-grandfather, grandfather and uncle, the prominent churchmen Henry, John and

Henry Venn. Generations of both sides of the family had written on religion in a variety of genres, including journalism, theology, novels and hymns.⁴ Woolf inherited many of their works with her father's library, and kept them throughout her life.

Through the Clapham Sect, Woolf's family had been deeply involved in key social, political and religious movements of the nineteenth century. The Stephens and Venns, along with the Wilberforces (who were related to the Stephens by marriage) and the Thorntons and Macaulays, made up this close-knit and deeply influential set of middle-class Evangelical families, committed to philanthropy and humanitarian causes, most significantly the fight against slavery. Their political commitment meant that they shaped the religious life of the nation, but as a strongly family-orientated religious practice, Clapham Sect values were deeply influential on the politics of the home. Woolf's family members had made significant contributions to its literature and doctrine: Henry Venn the elder, who according to Noel Annan 'can almost be said to have invented the Clapham Sect',⁵ wrote its key theological work *The Complete Duty of Man;* and Leslie Stephen's father Sir James wrote the history of the group in an article for the *Edinburgh Review* (subsequently collected in his *Essays in Ecclesiastical Biography*).⁶

A clue to Woolf's recognition of the importance of religion within her family background can be found in a diary entry from 1929, in which she recalls her teenage interests in reading and writing:

> I was then writing a long picturesque essay upon the Christian religion, I think; called *Religio Laici,* I believe, proving that man has need of a God; but the God was described in a process of change; & I also wrote a history of Women; & a history of my own family – all very longwinded and El[izabe]than in style. (*D3* 271)

This diary entry is the only reference we have either to her work of family history or to her essay on Christianity, written when she was '15 or 16'. It is appropriate, however, that Woolf should have been writing family history alongside an essay on Christianity, given the close connections between the two. It is also pertinent that Woolf was considering the history of women in tandem with these questions, not only because of the perennial gender debates within Christianity from its earliest days, but more specifically because writers within her own family had contributed to these discourses. The passage also suggests that Woolf was pondering theological questions, as she did in her letter to Violet, by asking why humankind needs a god and how it envisages the deity. The juxtaposition of concerns in this diary entry shows that the Woolf of 1929 (like the Virginia Stephen of 1897–8), was exercised by both the sociopolitical and the spiritual-theological aspects of Christianity.

Woolf was ambivalent about this heritage, often representing her family networks ironically. In 'A Sketch of the Past', Woolf presents her family background in a parody of a *Dictionary of National Biography* entry:

> Who was I then? Adeline Virginia Stephen, the second daughter of Leslie and Julia Prinsep Stephen, born on 25th January 1882, descended from a great many people, some famous, others obscure; born into a large connection, born not of rich parents, but of well-to-do parents, born into a very communicative, literate, letter writing, visiting, articulate, late nineteenth century world. (*MB* 65)

Instead of naming the influential circles to which she was connected, she refers to them obliquely in a flippant generalising style. She goes on to note that although she could write at length about various relatives, this would not be helpful in explaining her identity. She is ambivalent about her family, preferring to emphasise her own uniqueness.

However, a later passage suggests a more complex connection with her family past, as she mentions her grandfather as a possible hereditary cause of her 'shame' of mirrors, dress and appearance:

> I am almost inclined to drag in my grandfather – Sir James, who once smoked a cigar, liked it, and so threw away his cigar and never smoked another. I am almost inclined to think that I inherited a streak of the puritan, of the Clapham Sect.[7]

Woolf looked on her evangelical ancestry as a disadvantage, a source of inhibition, a fundamental conflict with the liberated Bloomsbury lifestyle, yet its influence was profound.

This chapter will set Woolf in a religious background rooted in a specifically Evangelical tradition that remained meaningful for some of her friends and family but also shaped the culture of her family home even after the underpinning of faith was lost. As we saw in the Introduction, the Clapham Sect was a particular manifestation of the Protestant work ethic described by Weber, but this chapter will demonstrate that the familial connection was an important focus for Woolf's social criticism. Her ancestors were particularly influential in the development of evangelical thought, which in turn shaped English political culture, but they also became active in national and colonial politics and the law, and Woolf critically engaged with them in her writings. The chapter will also show how theological debates, including those around salvation, remained a heated debate for the family, including Woolf.

Clapham commenced

The foundations for the moral code and Evangelical theology of the Stephen family were laid by Henry Venn's *The Complete Duty of Man, or a System of Doctrinal and Practical Christianity* (1763), which was one of Woolf's inherited books. Despite its very early date, its effects were long-lasting, as Leslie Stephen noted: 'For three generations it was the accepted manual of the sect and a trusted exposition of their characteristic theology.'[8] This close pairing of theological treatise and conduct manual, the interweaving of doctrinal and practical, meant that the social and cultural prescriptions would endure even after the agnosticism of later generations had dismantled the scaffolding of faith.

Venn's purpose is conversion and he is in no doubt about the inevitability of the Last Judgment and the realities of damnation and salvation. He saw the soul as a separate entity from the body that would continue after death in everlasting bliss or torment. Significantly, his views were counter-cultural for their time: as a leading figure in the Evangelical revival of the late eighteenth century, Venn provides a wake-up call to Christianity in general and presents his book as a corrective to harmful doctrinal trends.[9] He aimed to restore the doctrine of Justification by Faith, arguing that salvation could not be earned by good works or by one's own spiritual efforts, but by perceiving one's own unworthiness and weakness and recognising one's own need for the Trinitarian God, could only be known through reading the Bible 'correctly'.

Venn's theology, with the stakes for salvation set very high, serves to enforce his social teaching. Greater obedience to God's law and greater conformity to his nature could only be achieved through a Puritan turning-away from the ways of the world that Ian Bradley has labelled the 'call to seriousness'. The second half of Venn's book therefore presents practical guidance for daily living. Venn focuses on family and domestic life with marriage at the centre. Love and affection were emphasised but social order was essential too, so Venn therefore gave a particularly strong religious endorsement of gender relations: the husband would be guilty of desertion of duty if he failed to 'preside' over the home and the wife was deemed the 'weaker vessel', whose role was to support and obey her husband in turn for protection. Parenthood was a religious calling and parents had the weighty responsibility of leading their children to salvation. Woolf chose an easy target in 'Professions for Women' when she used Coventry Patmore's *The Angel in the House* as an example of the binding ideology of the separate spheres, for the theology was deeply engrained: Venn's book was the first of many conduct manuals became popular during the nineteenth century alongside works by William Roberts and Thomas Gisborne (who became a particular focus for Woolf's criticism).[10]

Venn also devised a devotional practice to reinforce his theology and conduct advice: his book is structured as a cycle of treatises to be read out by the paterfamilias, followed by prayers designed to encourage families to take the lessons to heart. This established a prayer life centred on the home rather than church: as Bradley has noted, the Evangelical movement tended to be anti-church.[11] Venn's prayerbook and another popular collection by Henry Thornton therefore took the place of *The Book of Common Prayer* for Claphamites. Family prayers remained common practice for several generations: Leslie Stephen and his siblings were brought up with them in the 1830s and 1840s.[12] Woolf recognises the persistence of this tradition in *Mrs Dalloway,* where Clarissa remembers family prayers from her youth in the 1880s and 1890s. It a significant piece of subversion that Sally Seton plans to denounce Hugh Whitbread for sexual harassment at family prayers, but equally indicative of the coercive power of these devotions that Clarissa talks her out of it *(MD* 238).

Clapham families were also encouraged to adopt a distinctive lifestyle that eschewed popular culture: novels, songs and plays were all seen as corrupting influences to be avoided. This counter-cultural, resistant mindset would prove long-lasting and become a trademark of the family through to Woolf herself. The Protestant work ethic was another aspect of Clapham mores that would prove to be deeply ingrained, and what was religious duty for Venn became compulsion for future generations: Sir James, Leslie and Fitzjames Stephen and Woolf herself were characterised by their prodigious hard work to the point of breakdown.

Venn also presented an account of the interrelationship between private and public life, something that would exercise future generations, including Woolf. Although Venn concentrated mainly on the private realm, he acknowledged that Christians had a wider social responsibility because only true believers could work for the welfare of society,[13] and their challenge was how to live in the world while preserving Christian values such as sincerity, justice, mercy, meekness and forgiveness. Venn highlights how authority figures had a responsibility to exercise justice in public life, as well as stressing that the wealthy should be mindful of their social duties and that tradesmen should behave honestly. Venn established the father's role in the private home as a blueprint for the role of the patriarch in the public world. He thereby established the paternalism that Woolf would criticise in *Three Guineas*. However, whereas Venn believed that a man should preside with justice over his private house as a springboard for just practice in the wider world, Woolf took a different view: that the authoritarian paterfamilias had the same motivations as the political tyrant, for 'the public and the private worlds are inseparably connected . . . the tyrannies and servilities of the one are the tyrannies and servilities of the other' (*3G* 214–15).

Stephens against slavery: James and Sir James Stephen

The next two generations would see the fuller development of a commitment to public life as the parental duty of spiritual care was extended into the paternal business of conversion, particularly in the colonies. Henry Venn's son John founded the Church Missionary Society in 1799 and his grandson Henry continued the work as its Secretary. However, a more fully worked-out public commitment to Christian duty was found in the Stephen family: in John Venn's contemporary James Stephen (John and James were to become Leslie Stephen's grandfathers), and Sir James Stephen (Leslie Stephen's father, brother-in-law to Henry the Younger). This was seen most specifically in their fight against slavery.

The life of James Stephen (1758–1832) is a colourful story of conversion to Evangelicalism through a political and religious commitment to ending slavery and an adoption of middle-class seriousness that saw him rise from debtor's son and dissolate youth to middle-class professional. Writing his *Memoirs* for his children at the age of 60, James Stephen employed tropes of confessional literature to

use his own life as testimony for the power of prayer and the action
of providence. As Canon Charles Smith notes in the Foreword to
the published edition: 'Nobody who has read the *Confessions* of
St Augustine will lightly bring the charge of hypocrisy against the
author of these *Memoirs*.'[14] James is frank about his shortcomings as
a young man and the deprivations of his early life.[15] Having had his
early education disrupted by his family's financial difficulties, including time in a debtors' prison, he completed legal training after inheriting money from his uncle William Stephen, a doctor and slave-trader
based in St Kitts in the Caribbean, but 'made no serious attempt
to get into practice' after qualifying preferring instead to continue
studying, collect law books and conduct relationships with both
'Maria Rivers' and Anna Stent.[16] He fathered a child with 'Maria'
but married Anna, a 'truly embarrassing and painful dilemma'[17] that
also brought financial responsibilities and prompted him to draw on
family connections to set up a legal practice in St Kitts in 1783. Hard
work and a boost to his business brought about by the outbreak of
war between England and France in 1793, which gave him a lucra-
tive practice of defending traders who had had goods seized for trad-
ing with the French colonies, enabled him to return permanently to
Britain as a much wealthier man in September 1794.

His years in the Caribbean therefore saw his conversion to the
Protestant work ethic, but also, more profoundly, his conversion to
the fight against slavery. In his *Memoirs* he claims that his first, highly
successful, anti-slavery speech came about by accident as he tried to
impress Anna and 'Maria' at a debating society at Coachmakers'
Hall, London. The real turning-point of his life, however, took place
on his journey to St Kitts when he stopped at Barbados and witnessed the unfair trial of four slaves accused of murder. Although
it was clear that they were innocent – and indeed a white man was
known to be the more likely culprit – the slaves were found guilty
and two were burned to death. At that moment, James vowed never
to own slaves himself.

James Stephen became actively involved in the anti-slavery campaign after meeting William Wilberforce on his only visit home during
his stay on St Kitts, in the winter of 1788–9. It was also his entry to
the Clapham Sect, for he settled in Clapham on his return to England
and subsequently married Wilberforce's sister Sarah. Stephen supported Wilberforce's campaign from St Kitts by supplying him with
first-hand information about the slave trade and the conditions of
slavery. Then, on his return to London, he wrote anti-slavery pieces

for London's *Morning Chronicle,* worked as a legal expert presenting evidence to the House of Lords in an attempt to abolish the slave trade off the coast of Sierra Leone, and served as a member of the London Abolition Committee from May 1804 until it achieved its goal in 1807. His involvement included drafting an Order in Council prohibiting the importation of slaves into Guiana and drafting a bill to abolish the slave trade in other dominions.

After the slave trade was abolished, James helped to enforce the law in Africa as a member of the African Institution. As an MP from 1808 to 1815, he promoted measures designed to lead to the freedom and emancipation of slaves (a goal that would not be achieved in his lifetime). He petitioned for the improved treatment of slaves throughout the colonies in the meantime, securing a landmark victory in March 1812 for the registration of slaves in Trinidad, shortly followed by Mauritius, St Lucia and Tobago.[18] He resigned from Parliament on principle in 1815 when it did not support Wilberforce's Bill for registering slaves. After leaving Parliament he continued his anti-slavery campaigning as a pamphleteer, public speaker and legal scholar. His magisterial work *The Slavery of the British West India Colonies Delineated,* which he started while living on St Kitts and continued to work on for thirty years, was published in two volumes of 1824 and 1830, at the request of the London Society for Mitigating and Gradually Abolishing Slavery, and became a major reference work.[19]

James Stephen was in many ways the sort of establishment figure that Woolf criticised in *Three Guineas.* His anti-slavery campaigning was paternalistic and also driven by a nationalistic desire to improve his country's morals on the grounds that slavery was an 'odious oppression which dishonours the British and the Christian name'.[20] He argued that ending slavery would entail

> redeeming the national conscience, and the national honour, by making some restitution, a tardy and imperfect one indeed, but all the restitution in our power, to seven thousand hapless human beings whom we have deeply wronged, the victims of our iniquitous slave trade.[21]

He uses the word 'hapless' frequently to describe the African slaves and his discourse is marked by what would now be seen as a drive to impose western culture on them under the ideology of civilising them. He was active in the Church Missionary Society and had a zeal for conversion, to rescue them from what he called the 'moral filth of slavery . . . the darkness of pagan ignorance' and 'idolatry'.[22]

He was also imperialist, arguing that slaves should be made subjects of the Empire as a route to emancipation and calling for a strengthening of Britain's control over the colonies in order to enforce the ending of slavery. In a pamphlet of 1826 significantly entitled *England Enslaved by her own Slave Colonies,* he decries that the mother country was held to ransom by the colonies. He resists any talk of independence, arguing that if the British government gave in to calls for 'no taxation without representation' then it would 'lay down the imperial sceptre at the foot of every petty assembly'.[23]

But James Stephen's legacy to Woolf was more mixed than this because his anti-slavery campaigning was counter-cultural. Even as an MP, his position as a campaigner placed him on the margins of the establishment: he rarely spoke in debate and when he did, it was mainly on anti-slavery issues and religion. He was not prepared to toe the party line and he resigned from Parliament on principle, frustrated by the government's unwillingness to take action over slavery. He also saw a radical potential in religion, for it was the Christian church in the West Indies that pressed for improved conditions for slaves and James frequently cites an incident in which white local governors in Bridgetown, Barbados destroyed a Methodist chapel as a protest against Christian attempts to reform slavery.

Slavery Delineated therefore exemplifies a working-out of Henry Venn's belief in resisting social forces on matters of conscience. James Stephen situates himself between worlds, for he was critical of the colonial governments (the Local Legislatures or Assemblies) for failing to implement the new laws but also critical of the British government for failing to enforce compliance. In a shrewd analysis of how slavery was upheld by economic forces, he identifies the difficulties of implementing laws to reform slavery. He notes that 'the assemblies, in the smaller islands at least, are generally composed of men dependent for their subsistence on the system proposed to be reformed.'[24] These were small groups of 20 people or fewer, consisting of planters who were in debt, or managers or other dependants of planters. In *England Enslaved,* he urges the electorate to vote out the government for continuing to leave the local Assemblies in the West Indies to implement changes, suggesting that Parliament was swayed by factions of English people who had invested too heavily in the sugar trade to countenance the end of slavery.[25] Invoking evangelical moral rhetoric, he condemns such people as mere gamblers, arguing that they cannot hope to make a living from the sugar industry and that the government should not bow to pressure from them. This pamphlet reflects his despair over the corruption of power, as he argues that Parliament and the local Assemblies had too many vested interests to improve the condition of slaves.

James Stephen's writings demonstrate that his anti-slavery views involved independence of mind and personal sacrifice. He disowned his slave-owning family members (remarking triumphantly that he had used his slave-trading uncle's inheritance against his intentions),[26] he broke with Parliament, and he renounced friends, clients and acquaintances in order to fight for abolition.[27] Stephen's book also gives personal testimony of how he put his politics into practice in his home life, for while living in St Kitts, he was unusual for employing (rather than owning) his domestic servants. When he used the labour of slaves who were let out for hire by their owners, he helped many purchase their freedom (either by paying the whole price, or by supplementing their savings), and in one case, he gave legal help to a slave who had been unlawfully denied freedom. Here, he acknowledges that the home is a microcosm of the wider political world and he reflects Henry Venn's values of remaining aloof from the world.

James Stephen's son Sir James (1789–1859) continued the fight against slavery: he wrote the Act abolishing slavery in British colonies in 1833 in his capacity as a lawyer in the Colonial Office. Ironically, James had died the previous year; Wilberforce died a few days after the Act was passed. Although Sir James was critical of Britain's historical abuses around the world – for example, congratulating himself on a career in which he had contributed to 'the mitigation, if not the prevention, of the cruel wrong which *our country has inflicted on so large a portion of the human race*',[28] Evangelical Christianity was by this time no longer counter-cultural, but integral to the establishment and imperialism. As Bradley notes, missionary zeal would 'shape Britain's attitude to the countries under its dominion and play a major part in determining imperial policy'.[29] Sir James became synonymous with British colonial power, through his nickname 'Mr Mother-Country Stephen', given to him by detractors who felt that he had come to hold too much power during his three decades in office (1813–47). His attitude towards the colonies was paternalistic, again in the spirit of seeing the wider world as an extension of the private house: justifying his decision to draft legislation granting independence to Canada while keeping other colonies under British government, he argued that '[w]e emancipate our grown-up sons but keep our unmarried daughters, and our children who may chance to be rickety, in domestic bonds'.[30] He argued that Britain needed to retain control over certain colonies in order to ensure the liberation of slaves, and like his father he wanted to use English colonial power to promote Christianity, convinced that 'he who should induce any heathen people to adopt the mere ceremonial of the Church . . . and to recognise the authority of its Divine head would confer on them a blessing exceeding all which mere philanthropy has ever accomplished.'[31]

Sir James embodied the Clapham Sect: indeed he cemented the group by marrying Jane Venn, granddaughter, daughter and sister of the three famous Venns. His Clapham work ethic was most famously exemplified in his drafting the Act for abolishing slavery in one sitting over the course of one weekend, breaking the Sabbath on one of only two occasions in his life.[32] He embodied middle-class seriousness and establishment values, working as a lawyer and colonial administrator for thirty-four years and then as a Professor of Modern History at Cambridge. His reverence for Venn and Clapham is clear. After buying copies of Venn's *Life* and *Complete Duty,* he wrote to his wife, 'Do you know that I never think of the writer of these books without a sort of awe to think that I am his grandson-in-law? He was a wondrous man.'[33] As well as writing the collective biography of the Clapham Sect in *Essays in Ecclesiastical Biography,* he cherished his connections with William Wilberforce, Henry Thornton, Thomas Bowdler, Thomas Macaulay, Thomas Babington and Thomas Gisborne.[34]

Sir James put Venn's prescriptions for household order into practice, too. He gave priority to the education of his three sons, Herbert, Fitzjames and Leslie, moving house (first to Brighton then to Eton) for the sake of their education, while his daughter Caroline Emelia was educated by a governess: a clear acceptance of the gender divide set out by Venn. Although his letters to his wife are amiable and his passing references to her as his amanuensis suggest that she had a lively engagement with his ideas, it is also clear that her role was to support him and create a safe domestic space for him to withdraw into.[35] Caroline Emelia Stephen gives insight to his gender values when describing his admiration for his sister-in-law Emelia Venn:

I think my aunt as nearly as possible fulfilled my father's ideal of the life most to be desired for a woman – combining many of the avocations of a Sister of Charity with the brightest domestic happiness, and a rare fullness of interest in the affairs of those she loved, and in the larger concerns of the outer world.[36]

Clapham continued: Fitzjames Stephen

One of Sir James's sons, Fitzjames, the lawyer and judge who shaped the Indian legal system, continued in the Clapham tradition of middle-class values, colonialism, paternalism and patriarchy, holding fast to these even as he drifted from Christianity in matters of faith: as James Colaiaco notes, he 'began as an Evangelical, grew to accept the views of the liberal Broad Church and, though retaining his belief in God and a future life, gradually lost faith in Christianity.'[37] Fitzjames asserted Christian views even as he began to engage with liberal ideas and he attended church until he was in his early forties. This meant that unlike Virginia and her siblings, Fitzjames's children, including Dorothea and Rosamond, were brought up as Christians. Like Sir James, Fitzjames had married into a clergy family: his wife Mary was the daughter of John William Cunningham, editor of the *Christian Observer,* who encouraged him in religious journalism, an interest that he pursued throughout his life, becoming increasingly controversial over the years.[38]

Fitzjames's adherence to the culture and mores of Christianity remained strong because he saw them as integral to his profession as a lawyer. Fitzjames regarded the law as a vocation: Sir James had wanted him to become ordained but Fitzjames considered this in a long manuscript in which he concluded that he could serve God as a lawyer better than as a priest. As Christopher Tolley notes, the method of determining life choices through a personal journal was itself in the evangelical tradition of self-reflection;[39] so his manuscript both continued and subverted the practices of his upbringing.

Fitzjames's vocational approach to the law was founded on a belief that he was upholding all that was right and true, and that these values rested in the joint authority of the church and the state. Challenging John Stuart Mill's *On Liberty* in a series of articles in the *Pall Mall Gazette* (published shortly afterwards as *Liberty, Equality, Fraternity*), Fitzjames argued that religious values should continue to dictate morals and to inform the law. In a healthy society, he argues, church and state should work in the same direction, for the 'spiritual and temporal powers differ not in the province in which they rule, but in the sanctions by which they rule it.'[40] The doctrines of salvation and damnation therefore continued to play an important role for him: while the state had the penalties of the courts, the church had punishment or reward in the afterlife. It is no coincidence that Fitzjames pictured the final judgement as a courtroom:

> I know not what can be a greater infringement of [Mill's] theory of liberty, a more complete and formal contradiction to it, than the doctrine that there is a court and a judge in which, and before whom, every man must give an account of every work done in the body, whether self-regarding or not.[41]

Although Fitzjames came to question the doctrine of eternal damnation and acknowledged that the concept of Judgment Day was open to debate,[42] he clung to a belief that the *possibility* of punishment after death should be enough to coerce people into keeping society's moral and religious codes.

One of the main reasons why Fitzjames maintained his nominal Christianity for so long was a fear that the loss of religion would cause a decline in values.[43] As Leslie Stephen commented, 'to destroy the old faith was still for him to destroy the great impulse to a noble life'.[44] It was an opinion that Leslie Stephen had sympathy with, having vowed to 'live and die like a gentleman' on renouncing his Holy Orders. Like fellow-doubter Matthew Arnold, Fitzjames feared that a rejection of religion would lead to anarchy, and both argued vigorously against disestablishment.[45] In the last years of his life, however, Fitzjames came to the conclusion that the law must replace religion. Pointedly using religious language, he wrote that

> the criminal law may be described with truth as an expression of the second table of the Ten Commandments . . . I think that there never was more urgent necessity than there is now for the preaching of such a sermon in the most emphatic tones.[46]

In other words, the power that had been vested in religion had now passed to the law.

The issue on which Fitzjames was most conservative (and which elicited his most trenchant criticism of Mill) was that of equality between the sexes. Asserting the supreme importance of 'the difference of age and sex', he reminds the reader that it was not for nothing that 'the best part of the human race' refers to God as Father.[47] He strongly defends marriage as an institution: speaking as a lawyer, but also tacitly invoking the marriage service from *The Book of Common Prayer*, he insists that it is the means by which society is ordered and passions are contained.[48] Likewise, he implicitly invokes the biblical injunction that wives should be subject to their husbands (Ephesians 5:22–4), to say that wives should defer to their husbands in cases of differences in opinion and that the best-regulated homes are ones in which the father is in absolute control.[49] Patriarchy clearly survived even as its religious foundations were crumbling.

Challenging the family script

We can therefore see that the culture of middle-class patriarchy that Woolf critiqued in her feminist essays was strongly influenced by Evangelical Christianity in general, and by the Clapham Sect and members of her own family in particular. Successive generations of male ancestors had played an integral part in developing the establishment: as public figures, they shaped the patriarchal, imperialistic, nationalist political climate that she consistently attacked; as patriarchs within the private home, they endorsed a domestic hierarchy underpinned by Christian ideologies. When Woolf attacked the values of the public world and the private house in *A Room of One's Own* and *Three Guineas*, therefore, she studied her own extended family very closely as a model.

Three Guineas is a pointed riposte to the men of Clapham. The essay is presented as a reply to a letter from a middle-class man who has sought her help in defending culture and intellectual liberty and preventing war. Her correspondent's career path (*3G* 89) is a model of Clapham life: he is a lawyer, like James, Sir James and Fitzjames, and as Thoby was expected to be; he exemplifies the Protestant work ethic, devoting himself to serious causes rather than enjoyment; he is a family man and enjoys the rewards of Providence: 'your prosperity – wife, children, house – has been deserved'. He has been educated at public school and university like the Stephens (and Woolf invokes the master of the family college Trinity Hall as a supporter of patriarchal values (*3G* 114)). It is significant that the middle-class professions that Woolf sees as forming a conglomeration to dominate public life, the law, the church, politics and the universities, were represented in her family (only the financial sector was not directly represented by the Stephens, though Woolf makes it clear that economics underpins them all). There is also a strongly personal dimension to the class of 'educated men's daughters' with which she identifies herself: the middle-class women who were denied the privileges their brothers enjoyed, often forced to make sacrifices to fund their brothers' education. Indeed, Woolf's definition of the term in her second footnote pinpoints the personal nature of this class to include women 'whose fathers have been educated at public schools and universities' (*3G* 218). Even the generic procession of middle-class men whom she watches askance, 'great-grandfathers, grandfathers, fathers, uncles' (*3G* 142), can be seen to have a familial relevance.

Three Guineas also makes a specific riposte to the writings of her forebears and their associates. Although it is informed by a vast range of reading and research, there are pointed references to works by members of the Clapham Sect that serve to situate that group as influential figures in a patriarchal culture that excluded women.

Sir James's *Essays in Ecclesiastical Biography* is a particularly significant intertext. Woolf first read this work at the age of 15, precisely at the age when she began to write her essays on Christianity, women, and her family (*D3* 271). Leslie Stephen brought the text to her attention, for she noted in her journal that 'father has given me Essays in Ecclesiastical Biography, which will do for me for some time' (*PA* 42). Since Leslie Stephen used to urge her to read books thoroughly and would question her on them,[50] she probably read this work in depth, but she would also have imbibed the healthy scepticism with which her father annotated the text, including remarks like 'hardly' and 'Oh! Oh!' and a cartoon on the flyleaf of a monkey riding a goat.

Sir James's essays construct a history through the exemplary lives of prominent men, many of whom are insiders to Cambridge, the legal profession and the government. Women are barely mentioned, except as distractions from seriousness. Woolf presents her alternative history of Sir James's culture as one that excluded and suppressed women. She consistently cuts down Sir James's heroes by denouncing them as misogynists. There is John Bowdler, whom Sir James had described in glowing terms ('The interior life of John Bowdler, if it could be faithfully written, would be a record which none could read without reverence, and few without self-reproach'[51]) but whom Woolf uses as an example of the educated man who forces his daughter to 'bolster' up the system and conform to patriarchal ideologies, in order to get married. Woolf quotes Bowdler's letter 'addressed to a young lady for whom he had a great regard a short time before her marriage', in which he insists on avoidance of 'anything which has the *least tendency* to indelicacy or indecorum'; in other words, stifling any wish to criticise patriarchal society (*3G* 228, n34).

Sir James hailed Thomas Gisborne for 'contribut[ing] largely to the formation of the national mind on subjects of the highest importance to the national character',[52] but Woolf incorporates him into a different historical narrative as a patriarch who was influential in determining the position of women. Quoting from his advice on teaching women the art of religious devotion in *The Duties of the Female Sex,* Woolf construes that he saw that 'the female sex was to be "taught habitually to contemplate in the works of creation, the power and wisdom and the goodness," not so much of the Deity, but of Mr Gisborne.' Woolf continues, with a satirical compound reference to Sir James's *Essays* and her father's famous work, the *Dictionary of National Biography*: 'And from that we were led to conclude that a biography of the Deity would resolve itself into a Dictionary of Clerical Biography' (*3G* 224, n20).

Woolf therefore argues that patriarchy has constructed its own notion of God to support its own power, arguing that unwritten laws of behaviour that had been thought of as 'natural' or 'God-given', can now be seen to be produced and reproduced by those in power: 'it is beginning to be agreed that they were not laid down by "God", who is now very generally held to be a conception, of patriarchal origin, valid only for certain races, at certain stages and times' (*3G* 250, n42). This point is a mature articulation of the argument that the young Virginia had made about the idea of God being 'in a process of change' in the essay she wrote at around the time she read Sir James's *Essays*.

Woolf critiques the Evangelicals' use of the Bible for the same reason. They had hailed it as the word of God: it was an important part of Venn's teaching in *The Complete Duty of Man*; James Stephen and the Venns had promoted it internationally through the Bible Society; and Sir James had commended Evangelicals as 'restorers' of the faith for their emphasis on the importance of Scripture.[53] Woolf, by contrast, argues that these evangelical patriarchs have used the Bible to support their views and to subjugate women: she argues that 'the fact that Mr Gisborne and his like – a numerous band – base their educational theories upon the teaching of St Paul' indicates that they want to bring up their daughters to worship men, not God (*3G* 224, n20). Woolf particularly attacks St Paul as an influence on the subjugation of women. She blames his epistles to Titus and Corinthians – which she sees as expressions of his own pathological misogyny – for her society's hypocritical emphasis on female chastity in the face of sexual double standards where male lust was not condemned. She shows how patriarchy has been happy to adopt his notion of chastity to enforce the subjugation of women in society, especially in marriage and in affirming the separate spheres: 'Such a conception when supported by the Angels, nature, law, custom and the Church, and enforced by a sex with a strong personal interest to enforce it, and the economic means, was of undoubted power' (*3G* 236, n38). Woolf therefore reduces biblical authority both to an ideology and to an expression of pathological male psychology.

Woolf sees the evangelical construction of chastity not as a virtue but as fear and misogyny. She had satirised this attitude earlier in the sex-change scene in *Orlando,* where she presents a masque, in which the ladies of Purity, Chastity and Modesty contest with the trumpets of Truth to dramatise how the narrator struggles with the dilemma of speaking truthfully about matters deemed to be offensive. The narrator is a parody of the nineteenth-century biographer, but the stand-off can be read more specifically as an allusion to Sir James's apostrophe to Henry Thornton's honesty: 'Truth, the foe of falsehood – truth, the antagonist of error – and truth, the exorcist of ambiguity – was the object of his supreme homage.'[54] The ladies' attempt to throw a veil over Orlando, can be read as an allusion to Sir James's discomfort at the youthful passions of the otherwise impeccable Henry Martyn:

> The writer of his Life, embarrassed at the task of reconciling such an episode to the gravity befitting a hero so majestic, and a biography so solemn, has concealed this passage of his story beneath a veil at once transparent enough to excite, and impervious enough to baffle, curiosity.[55]

However, although Woolf satirises particular patriarchs in *Three Guineas* (St Paul, Sir James, Bowdler and Gisborne), she does not discredit evangelical values completely: instead, she co-opts these views to propose the moral argument that women should resist patriarchy by practising the virtues of poverty, chastity, derision and freedom from unreal loyalties. She recasts chastity not as marker of sexual behaviour (itself provoked by male lasciviousness) but as an attitude of mind or 'mental chastity' (*3G* 163) by which women can distance themselves from patriarchal attitudes and expectations.

Such resistance is in tune with the turning-away from the ways of the world that marked Clapham from the start. As Henry Venn had argued, 'to preserve chastity of mind, is a fruit of faith in Christ, and a part of self-denial indispensably required from all Christians'.[56] The concept of the Outsiders' Society can therefore be seen as a re-appropriation of Venn's principles, later practised by James Stephen in his resistance of the slave-owning culture.

Woolf's definition of the virtue of poverty can similarly be seen as a reappropriation of the ideas of her Clapham ancestors. In *Slavery Delineated*, James Stephen had analysed the ways in which ordinary citizens were bound into a culture that supported slavery simply by being part of the economic system. Just over a century later, Woolf showed how women's economic dependence upon men locked them into a system that supported war, meaning that they were 'consciously and unconsciously in favour of war' (*3G* 121). She urges women to step outside the system and criticise it by adopting an attitude of poverty and resisting the patriarchal shilling. Just as James Stephen resigned from Parliament in order to pursue his campaign against slavery, so Woolf urges women to resist patriarchal politics from the outside.

However, Woolf crucially reconfigures anti-slavery discourse by showing that women have been enslaved and disenfranchised by patriarchy. She defines slavery as financial dependence on men and points out that women, like slaves, were denied citizenship:

> 'Our' country ... throughout the greater part of its history has treated me as a slave; it has denied me education or any share in its possessions. 'Our' country still ceases to be mine if I marry a foreigner. (*3G* 185)

The solution, however, is not for women to bow to paternalistic attitudes and accept solutions provided for them by patriarchy (as James, Sir James and Fitzjames had done with the colonies), but rather, that women should declare themselves 'outsiders' to the establishment and to the nation as a whole: '"For," the outsider will say, "in fact, as a woman, I have no country. As a woman I want no country. As a woman my country is the whole world"' (ibid.).

This famous statement takes and recasts a notion of world citizenship, which Sir James had applied to the hymn writer Isaac Watts: 'As a citizen of the world, he called on earth and heaven to stay the plagues of slavery and the slave-trade, and advocated the independence of America, with such ardour as to sacrifice to it his own.'[57]

Woolf's representation of women as the slaves of patriarchy therefore arises out of her critique of her ancestors and their values. It exposes the hypocrisy of their attempts to free one part of the human race while at the same time taking a paternalistic approach to the rest of the world, also showing that attitudes to world politics redound upon the private house. Simultaneously, however, she harnesses their rhetoric to promote a new cause: the liberation of women.

Woolf was often satirical about her family's history of authorship: she commented that the 'Stephen family seems to think no controversy complete without their printed opinion. A wonderful race!' (*L1* 206), and yet she herself continued in that tradition with her polemical essays. The Clapham Sect heritage therefore was highly ambivalent for Woolf: it epitomised many of the values she pitted herself against, as well as ones that influenced her. She was part of a milieu in which writing was a way of life, as well as one that had established a family script that she would challenge.

The drift from faith

The establishment figures and polemic writers of the Clapham Sect presented Woolf with relatively easy targets for criticism, but the gradual retreat of faith in later generations of her family took place in a way that left more subtle and complex traces of belief and cultural practice that would prove much harder to eradicate. The bedrock of Evangelical faith was beginning to crumble even during Sir James's lifetime. *Essays in Ecclesiastical Biography* ended with a controversial chapter that expressed doubts about eternal damnation and this direct refutation of the theology of Henry Venn senior earned him a rebuke from Henry Venn the younger and brought him close to losing his Chair in History at Cambridge. (He only kept his tenure by claiming that a historian should not be expected to be an expert in theology: F. D. Maurice lost his Chair in Theology for disputing eternal damnation four years later, as he was deemed to be at risk of misleading young minds.) Sir James also engaged in religious debates with his correspondents, including Thomas Carlyle, who provoked him by suggesting that their views were not dissimilar.

Sir James was also accused of having a family life that did not match his public Evangelical pronouncements and there was some truth in this. Although he gave his children an approved education (Fitzjames and Leslie attended a school in Brighton run by Rev. Benjamin Guest recommended by Jane Stephen's cousin Henry

Venn Elliott, where according to Leslie there was 'rather an excess of evangelical theology'),[58] none of them continued in the faith. Herbert was already questioning biblical truth by the time of his premature death at twenty-hour and Fitzjames asked challenging questions from childhood onwards, surprisingly earning his mother's approval for his precociousness.[59] Leslie's retreat from religion occurred later in life, of course, and he became as prominent a spokesperson for agnosticism as his family had been for Anglicanism. Caroline Emelia remained a person of faith but renounced Anglicanism to become a leading figure in modern Quakerism.

This detachment from the tenets of faith actually served to reinforce the family's evangelical identity as a matter of culture rather than belief. As Leslie Stephen noted,

> The line between saints and sinners with the Church and the world was not so deeply drawn as in some cases. We felt, in a vague way, that we were, somehow, not quite as other people, and yet I do not think that we could be called Pharisees.

The family did not go to the theatre or to balls, he says, out of custom rather than due to moral objections.[60] Likewise, Caroline Emelia notes that she was not debarred from parties and balls but that her parents were happy that she was not interested in them.[61] Here, perhaps, lie the origins of Woolf's 'puritan streak' and her dislike of dress and a focus on appearance (*MB* 68).

Christian culture influenced the family in subtler ways, too. Family prayers had established a practice of recitation that entailed hearing scripture read aloud, savouring the spoken word and committing words to memory. While Sir James continued this practice, Jane Stephen encouraged her children to love memorising and reciting literature. Leslie Stephen recalls this as a key memory of his childhood: 'she could repeat Cowper and Wordsworth and Campbell and Scott, and her children learned "The Merriness of England" and "The Death of Marmion" from her lips almost before they could read for themselves'. He adds that her choice of reading material showed that she had accepted her family's religious opinions in 'a comparably mild form'.[62] The practice may have equipped Leslie for taking Chapel services during his brief time as a minister, but literary recitation remained a lifelong habit that he shared with his own children. Some of his recitations even took on a semi-liturgical pattern, such as his habit of reciting Milton's *Ode on the Morning of Christ's Nativity* at Christmas. Stephen's recitations were delivered in such a heartfelt way that Woolf felt he was passing on 'what he himself felt and knew', so that his favourite poems were imbued with his 'teaching and belief'.[63] Literature therefore took the place of the Bible in Woolf's upbringing.

Leslie Stephen's departure from faith can be read as a reaction-formation against his Evangelical upbringing. Like Fitzjames, who used the practice of journaling to decide against ordination, Leslie used *The Mausoleum Book* as a spiritual autobiography, in which his conversion experience was his discovery of Comte and rejection of the notion of biblical truth. Stephen writes that Comte convinced him 'among other things that Noah's flood was a fiction (or rather convinced me that I had never believed in it) and that it was wrong for me to read the story as if it were a sacred truth.'[64] Stephen is here taking one side in a controversy that Norman Vance has described as being based on an 'artificial polarity: either the bible was literally true or it was completely untrue. No scope was allowed for intermediate possibilities.'[65] Yet, Stephen's statement can be read as an ironic appropriation of the language of Evangelical Christianity: because truth was of great importance to the Evangelicals, as we have seen, Stephen castigates them for dealing in falsehoods.

Comte's ideas were built on the principles of primitive Catholicism, and Stephen's adoption of these can be seen as a specific reaction against his father's Protestant prejudices (Sir James dismissed 'Popery' as a mixture of Christianity and 'idolatry, in which the carnal life expands itself with greatest force').[66] This was a crucial turn: where the family theology had emphasised the depravity of human nature and the need for grace, Comte encouraged the celebration of human goodness. Comte's religion of humanity made saints of ordinary people and saw sanctity in ordinary relationships. This partly helped Stephen resolve the dilemma that a loss of faith might lead to a loss of values, as can be seen in his essay 'Forgotten Benefactors', where he seeks to extract an ethical code from Christianity that does not rely on the person of its founder or on superstition, but on a body of people acting ethically. Christianity succeeded, he argues,

> so far as it corresponded to the better instincts of great masses of men, struggling blindly and through many errors to discover rules of conduct and modes of conceiving the universe more congenial than the old to their better nature.[67]

All religions are part of the 'advance of ethical ideas', he argues, and this gives 'solid ground for the hopes of humanity'.[68]

Stephen's Comtean ethics exalted women as moral beings, cementing the separate-spheres ideology by casting woman as the Angel in the House. Stephen admires people who acted with kindness and self-sacrifice:

> such persons appear to be formed by nature for ministering angels, and move among us unconscious of their claims to our devotion, and bringing light into darkness by their simple presence with as little thought that they deserve our gratitude as that they ought to emerge from obscurity.

Every religion has its saints, he says, 'but that man is unfortunate who has not a saint of his own'.[69] For Leslie, this saint was Julia Stephen: he hailed her as such in the *Mausoleum Book* and elided her with the Madonna.[70] While Stephen had distanced himself from his family faith, then, he had endorsed and actually enhanced the role of womanhood found in Evangelical Christianity. This provided Woolf with an even more complex image that she would resist throughout her life, as we will explore in Chapter 6.

Julia Stephen's departure from Christianity was more guarded than her husband's, and she too sought to preserve its ethical values as a way of life. As Woolf recalls in 'A Sketch of the Past', her change of heart was more sudden than Leslie's, dating almost certainly from the tragic death of her first husband; it caused a breach with her family, for it grieved her religious mother. Yet Woolf also remembers Julia Stephen continuing to read the Bible, strangely speculating that this might have provided her with a link with her late husband, whom the young Virginia imagined to have been a clergyman (*MB* 82). In her essay 'Agnostic Women', Julia held back from identifying herself as one, again through fear of social unrest: 'I know no such pariahs'. And it was she who owned a signed copy of Patmore's *The Angel in the House* that was ultimately inherited by Woolf. Clearly, then, Woolf was brought up in a home where the social prescriptions, customs and practices of Evangelical Christianity were deeply ingrained, despite her parents' scepticism.

Clapham reconfigured: Caroline Emelia Stephen

The last figure we will consider here was also the most significant: Caroline Emelia Stephen was a mentor, a confidante and a spiritual influence for Woolf, and she played a key role in mediating the

Clapham tradition to her. Caroline Emelia was introduced to Quakerism by Leslie Stephen's first wife Minny and found it a blissful alternative to church. She preferred silence to the word-laden liturgy and loved the personal engagement with God as an alternative to the intercession of the male clergy. She also carved out an alternative lifestyle: having dutifully cared for her parents until their deaths, she went on to establish herself as a single woman living a celibate, monastic life in The Porch in Cambridge. She was committed to pacifist causes and she established Metropolitan Society for Befriending Young Servants with her cousin Sarah Stephen.

Jane Marcus, in her seminal study of Caroline Emelia's influence, suggests that she offered Woolf an alternative inheritance to patriarchy,[71] but her position is more ambiguous than this because her shift away from Evangelical Christianity was measured and incremental and her relationship to patriarchy was complex. Caroline Emelia contributed to the revival of Quakerism at the turn of the century and helped to define its identity and practices at the time, but significantly she defined her faith as 'a Christian profession' and aligned it with the range of Nonconformist denominations that were active at the time.[72] Although she critiqued the Evangelicals' emphasis on the Bible as the sole source of divine inspiration, her writing is peppered with biblical allusions and the crucifixion is central to her thinking. One reason for her continued interest in Evangelical Christianity was a particular closeness to her father: as her niece Katharine Stephen noted, she had 'much natural sympathy' with Sir James and 'his influence over her was very powerful'.[73] Furthermore, she did not distance herself from patriarchal institutions as radically as has been suggested, for she had a lively interest in Cambridge University, hosting meetings for male and female Quaker students at The Porch and giving lectures at women's colleges.

Woolf's reaction to her aunt was consequently ambivalent. Woolf often disparaged her, nicknaming her 'the nun', the 'Quaker' and even the 'quacking Quaker' and describing her as 'soporific, and leisurely to an excess and my desire begins to be to blow her up with gunpowder and see what would happen' (*L*1 144) (an ironically violent image to use for a pacifist, though perhaps explained by Virginia's youth at the time of writing). On the other hand, there is evidence of great warmth and affection, for Woolf enjoyed conversing with her aunt for eight or nine hours at a time and found her 'charming and wise and humane' (*L*1 230). This attitude has the hallmarks of the ambivalence that Marion Dell has detected in Woolf's reaction to many of her female precursors,[74] but an important reason for Woolf's reaction in this case was her perception that Caroline Emelia was too closely implicated in the Victorian world of the Clapham Sect. Marcus notes in passing that Woolf was concerned about 'the work of female family as collaboration' with patriarchy,[75] and this can be seen in Woolf's disparaging comments on her aunt's edition of Sir James's *Letters* (1906): 'the Quaker has a well worn semi religious vocabulary; left her by the late Sir James, I think' (*L1* 235).

Woolf did not adopt Caroline Emelia Stephen as a positive model for a radical rejection of patriarchal religious values, but rather saw her as someone who was engaged with a shared problem of how to negotiate such values. Kathleen Heininge hints at the commonality between them when she argues that 'the family alignments and influences, the biographical details, the works of both women, and the historical moment combine to create a compelling argument that Woolf's spirituality was deeply influenced by her Quaker aunt'.[76]

Heininge places Woolf and Caroline Emelia in the same 'historical moment': despite being born almost half a century after her aunt, Woolf saw herself as being shaped by the same constraints. Heininge adds that they shared the same educational background for the 'urge to align truth and mysticism, to find such truth without the paradigm of authority under which they were both educated, was powerful for both women.'[77] The educational background was, of course, a compromised one, for both women were home-schooled while their brothers went to public school and Cambridge: they were both therefore 'educated men's daughters' (and educated men's sisters).

This idea comes more clearly into focus when we appreciate that, although members of different generations, Woolf and Caroline Emelia Stephen were also contemporaries. Their lifetimes overlapped by twenty-seven years, from Woolf's birth in 1882 to Caroline Emelia's death in 1909: years that were particularly formative for Woolf. Although Caroline Emelia was somewhat distanced from Leslie and his family when Woolf was born,[78] she paid two memorable visits to the family holidaying in St Ives in 1888 and 1889 and shared Woolf's fascination with the Godrevy lighthouse. Woolf's mature relationship with her aunt began a decade later when Vanessa and Virginia visited her at The Porch in 1898 and again in 1902. Significantly, Woolf stayed with Caroline Emelia in the autumn of 1904 while recovering from her breakdown following Leslie Stephen's death, during which time her aunt gave her a safe space and a peaceful environment and encouraged her as a writer. It is appropriate that Woolf was staying with her aunt when one of her first articles appeared in print: a piece on the Brontës in the clergy journal, *The Guardian*. Woolf visited her aunt frequently after this, and she and Adrian briefly moved in with her after Vanessa's marriage. Woolf was one of very few people to attend Caroline Emelia's funeral and if economic generosity can be taken as a measure of affection, Woolf's inheritance of £2,500 from her aunt (in contrast to bequests of just £100 each for Vanessa and Adrian), suggests particular closeness. Woolf acknowledges Caroline Emelia in the aunt's bequest in *A Room of One's Own* (*Room* 29–30).

The relationship between Woolf and Caroline Emelia can therefore be read in terms of the concept of the transpersonal: a horizontal relationship of writers working side-by-side rather than a vertical or hierarchical one of inheritance. It is a model of intellectuals working collaboratively and in dialogue, so that similarities between their works are read in terms of synergy and correspondence rather than through linear or hierarchical dynamics of influence.[79] This can be seen through a study of Caroline Emelia's writings during the period of her relationship with Woolf.

A starting point for this exploration is Caroline Emelia Stephen's *Quaker Strongholds* (1890) which, though it pre-dates their close relationship, is significant because she gave it to Virginia as a present during her first visit to The Porch in 1898. The book gives evidence of how Caroline Emelia defined her religious views through a critique of her evangelical background. The task she sets is to liberate the faith from what the church had made it. So, she argues: 'Are there not many, in these days especially, who would willingly listen to the Christianity of Christ himself, could they but find it disentangled from the enormously "developed" Christianity of the dominant churches?'[80]

There are echoes of this idea in *The Voyage Out,* in the scene where Rachel attends a church service and discovers that she does not believe. As Heininge has noted, there are parallels between this scene and Caroline Emelia's account of her own conversion on attending a Quaker meeting, but it is significant that, although Woolf is critical of the minister she nonetheless shows the appeal of 'the sad and beautiful figure of Christ' (*VO* 263). When Woolf criticised the clergy for excluding women from public life and for aggrandising war in *Three Guineas,* she also argued that they were being anti-Christian in doing so, for they were appealing not to the 'mind of the founder' but to the 'mind of the church' (*3G* 197). Both writers, therefore, argue that the established church had constructed Christianity as a religion that suppressed women, and both sought to liberate Christ's teachings from what the church had made of them.

While Woolf is unlikely to have read *Quaker Strongholds* until a few years after its publication, she had first-hand knowledge of the compilation of the letters of Sir James Stephen, as Caroline Emelia was bringing the project to its completion during the time of Virginia's formative visits between 1904 and 1906. Significantly, Stephen drew Woolf into a parallel project by providing her with materials for the sketch of Leslie Stephen for Maitland: both works were published in 1906. Both projects involved producing private, personal views of their fathers as a counterbalance to well-known conventional, public images. In editing Sir James's letters forty-seven years after his death, Caroline Emelia memorialised him and sought common ground with him. In doing so, she claimed her father an antecedent for her Quakerism. She emphasises his pacifism, claiming that 'no Quaker could entertain a more intense horror of war',[81] citing the example of his distaste on visiting the Waterloo battle-site with his sons but downplaying his comments that the Crimean War may have been a necessary evil. In the latter part of the volume, Caroline Emelia uses his letters on religious debates from his years in Cambridge to argue that his views were relevant to the present time of religious change, thus preserving her father as a contemporary.

As Tolley has argued, this volume reflects the Clapham Sect's interest in autobiography, biography and collective biography, a trait that would continue into Bloomsbury. In encouraging Woolf to write her piece for Maitland, Caroline Emelia drew Woolf into the Clapham tradition of domestic biography, helping her to produce a daughter's-eye view showing the private side of a public literary figure. Like Caroline Emelia, Woolf's memoir seeks to establish the contemporaneity of her father, noting the feeling that he seemed to be 'not much older than we were'; and sharing common ground, not of religious faith but of their shared love of books and recitation.[82]

Caroline Emelia's later works – *Light Arising* (1908) and the posthumously published selection of essays *The Vision of Faith and Other Writings* (1911) – showed a desire to free herself spiritually by defining her own faith position clearly and with confidence in the context of rapidly changing attitudes to religion. In *Light Arising*, she wrote about a 'sense of absolute freedom in the search for truth; freedom being, as I suppose we shall all agree, not lawlessness, but the absence of external restraint, a state of being controlled only from within'.[83] In *The Vision of Faith* she notes that the 'flood of free thought' had made it impossible to 'formulate opinions' about higher truths that are both 'correct and adequate', and continues:

> I suppose this is a mild form of agnosticism, but I don't think it is any the worse for that. Agnosticism with mystery at the heart of it seems another description of the 'rational mysticism' which is my favourite expression of my own ground.[84]

It is crucial to note that her thought is both rational and mystical, for *The Vision of Faith* is a dialogue with agnostics, implicitly with Leslie and Fitzjames. Jane Marcus has described mysticism as a subversive feminist discourse, 'the purest religious concept' that 'allows access to the community of saints without the dogmas and disciplines of organized religion' and a 'refuge of silence'.[85] However, Caroline Emelia did not seek escape and refuge but she wrestled with dogma, and she did not dispense with words but used them wisely, as Woolf wrote in her obituary: 'She was one of the few to whom the gift of expression is given together with the need of it, and in addition to a wonderful command of language she had a scrupulous wish to use to accurately' (*E1* 268). Woolf, too, we should note, wrote very eloquently about silence.

Caroline Emelia wrestled particularly with the concepts of salvation and damnation, which had been used for generations to enforce compliance. She challenged such views by arguing that unbelievers who have lived a good life are worthy of salvation. Clearly this has a personal dimension: *The Vision of Faith* was written after her brothers had died, and she sought to reconcile her faith with their doubts, making a sensitive and painstaking effort to retain a belief in salvation without condemning her loved ones. Caroline Emelia found Dante particularly helpful in her thinking here. She had discovered him through the religious culture popular at the time, noting that she was reading Dante 'like everyone else'. She records feeling 'deeply edified' by his work, being left with 'a more distinct impression of the nature of salvation through this noble picture of it . . . It stays with me like a map of eternal things and a strong reinforcement of trust.'[86] Caroline Emelia gave Woolf a copy of *The Divine Comedy* in 1898 and, although the pristine state of this copy in Woolf's library at Washington State University suggests that she made little use of this particular edition, we do know from Woolf's diaries, and from annotations in her other editions of Dante, that she wrestled with *The Divine Comedy* throughout her life, reading it in English, translating it from the Italian, and quoting it in both *The Waves* and *The Years*. In *The Waves* in particular, that 'mystic', 'spiritual' book (*D3* 114), Woolf explored 'lives together', an early instance of that 'new religion' that binds people together ensuring continuance of the self in the collective being of a group while also having resonances with the Christian narrative through the Edenic childhood garden, presided over by a woman writing; and the Christlike Percival who has his last supper and whom Bernard continues to look on, in apocalyptic terms, as a 'judge'.

From the Clapham Sect to a 'new religion'

We cannot know what Woolf and Caroline Emelia Stephen discussed during their lengthy conversations, but in tracing their relationship through the books they wrote and the books they shared, we can see that they embarked on a shared journey of detaching themselves from the evangelical values that had continued to permeate English society. Woolf's crucial argument in the conclusion of *Three Guineas* can now be read in part as a tribute to her aunt:

> By criticizing religion [the daughters of educated men] would attempt to free the religious spirit from its present servitude and would help, if need be, to create a new religion based it might well be upon the New Testament, but, it might well be, very different from the religion now erected upon that basis. (*3G* 189)

The ideology that continued to hold Christianity in thrall was the middle-class, Evangelical heritage of the Stephen family, whereas the 'new religion' that Woolf proposes has many of the hallmarks of the Quakerism of Caroline Emelia Stephen. Both Woolf and Stephen were therefore reaching towards a 'new religion', a form of thought and spirituality that was more conducive to women than the established church could offer.

Virginia Woolf and Christian culture

The Christian culture which Woolf experienced first-hand, and against which she reacted, was therefore essentially evangelical in nature. Its doctrines had influenced ideologies of Empire and nation, shaping the public schools, universities, legal system and Parliament itself. *Three Guineas* is Woolf's most explicit riposte to these values and, as we have seen, she shows herself to be particularly well informed about the theological writings that had contributed to it, to the extent of critiquing and appropriating them for her feminist purposes. *Three Guineas* also examines how public values are reflected in the private home – a theme she also pursues in *A Room of One's Own* and 'Professions for Women' – and again evangelical ideas are among her most prominent targets.

However, this account of Woolf's heritage also reveals some more subtle ways in which the customs and attitudes of Evangelical Christianity had influenced her practices as a writer. The home was an important locus for religious practice for the Clapham Sect – it became even more so for Caroline Emelia Stephen – and this would inform Woolf's emphasis on the need of a room of one's own. Woolf's practice of reciting literature had derived from the practice of family prayers. She kept a diary throughout her life – a derivation of the evangelical practice of keeping a spiritual journal – and this came to fruition in the final years of her life when she collected her memoirs and reflected on her life in 'A Sketch of the Past'. Woolf continued the Clapham tradition of domestic biography by memorialising family and friends in her novels: *The Waves* in particular, with its emphasis on 'lives together', echoes the principle of the collective biography. Finally, however, Woolf's relationship with Caroline Emelia Stephen shows the importance of women to her spiritual experience, for she was one of several important female influences: we will explore more of these in the next chapter.

Notes

1. McIntire, 'Notes Toward Thinking the Sacred', p. 1.
2. Lee, *Virginia Woolf*, p. 56.
3. Leslie Stephen, *Life of Fitzjames*, p. 33.
4. In addition to the figures discussed in this chapter, the family included religious novelists George Stephen (*A Jesuit at Oxford*) and Sarah Stephen (*Passages from the Life of a Daughter at Home*) and hymn-writer Charlotte Elliott.
5. Annan, *Leslie Stephen*, p. 10.
6. Sir James is often credited with coining the term: see, for example, Kupar, *Incest and Influence*, p. 137. However, the title was an editorial invention and Sir James was embarrassed by it for its implications of dissension (Tolley, *Domestic Biography*, p. 3).

7. *MB* 78–9. Leslie Stephen recounts the anecdote about his father's dislike of mirrors and his liking for cigars in the *Life of Fitzjames,* pp. 51 and 61.
8. Leslie Stephen, *Life of Fitzjames,* p. 34.
9. Venn, *Complete Duty,* pp. xii–xiii. As Bradley notes, the Evangelical revival was 'a reaction against the worldliness and complacency of eighteenth-century England', specifically against the 'prevailing attitude towards religion and morality' (*Call to Seriousness,* p. 19).
10. See Bradley, *Call to Seriousness,* pp. 148–9 for an overview of these conduct books.
11. Bradley notes that Evangelicals, though loyal members of the Church of England, preferred to exercise ministry outside the church or, if they were clergy, to be deeply critical of their colleagues (p. 57).
12. Leslie Stephen, *Life of Fitzjames,* pp. 62–3; C. E. Stephen, *The First Sir James Stephen,* p. 296.
13. Venn, *Complete Duty,* pp. 294–5.
14. James Stephen, *Memoirs,* p. 10.
15. Since this book will discuss several members of the Stephen family, they will be referred to by their first names.
16. James Stephen, *Memoirs,* p. 415.
17. Ibid.
18. Lipscomb, 'James Stephen'.
19. Ibid.
20. James Stephen, *Slavery Delineated,* p. iii.
21. Ibid., p. xli.
22. James Stephen, *England Enslaved,* p. 3.
23. Ibid., p. xxii.
24. James Stephen, *Slavery Delineated,* p. xiii.
25. James Stephen, *England Enslaved,* pp. 14–15.
26. James Stephen, *Memoirs,* p. 42.
27. James Stephen, *Slavery Delineated,* pp. lvi–lvii.
28. C. E. Stephen, *The First Sir James Stephen,* p. 45, emphasis added.
29. Bradley, *Call to Seriousness,* p. 74.
30. C. E. Stephen, *The First Sir James Stephen,* p. 144.
31. Quoted Shaw, 'Sir James Stephen'.
32. Leslie Stephen, *Life of Fitzjames,* p. 48.
33. C. E. Stephen, *The First Sir James Stephen,* p. 66.
34. Ibid., p. 46.
35. Leslie Stephen, *Life of Fitzjames,* p. 41.
36. C. E. Stephen, *The First Sir James Stephen,* p. 83.
37. Colaiaco, *James Fitzjames Stephen,* p. 167.
38. Smith notes that he 'gained a reputation for religious controversy' for his articles in the *Saturday Review* ('Sir James Fitzjames Stephen', *ODNB*).
39. Tolley, *Domestic Biography,* pp. 67–8.

40. Fitzjames Stephen, *Liberty, Equality, Fraternity*, p. 106.
41. Ibid., p. 11.
42. Fitzjames Stephen, Letter to Emily Cunningham 23 September 1874, quoted in Colaiaco, *James Fitzjames Stephen*, p. 186; *Liberty, Equality, Fraternity*, p. 11.
43. See also Colaiaco, *James Fitzjames Stephen*, p. 190.
44. Leslie Stephen *Life of Fitzjames*, p. 10.
45. Fitzjames Stephen, *Liberty, Equality, Fraternity*, p. 65. Matthew Arnold's objection to disestablishment runs as a theme throughout *Culture and Anarchy*.
46. Fitzjames Stephen, *History of the English Criminal Law*, 3, 366–7.
47. Fitzjames Stephen, *Liberty, Equality, Fraternity*, pp. 210, 211.
48. Ibid., p. 223.
49. Ibid., pp. 217, 231.
50. Maitland, *Life and Letters*, p. 474.
51. Sir James Stephen, *Essays in Ecclesiastical Biography*, p. 580.
52. Ibid., p. 533.
53. Ibid., p. 467.
54. Ibid., pp. 525–6.
55. Ibid., p. 557.
56. Venn, *Complete Duty*, p. 414.
57. Sir James Stephen, *Essays in Ecclesiastical Biography*, p. 541.
58. Leslie Stephen, *Life of Fitzjames*, p. 73.
59. Ibid., p. 70.
60. Ibid., p. 62.
61. C. E. Stephen, *Vision of Faith*, p. cxxiii.
62. Leslie Stephen, *Life of Fitzjames*, p. 40.
63. Maitland, *Leslie Stephen*, p. 476.
64. Leslie Stephen, *Mausoleum Book*, p. 6.
65. Vance, *Bible and Novel*, p. 35.
66. C. E. Stephen, *The First Sir James Stephen*, p. 262.
67. Leslie Stephen, *Social Rights and Duties*, 2, 232.
68. Ibid., p. 233.
69. Ibid., pp. 257, 264.
70. Leslie Stephen, *Mausoleum Book*, p. 31.
71. Marcus, *Languages of Patriarchy*, pp. 75–95.
72. C. E. Stephen, *Quaker Strongholds*, p. 13. Weber similarly classifies Quakerism as a Protestant denomination. This position differs from that of the twenty-first-century Quaker movement, which states: 'Although we have our roots in Christianity, we find meaning and value in the teachings and insights of other faiths and traditions.' Quakers in Britain, 'Our Faith', <http://www.quaker.org.uk/about-quakers/our-faith> (last accessed 4 June 2016).
73. C. E. Stephen, *Vision of Faith*, p. 13.
74. Dell, *Virginia Woolf's Influential Forebears*, pp. 159–61.

75. Marcus, *Languages of Patriarchy*, p. 81.
76. Heininge, 'The Search for God', p. 21.
77. Ibid.
78. Raby, *Wise and Witty Quaker Aunt*.
79. Mills uses this model for Woolf's relationship with Jane Harrison in *Spirit of Modernist Classicism*.
80. C. E. Stephen, *Quaker Strongholds*, pp. 95–6.
81. C. E. Stephen, *The First Sir James Stephen*, p. 81.
82. Maitland, *Leslie Stephen*, p. 474.
83. C. E. Stephen, *Light Arising*, pp. 26–7.
84. C. E. Stephen, *Vision of Faith*, p. cxi.
85. Marcus, *Languages of Patriarchy*, p. 120.
86. *Vision of Faith*, p. xcviii.

Chapter 2

Contemporary Conversations

It is to the Greeks that we turn when we are sick of the vagueness, of the confusion, of the Christianity and its consolations, of our own age.

Virginia Woolf, 'On Not Knowing Greek' (1925; CE1 13)

What I seek to show in this book is that the civilization in which we live is a Christian civilization and that it can be understood only if we are prepared to think of it in those terms.

John Middleton Murry, *Heaven – and Earth* (1938, p. 7)

Just as Virginia Woolf grew up in an extended family that was more Christian in character than has been assumed, we need also to recognise that she lived and worked in a culture that owed more to Christianity for its identity than one might expect. Woolf recognises 'Christianity and its consolations' as characteristics of the 1920s: Christianity was still sufficiently pervasive as a worldview that classical Greek literature could be seen as a refreshing alternative, not least for the consolations it offered on the question of life after death, with Thessaly providing a substitute for heaven.[1] Writing over a decade later, Bloomsbury acquaintance John Middleton Murry could still declare himself to be living in a 'Christian civilization'. Indeed, he was commenting on an era when Christianity was making a resurgence: though Murry had been critical of religion, by the 1930s he had converted, one of many intellectuals to have done so. E. M. Forster noted the increased prominence of religion the following year, speaking as an opponent: 'I do not believe in Belief. But this is an age of faith, and there are so many militant creeds that, in self-defence, one has to formulate a creed of one's own.'[2] By that time, too, churchmen were becoming increasingly vocal on social and political issues, the spectre of war in particular: it is no coincidence therefore that Woolf's *Three Guineas*, with its trenchant criticism of the political involvement of the church, appeared in the same year as Murry's *Heaven – and Earth*.

These examples, markers of two different periods in Woolf's life, provide further evidence against the 'secularisation thesis': rationalism and secularism had not triumphed, for critics of religion like Forster still had to do battle with Christianity. Indeed, the examples show that Christianity was an ongoing and active way of life but also that it was being reinvigorated in significant ways.[3] The influx of emigrés from the Russian Revolution early in the modernist period brought a wave of Orthodox Christianity into Britain. It is well known that modernism acquired an impetus by the arrival of the Russian ballet and literature and that Woolf's thoughts on literature were inspired by reading Chekhov, Dostoevsky and Tolstoy, but the influx brought greater awareness of their religious ideas too; for example, the Woolfs published Jane Harrison's translation of the autobiography of the Archpriest Avvakum at the Hogarth Press in 1924. The wave of conversions in the late 1920s and 1930s was also significant to the reinvigoration of Christianity: alongside Murry and T. S. Eliot, C. S. Lewis adopted Anglicanism, while Gwen John, G. K. Chesterton, Graham Greene, David Jones, Fredegond Shove and Evelyn Waugh became Catholics (Vita Sackville-West became deeply interested in Catholicism, though she did not convert). It is therefore more accurate to see the religious climate of the early twentieth century as one of competing dynamics: challenges to Christianity did not overwrite or erase earlier understandings, but existed in competition and dialogue with them, while new expressions of Christianity arose to challenge rationalism.

It is also important to note that Christianity was not a uniform movement, for it presented an increasing range of identities within the early twentieth century, with denominational differences becoming more pronounced in Britain. Nonconformist churches (such as the Baptist, Methodist and Congregationalist churches) were gaining in strength and influence; the most significant of these for Woolf was Quakerism, which was revived in the early twentieth century under the impetus of Caroline Emelia Stephen and continued to thrive.[4] The Catholic Church steadily gained in numbers and prominence, while Anglo-Catholicism emerged as a strong movement within Anglicanism. The Church of England, meanwhile, remained the established church and the focal point for many social and civic functions (as the presence of Rev. Streatfield and the 'dear old church' in *Between the Acts* attests).

An awareness of this wide diversity of Christian beliefs and practices leads us to a more nuanced account of intellectual and religious
development in the modernist period. If we recognise the diversity
of Christianity at this time, it becomes harder to generalise about
Woolf's position towards it. Woolf responded to a variety of different stimuli and her responses varied. This chapter will therefore
explore more closely how Woolf responded to particular manifestations of Christian belief and culture across her career. Since religion
is interpersonal as well as social and cultural, this account will also
examine how Woolf reacted to the faith and practice of the groups
and the people with whom she had significant contact during these
periods: many of these people were women and the three with whom
she had intense relationships (Violet Dickinson, Vita Sackville-West
and Ethel Smyth) were particularly important.

In order to home in more closely on the texture of the religious
climate in which Woolf wrote, the chapter will consider her life and
career in stages, looking at her engagement with different manifestations of Christian culture over the decades. The chapter will consider her career in four phrases: the years of Woolf's adult life before
the First World War (1900–14); the war years; the 1920s; and the
1930s. The significance of Christianity within British culture shifted
over the course of these time periods, and Woolf's attitudes changed
markedly too: in particular, while Woolf was drawn more towards
Christianity at the start of the century, her work became explicitly political and markedly anti-religious in the 1930s, partly as a
response to the way in which churches had become more involved
in the political crisis.

Theological debates

Before we turn to this study of Woolf's contemporary conversations
with Christian culture, however, it is important to note that these
encounters also involved theological discussions, for the twentieth
century brought intense debates about the nature of God, and Woolf
herself was interested in these questions. Just as it is important to
note the denominational variations in religion, so it is also important
to note that the lines of orthodoxy and heresy were no longer clearly
drawn, because some churchmen and theologians were embracing
rationalist ideas and seeking to incorporate them into mainstream
beliefs: as David L. Edwards notes, the early twentieth century saw

some clergy and many laypeople tentatively asking questions 'about the virgin birth, the miracles and the physical resurrection of Jesus and about the whole historical basis of Christianity.'[5] R. J. Campbell, a controversial Congregationalist preacher who later converted to Anglicanism, was influential in arguing that churches existed to reconstruct society and that, if Jesus is God, then so are we.[6] The Catholic Church underwent its own 'modernist' movement spearheaded by Baron Friedrich von Hügel, who questioned concepts of truth ('the deeper we get into any reality, the more numerous will be the questions we cannot answer').[7]

The First World War provoked widespread doubts about the supremacy of a loving God who could allow such things to happen. The church did not provide a unified response for, as Edwards has shown, theologians adopted different approaches, variously emphasising God's transcendence (God was beneath it all but not active in history), or the 'suffering God' (God suffers with us), or faith in God after the failure of faith in progress.[8] Woolf was exercised by the problem of pain, and regularly challenged her Christian friends about how suffering could be reconciled with the idea of a loving God.

Debates about the nature and existence of God and the role he played within the world and the nature of his relationship to humankind and the individual remained lively into the 1920s, and both Leonard and Virginia Woolf engaged in these discussions. One sceptical argument, which particularly attracted Woolf, was drawn from the work of Jane Ellen Harrison. In the *Epilegomena* (1921), which the Woolfs owned, Harrison discusses the implications for contemporary religion of recent anthropological research (including her own work in the *Prolegomena*). Citing the example of Buddhism, Harrison argued that 'we must face at the outset the fact that religion does not presuppose a god', challenging Christianity by arguing from anthropology and psychology that humans created the idea of god, rather than the other way around.[9] She points out that rituals do not presuppose an object of worship but that with the rise of heroes and monarchies the idea of god becomes humanised, and is no longer unknown or unseen, therefore challenging the doctrine of the incarnation. Harrison influenced Virginia Woolf's interest in 'proving that man has need of a God' (D3 271), and her later argument in *Three Guineas* that God was a 'conception, of patriarchal origin' (3G 250). As Jean Mills has argued, too, Harrison was influential on Woolf's interest in Greek religion as an alternative to Christianity: not as an elevation of god/hero figures, as with male modernists, but by emphasising female community and elevating female characters to godlike status.[10]

Woolf also had insight to a range of views on religious matters through a research project that Leonard Woolf set up on contemporary views on religion in 1926, with the question 'Do you believe in a personal God?' as a leading line of enquiry. Virginia Woolf followed the progress of Leonard's questionnaires and discussed them with visitors (*D3* 108, 162). Leonard issued the questionnaires to readers of two publications: the *Nation and Athanaeum*, as a representative group of 'educated' readers, the majority of whom stated that they did not believe in God; and the *Daily News*, with a liberal but more general readership, the majority of whom stated that they did.

Leonard commissioned one of his fellow Cambridge Apostles, Richard Bevan Braithwaite of King's College (*D3* 16, n6) to study the results and draw conclusions, which were published by the Hogarth Press in February 1927. Braithwaite concluded that the figures 'do not warrant the generalization that the educated classes of this country are no longer concerned with Christianity',[11] and he found that there was a strong adherence to it as a moral force, despite a decline in belief in traditional doctrines such as the divinity of Christ and scripture as the word of God. He found that a decline in belief in the explanations provided by Christianity did not seem to give rise to alternatives but to an 'increasing conviction that ultimate explanations of the universe are impossible.'[12] Braithwaite also uncovered an open-mindedness towards religion, in that 'the agnostics today' are 'less prone to sneer at religious and mystical experience' than those of an earlier generation;[13] as Adrian Hastings reflects retrospectively, in his religious history of the 1920s, it was not a contradiction in terms for an agnostic to be a churchgoer: 'Agnostics could tell a good sermon from a bad one, subscribe to Church funds, read the lesson and take participation in the public rituals for granted.'[14] Again, the lines between belief and doubt become blurred: a condition that Woolf recognises when she has Neville note that Percival, who regards the school chapel with 'pagan indifference' would make 'an admirable churchwarden' (*W* 27).

Along with debates about the existence of God, the concept of the afterlife came into question: already subject to debate in the nineteenth century as we have seen, it became regarded as even less of a certainty. There was a decline in belief in an afterlife and in Heaven as a place; there was also a corresponding decline in belief in hell, particularly again with the First World War when, as Edwards notes, the battlefield was hell enough.[15] Apocalyptic thinking was on the rise, manifested among other ways in a renewed interest in Dante. But just as hell and the apocalypse were seen to be manifested in the present day, then redemption came to be seen as possible in the present day too. As C. F. G. Masterman showed in his influential study of religion in Britain in 1910, without the hope of redressing injustice in a future world, people worked to improve life in the present, so that 'tolerance, kindliness, sympathy, civilization' continually improved, as beliefs in 'otherworldliness' faded.[16] This approach was seen among churchmen, too, as some churches placed increased emphasis on attending to social welfare, through the doctrine of realised eschatology.

In this respect, some key features of modernist aesthetics can be seen to have a place within a range of religious debates in the twentieth century. David McMahon has argued that a 'key feature of modernity' is 'a new kind of world-affirming attitude that began with the Reformation and continues to our time.'[17] Although rationalism had brought disenchantment, the Romantics and some twentieth-century artists, writers and thinkers sought to 'recover a sense of lost meaning in things', to 'assert that an ultimate significance dwells in the quotidian particulars and events that we experience every day.'[18] Literary modernism therefore 'took up the emphasis on making an ordinary thing or situation extraordinary in an entirely new key': Joyce's epiphanies, Proust's moment with the madeleine, and Woolf's moments of being are examples of this. As a result they succeeded in 'resacralizing the world'.[19] Read in this way, we can see parallels between some of the more radical Christian discourses and key modernist concepts. The increased emphasis on the spiritual dimensions of everyday life within contemporary thinking became important to modernist experimentation. The emphasis on the present day also, of course, strongly influenced the modernist treatment of time: besides responding to philosophical and scientific advances in the conception of time (which have been well documented), modernism explored the spiritual dimensions of transcending clock-time to 'partake of eternity' (to paraphrase Mrs Ramsay's observation in *To the Lighthouse*). It also expresses a desire to redeem the past within the present moment, abandoning teleology and notions of progress as Walter Benjamin's concept of 'Messianic time' suggests: as Owen Ware notes, 'messianic time breaks from any faith in the imminence of future salvation, and directs all its energy to redeeming the past that lives immanently in the now-time.'[20] We will analyse this treatment of time further in later chapters; however, we will note the germination of these ideas as we now turn to examine Woolf's conversations with Christian culture and ideas over the course of her career.

Faith before the deluge: pre-war Britain

The years that saw Woolf's entry into journalism, her move to Bloomsbury, her marriage, and the writing of her first novel were not marked by popular indifference towards religion but rather by its opposite. Although attitudes towards religion changed profoundly after the war,[21] Christian culture had a strong claim on the popular imagination in the years leading up to it. As Kenneth Hylson-Smith notes, Christianity contributed to 'a sense of national identity, which was still as strong in the Edwardian and immediate post-Edwardian world as it had been in late Victorian times', finding particular expressions in muscular Christianity, Gothic architecture and choral evensong.[22] Christianity was integral to education: Christian 'religious education' was part of the school curriculum,[23] and many public schools, colleges and universities had religious foundations, as Woolf notes of Oxford and Cambridge in *Three Guineas*. Leonard Woolf attended St Paul's School and Adrian Stephen went to Westminster Abbey School. Thoby Stephen wrote a pamphlet objecting to the practice of compulsory chapel at Cambridge and the centrality of Christianity to university life is seen in the way he defends agnostics as a minority group.[24] Woolf shows the religious influence on education during this period, as well as its lasting effects, in her accounts of the childhoods of some of her characters: in *Jacob's Room,* Jacob and Timmy Durrant sing hymns on a sailing trip to pass the time (*JR* 66–7), the children in *The Waves* learn hymns and say prayers at school (*W* 19), and characters in both novels attend college chapel services.

Although definitive statistics are hard to find, it appears that a significant proportion of the population attended church regularly in the pre-war years.[25] Rites of passage certainly boosted figures for church attendance: the Stephen–Duckworth family used St Mary's for their 'conventional marriages' (*MB* 119) and when Stella Duckworth married Jack Hills, not only did the whole family go to church for the wedding, but the siblings attended a Sunday service to hear the banns read. (Although this was for the third time of asking: Virginia recorded their failure to attend on the previous two occasions (*PA* 61, 54, 57).) In *The Voyage Out,* Woolf presents church attendance as relatively normal when she has British tourists observing Sunday by attending a chapel service at their hotel in South America.

Woolf came to see her move to Bloomsbury in 1904 as a rejection of the Puritan values of the Victorian and Edwardian worlds of her youth: 'the gulf which we crossed between Kensington & Bloomsbury was the gulf between respectable mum[m]ified humbug & life crude & impertinent perhaps, but living' (*D1* 206). However, this process was more incremental than we might assume: as she shows in her memoir 'Old Bloomsbury' (1921/2), the group evolved in stages, the first of which was overshadowed by Hyde Park Gate (*MB* 182). The Thursday evening gatherings that she identifies as the origin of the group evolved from the Stephens' pattern of visits and visiting, moving from small talk to discussion of aesthetics, then homosexuality and finally sexual liberation as a replacement for the 'old sentimental views of marriage' of her upbringing (*MB* 196). Yet Woolf later admitted to Ethel Smyth that she was reluctant to embrace these mores: she admits to always being 'sexually cowardly' (*L4* 180) and to having an ancestral influence that prevented her from taking homosexuality seriously (*L4* 200). Leonard's cultural and religious otherness was a shock, and she recalls being intrigued by Thoby's account of 'that violent trembling misanthropic Jew who had already shaken his fist at civilisation and was about to disappear into the tropics' (*MB* 188), and on telling Violet Dickinson of her engagement, she 'confess[ed]' that she was going to marry a 'penniless Jew' (*L1* 500). Although the first of these quotations is a tease (Leonard was after all, in the audience when the memoir was read out), and the second a sign of embarrassment, Leonard and Virginia Woolf often played up their cultural differences and Leonard remained 'my Jew'.

Woolf's move to Bloomsbury also took place against the background of an ongoing influence of Quakerism forged through her regular visits to Caroline Emelia Stephen between 1898 and 1909, and her intimacy with Violet Dickinson from 1902 until 1911.[26] Indeed, both these women played significant roles in Woolf's move to Bloomsbury, for while Vanessa dismantled their childhood home and set up the *ménage* at 46 Gordon Square, Virginia was taking sanctuary first with Violet and then with Caroline Emelia as she recovered from a breakdown. The importance of Caroline Emelia was discussed in the previous chapter, but we can now note the significance that the writings in which she freed herself from her Evangelical past and defined her own faith position, her 'Vision of Faith' essay and *Light Arising* were written during the period of Old Bloomsbury (1906 and 1908 respectively).[27] Alison Lewis has noted that Woolf, like Caroline Emelia, was engaged in the process of 'casting off the external restraints of family history and societal expectation' and also in gaining 'a sense of freedom in seeking for the truth': the latter informed Woolf's modernism for this quest 'permeated [her] writing career, as she sought out new ways of expressing the true essence of the person to whom things happened.'[28]

Violet Dickinson was also significant to the development of Woolf's religious views, and this happened through the influence of their close personal relationship. Violet was introduced to the Stephen family as a friend of Stella Duckworth, but she came to assume a maternal role for the Stephen siblings after Stella's death in 1897 and Violet and Woolf became close during Leslie Stephen's terminal illness in 1902–4. Violet was a frequent and welcome visitor to Hyde Park Gate at the time and Woolf corresponded with her almost daily, writing far more letters to her than to anyone else. Woolf's letters display her characteristic trait of picking up on her correspondent's own register, for they have a religious inflection such as expressing thanks in phrases like: 'Blessings for all you have done' (*L*1 120). Woolf sometimes writes what she thinks Violet will want to hear, such as her fantasy about marrying a clergyman: 'I am training for a curate and 11 children. Curate first children after *of course*' (*L*1 55). Some of her comments, like this one, are tongue-in-cheek, such as when she teasingly imagines Violet writing 'about 6 pages to celebrate the Sabbath' (*L*1 54). She sometimes implies that Violet's faith is a stumbling-block between them, warning her 'Dont get too Holy' and 'don't get too pious' (*L*1 58, 73).

More seriously, this correspondence became a particularly important forum for Woolf to speculate about the nature of God. The words God, Creator and Almighty all become part of Woolf's vocabulary at this time and although the tone is sometimes flippant there are often serious undertones. At times, the correspondence shows Woolf making a subtle shift away from her father's agnosticism towards her friend's religiosity: 'The only reason I have to believe in a God is that *some* life grows in one and out-grows most things. But otherwise – it seems to me he has a heavy hand' (*L1* 85). The comment tests out the idea that there might be a life-force within and beyond the individual; and the perennial question that if that force is omnipotent then it is cruel. A fortnight later, after describing Leslie Stephen's further decline, she uses religion almost as a retreat from intellect: 'its no use thinking about things, and mercifully the creator hasn't contrived us with that capability' (*L1* 87). And in September 1904, after Leslie Stephen's death and while Violet was helping her with the move to Gordon Square, she writes: 'Oh my Violet, if there were a God I should bless him for having delivered me safe and sound from the miseries of the last six months' (*L1* 143). This correspondence suggests that Woolf recognised and responded to Violet's intention to bring her spiritual comfort, even though she was never convinced by her friend's beliefs.

Violet gave Virginia religious books, including an inscribed copy of the Bible presented on Woolf's twenty-fifth birthday and a tract *These thoughts were written by Anthony Harte*, in (1906). This turned out to be written by Violet herself, and no doubt there are personal overtones in the tract's injunction for the sufferer to show thankfulness to the carer, but Violet's assurance that 'life may still be trimmed with beautie even though [the] body be full of miserie' is picked up by Woolf in her exploration of the creative undertow of illness in her essay 'On Being Ill'.

Woolf's short story 'Memoirs of a Novelist' (1909) reflects the important role played by religion in fostering intimacy between women. Her relationship with Violet is echoed in that between eighteen-year-old Frances Willatt and her 'dearest friend' Ellen Buckle. Miss Willatt addresses all her early letters to Miss Buckle, sharing her deepest thoughts about her depression with the wrongs of the world. Like Violet, Miss Buckle lends Miss Willatt religious books that offer her a different moral perspective, as Miss Willatt gives up reading histories and the Waverley novels and learns 'with relief how one may escape the world, and at the same time earn everlasting joy' (*CSF* 96). Significantly, the books that Miss Willatt rejects are ones that Woolf associated with Leslie Stephen, and they are replaced by the kind of works that Violet had introduced her to: an echo of how Violet nudged her to think beyond agnosticism. The Misses Willatt and Buckle put the world to rights together and share experiences that are both profoundly spiritual and deeply intimate. They 'imagined a state in which the soul lay tranquil and in bliss, and that if one could reach it one was perfect'. It is a dream that puts them in

'trances' where they cease to be aware of their surroundings, allow-
ing themselves just one pleasure: that of 'submission' (*CSF* 97). That
submission implies both a religious self-abnegation to a higher being
and the self-giving of one lover to another.

The story is therefore ambiguous about whether the object of worship is the lover or a deity and Woolf similarly transmutes Violet's religious discourses by starting to ascribe a sacred nature to Violet herself:
an early instance of her modernist concern with perceiving the holy
in the present moment. Early in their friendship, Violet had a cottage
built for herself at Welwyn and began to establish a garden there, and
Woolf imagines this as a holy place, perfect like Eden (*L1* 89), with
Violet going about 'naked like Eve' (*L1* 60). This sketch of prehistory
illustrates the process noted by Suzanne Raitt, whereby 'lesbian poems
and autobiographies reach back to a world before the assumption of
heterosexuality, a world in which the women – and particularly the
mother – collude to keep men out'.[29] Same-sex attraction and resistance of male influence were therefore important to the development
of Woolf's spirituality, and would become increasingly so.

Woolf ascribes a similarly sacred character to Lady Katherine
Thynne, for whom she also had great affection: 'I think of Katie as
Heaven and Peace', she writes, and describes a visit to her as a pilgrimage (*L1* 80). Woolf goes further to make both Violet and Katie
divine figures to displace conceptions of God. In a letter written to
Violet on Good Friday 1903 (a holy day that Woolf notes, but dismisses by saying that she will mark it with champagne rather than
the traditional fast), she concludes: 'I get born anew into the bosom
of my God once a year – a God half Katie and some rakish old Pagan
like you' (*L1* 73).

The complex dynamics of Woolf's reactions to Violet – teasing
her for her religion, acknowledging and responding to her religiosity,
and making her an object of worship – can also be seen in Woolf's
tribute to Violet, *Friendship's Gallery* (1907). The first two of its
three chapters tell Violet's life story in a comic way, parodying biographical convention to mock the pious domestic biographies of the
Clapham Sect. The narrator reminds us that 'after all our concern is
with her spiritual progress' (*FG* 276), giving a comic account of Violet's baptism and a discourse on the significance of having a Christian
name. As the narrative progresses, there are teasing suggestions that
religion is a quirk of Violet's psychology and that her Puritan distrust
of beauty is a genetic disorder (*FG* 287).

Friendship's Gallery pays tribute to Violet by using biblical allusions but Woolf plays fast and loose with the original texts: the Good

Samaritan is said to help a leper (rather than a victim of robbers), and Woolf gives a saucy parody of the story of Elijah when she has Violet's grandmother describe her grandfather as

> 'a man like Elijah in his burnin' mantle' who gave her 'fire to drink and the flesh of wild goats and spake to me with the voice of the wind and the rain. And it was like the voice of none other; for he did the things he spake of, and lifted me in his arms and drave me behind wild beasts like a God to the little house in the valley and there he married me.' (*FG* 282)

Violet's life story is written large as it is overlaid with a wider historical narrative of religious change, so that Woolf's description of her having a house and garden built for herself at Welwyn aligns it with the historical moment in which Christianity overtook paganism as Violet tames the 'wild wood' and dislodges the fauns by holding Christian services.

The third chapter of *Friendship's Gallery* is a full-blown fantasy, as Woolf appears to leave the Violet narrative to recount what she describes as a Japanese bedtime story. Here Woolf starts to speculate about female divinity, introducing two sacred princesses who act as fairy godmothers, blessing babies with good fortune and eventually defeating a sea monster to ensure peace in the land. One of these princesses, a giantess, is clearly based on the unusually tall Violet Dickinson; the other, the 'Mistress of the Magic Garden', may well be based on Katie Thynne. The fantasy celebrates the triumph of female power over evil, with the fantastic creation of female superheroes who save the day, thereby supplanting the problematic concept of a God who allows or inflicts suffering.

The works that Woolf wrote under the inspiration of her relationship with Violet Dickinson establish a key motif within her work, whereby love between women assumes a particularly spiritual character. The relationship between Miss Buckle and Miss Willatt in 'Memoirs of a Novelist' foreshadows that between Clarissa Dalloway and Sally Seton in *Mrs Dalloway*: both couples put the world to rights together and share spiritual experiences. Sally's kiss is one of Clarissa's most important memories and significantly it is a 'religious' experience:

> Sally stopped; picked a flower; kissed her on the lips. The whole world might have turned upside down! The others disappeared; there she was alone with Sally. And she felt that she had been given

a present, wrapped up, and told just to keep it, not to look at it – a
diamond, something infinitely precious, wrapped up, which, as they
walked (up and down, up and down), she uncovered, or the radiance
burnt through, the revelation, the religious feeling! (*MD* 32)

The secret that has to be 'wrapped up' is not shameful but precious
and sacred, as Woolf's alliterative trio of 'radiance', 'revelation' and
'religious' stresses. The scene with Sally bears out Luce Irigaray's
observation that there is 'nothing more spiritual . . . than female
sexuality.'[30] By the time Woolf wrote *Mrs Dalloway*, of course, she
had begun a relationship with Vita Sackville-West, but there are
powerful overlaps between her representations of these two women:
Friendship's Gallery in turn foreshadows *Orlando*, with its mock-
ing of the biographical style, its use of biblical allusions that would
become literary allusions in *Orlando*, and its use of overlapping
timeframes, whereby one life is written onto a wider historical narrative. In both these novels, Woolf experiments with ideas of female
omnipotence and a desire to transcend time; in both cases presenting alternatives to the cruel god Woolf had identified in Christian
discourse.

'I owe God a grudge': the First World War

While Woolf's attitude towards religion in the early years of the century was formed by personal influences, her views on religion and
the Church during the war years were also partly shaped by current
affairs. The war put an end to the Christian culture that had pre-
vailed in the early years of the century: as Edwards writes, 'here was
the end of an England – for here was a horror to which conventional
piety and morality seemed largely irrelevant.'[31] The war precipitated
a decline in church attendance, which became even sharper in the
post-war years,[32] and the Church of England publicly acknowledged
in 1919 that it was out of touch.[33] One reason for its unpopular-
ity was its support for military action. Although Christian groups
had been involved in peace efforts in the run-up to war, once war
broke out church leaders of all the major denominations spoke in
favour of it: only the Quaker movement continued to promote a
pacifist message, and even then some individual Quakers signed up.
A popular rhetoric was to see the war as a crusade against evil forces,
a view famously summed up by Arthur Winnington-Ingram, the

Bishop of London: 'What the Church is to do. I answer. MOBILISE THE NATION FOR A HOLY WAR',[34] and sermons were preached encouraging enlistment.

Woolf's diaries from this time show that she recognised the association between Christianity, militarism and jingoism. At Hogarth House on Sunday 4 November 1917, she noted that

> writing has the advantage of making a weekday out of the Sabbath, in spite of the clamour & blare of military music & church bells which always takes place at about 11 – a noise which the other people have no right to inflict. (*D1* 71)

Here she displays a particular form of passive resistance: deliberately refusing to observe Sunday as a day of rest let alone a day for worship, and objecting to a soundscape that fused jingoistic celebration with religious observance in popular culture.

Woolf would critique this fusion of the military and the ecclesiastical more fully later in her career. She returns to it in *Jacob's Room,* where she shows how the religious values of Cambridge have trained undergraduates to be soldiers, and again in *Three Guineas.* However, Woolf did not always regard the church as powerful during this period, and indeed she often saw it as irrelevant. Although, as Arthur Marwick points out, churches 'seemed a natural focal point of Armistice celebration and thanksgiving',[35] including a national commemoration at Westminster Abbey, Woolf's account of the official Peace celebrations on Saturday 19 July 1919 appears to separate church from state. The event is 'a servants festival; some thing got up to pacify and placate "the people"' (*D1* 292). Summarising a report from her servant Nelly Boxall, she describes an entirely secular procession: 'Generals & soldiers & tanks & nurses & bands took 2 hours in passing. It was they said the most splendid sight in their lives.' This time, it is the Saturday-night fireworks that provide the noise pollution that Woolf resents, while the Sunday-morning church bells are muted and irrelevant: '(And now, in the rain, under a grey brown sky, the bells of Richmond [are] ringing – but church bells only recall weddings & Christian services.)' (*D1* 293) Woolf is also understated on the position of the church in relation to female suffrage, which came about as an effect of the war, and its widening opportunities for women. Noting the passing of the Act enabling women to become MPs on 24 October 1918, she imagines 'some retired cleric in the vales of Westmorland' denouncing it in a sermon as 'the death knell of liberty' (*D1* 207). Objections come from a marginal figure: in the immediate post-war period, at least, Woolf imagined that the views of the church were becoming irrelevant.

Woolf was far more exercised, however, by the religious opinions of people she knew. In July 1918, Woolf invited her brother Adrian to give a talk on peace to the Richmond branch of the Women's Co-operative Guild, of which she was president. The group responded enthusiastically, although Woolf felt that they had not considered the issues carefully enough, dismissing them as ignorant and too focused on peace at any price. She also found them hypocritical: when they discussed taking part in a Peace Meeting to be held by the British Workers' League in Hyde Park, their most vocal member, a Mrs Langston, declined on their behalf because she objected to its being held on a Sunday. This infuriated Woolf and she directed her anger towards Christianity in general:

> What a terrible grip Xtianity still has – she became rigid & bigoted at once, as if God himself had her in his grasp. That I believe is still the chief enemy – the fear of God. But I was tactful enough to keep this view dark. (*D1* 165)

Two days later, she remarked that 'I owe God a grudge for his effect upon the Guild' (*D1* 166). This in turn spilled over into her reading of Christina Rossetti, three weeks later: 'if I were bringing a case against God she is one of the first witnesses I should call' (*D1* 178), arguing that Rossetti turned to religious poetry after the failure of a love affair due to denominational differences (Woolf describes her suitor as having 'developed a case of Roman Catholicism & was lost', as though he had been struck down by illness). Yet, this view of Rossetti was an over-reaction to the Guild, for Woolf later praised Rossetti in *A Room of One's Own* (10–12) and, on her centenary in 1930, wrote that her 'instinct was so sure, so direct, so intense that it produced poems that sing like music in one's ears' and that her faith gives her poems their distinctive 'solidity' and 'sadness' (*CE4* 58–9).

These diary entries show that Woolf was exploring theological questions. Intriguingly, she refers to God as an entity (so that she does not actively dispute his existence) and she capitalises his name. Yet neither is she reverential: she expresses her grudges against God, puts him on trial, and blames him as a bad influence on human affairs. God is powerful because he continues to claim human imagination and because religious bigotry, in turn, has had a major impact on world affairs: it is no coincidence that the 'fear of God', which in biblical terms is 'the beginning of wisdom' (Proverbs 9:10), is for Woolf the 'chief enemy' and therefore an impediment to peace.

Woolf's diary entry about the 'grudge against God' takes the discussion much deeper than a personal irritation with the Guild. She had been following with amusement the correspondence in *The Times,* in which the Duke of Rutland had urged the clergy to pray for rain to save the harvest,[36] but in fact the drought had given way to storms: 'God being, as usual, spiteful in his concessions, & now threatening to ruin the harvest' (*D1* 166). Again Woolf probes the relationship of God to the world, satirising ideas about the power of prayer, and speculating that God may be a vindictive force. Woolf's speculations chime with wider cultural debates about how a loving God could allow the horrors of war, but unlike the theologians who sought to explain that God was not active in history or that he was suffering with humankind,[37] Woolf makes no such concessions: God can be active and he can make atrocities happen, just as he can make people ill.

However, Woolf was equally sceptical about the movements that arose during the war as a challenge to the organised churches: folk religion, folklore and spiritualism.[38] In her diary she provides an acid account of a visitor, John Mills Whitham, a 'self-taught working man', who 'went on about spiritualism': he had

> dabbled in mysticism, & had made tables walz [*sic*] & heard phantom raps & believed it all, but was too much afraid of the results upon his character to go in for it seriously. I thought this showed weakness, and I expect he hasn't a good head on his shoulders. (*D1* 113–14)

In 'Kew Gardens' (1919), Woolf represents such attitudes as the view of an elderly man suffering from what we would now recognise as dementia, who listens to spirits telling him about Heaven, hears 'spirit matter . . . rolling between the hills like thunder' and talks of a machine that will capture these voices (*CSF* 122). However, 'Kew Gardens' touches upon a more serious issue of how the massive losses during the war had brought about increased need to acknowledge the existence of the dead, and the Protestant churches were forced to bring back prayers for the dead, for pastoral reasons.[39] She would revisit this particularly in the traumatic haunting of Septimus Warren Smith by his friend Evans, which is presented as a very real experience indeed.

The 1920s: public religion, private faith

One might expect there to be very little connection between Woolf and Christian culture in the 1920s. Many church historians regard the 1920s as one of the least interesting decades of the twentieth century and consequently pass over it briefly. Church attendance declined in the post-war years and churches became more inward-looking: the Anglican Church focused its intellectual and political energies mainly on church organisation, such as attempts to revise *The Book of Common Prayer*. Matters of belief became rather more of a private issue: as Hylson-Smith notes, religious practice came to centre on the home, focusing on the mother in particular,[40] a view that accords with Pericles Lewis's argument that religion became privatised.

However, as with many attempts to identify trends within religion, this is only partially true, for the Christian church during the 1920s did become concerned with social problems, pursuing a broadly socialist line, albeit one that became more guarded with the rise of Communism.[41] For example, during 1924, the year of Britain's first and short-lived Labour Government, the Conference on Christian Politics, Economics and Citizenship (COPEC) was held in Birmingham in April, chaired by William Temple, Bishop of Manchester and first president of the Workers' Education Association (WEA). It made a systematic critique of social problems and urged the church and its clergy to tackle them.[42] Though it lacked immediate impact in Britain (and the movement folded within two years), its long-term effect was, as Hastings notes, to 'wean' the church from 'high Tory attitudes to an acceptance of the Christian case for massive social reform and the development of a welfare state.'[43] Slum clearance and social housing were two particular projects to arise from this. These liberal movements provoked a reaction from more conservative voices championing patriotism, supporting eugenics, and fearing the rise of an educated working class as a threat to the middle classes. A figurehead for this school of thought was Dean Inge of St Paul's Cathedral, whom Woolf critiqued in both *A Room of One's Own* and *Three Guineas*.

Virginia Woolf reflects this climate of debate in *Mrs Dalloway* by articulating a series of positions on whether Christianity can contribute to social justice. In one camp, Miss Kilman represents the Christian social conscience: having been excluded from the teaching profession due to her Germanic surname, and having been converted by a powerful clergyman, she espouses 'causes' to help deprived groups: the Armenians and the Russians. By contrast, Clarissa's scathing view of these causes ('Miss Kilman would do anything for the Russians, starved herself for the Austrians' (*MD* 10)), puts her in the conservative camp: Woolf makes an implicit judgement on Clarissa's ignorance and on society's marginalisation of those who are suffering, a theme that is brought out in the novel's depiction of Septimus's suffering as the shell-shocked veteran. Yet Clarissa has her own moral high ground too: an 'atheist's religion' that leads her to do good works such as visiting the sick without the impetus of a religious creed. Clarissa's views reflect the cultural trend noted by Masterman: a desire to improve life in the present rather than hoping for a redress in the hereafter.[44] (Mrs Ramsay reflects a similar stance, in her care for the sick and her researches into improving the conditions of the poor.) Elizabeth Dalloway presents a third perspective on the debate when she asks whether Christians or politicians are the more effective in social reform, and indeed whether either can make a difference:

> If it was being on committees and giving up hours and hours every day . . . that helped the poor, her father did that, goodness knows – if that was what Miss Kilman meant about being a Christian; but it was so difficult to say. (*MD* 122)

Virginia Woolf had some personal experience of working with socially engaged churchmen during the 1920s through Leonard's involvement with the Labour Party. Leonard had been instrumental in setting up the League of Nations, which had the backing of the Archbishop of Canterbury, Randall Davidson. The Woolfs came into contact with Davidson through their mutual support of the General Strike of May 1926. Although Davidson had initially spoken out against the strike, he changed his mind after receiving a delegation from churchmen, including Canon Kirk of the Industrial Christian Fellowship. Davidson published *The Crisis: Appeal from the Churches*, in which he called for an end to the strike in exchange for government assistance for the coal industry and an end to the new wage scales that had prompted the strike.[45] The government resented Davidson's intervention and the BBC refused to broadcast his appeal after pressure from Chancellor of the Exchequer Winston Churchill. However, the Woolfs vigorously backed Davidson, collecting signatures in support of his proposal, with Virginia urgently typing copies for circulation.[46] It may seem surprising to see Woolf on the same side as an Archbishop of Canterbury, in view of her critique of the church in *Three Guineas*, but as we will see later, both her views and the political and religious landscape were very different by the late 1930s.

It is also remarkable that Virginia Woolf expresses interest in a specifically faith-based response to the strike. On the second day of the strike (6 May 1926) she noted in her diary that 'What one prays for is God: the King or God; some impartial person to say kiss & be friends – as apparently we all desire' (*D3* 78). The following day she reported the 'only news that the archbishops are conferring, & ask our prayers that they may be guided right.' Even if she were absorbing commonly held views into her free indirect discourse here, she makes no attempt to challenge them. A humorous additional comment suggests that she recognised the dispute to be been drawn on religious lines: 'L. says if the state wins & smashes T[rades]. U[nion]s he will devote his life to labour: if the archbishop succeeds, he will be baptised.' And two days later, Leonard and Virginia quarrelled over the strike on points of religion, with Virginia cast into the Christian camp: 'I dislike the tub thumper in him; he the irrational Xtian in me' (*D3* 78, 80, 80–1).

As events transpired, Leonard did not have to fulfil either of his wagers, for the strike came to an end with the question of miners' pay still in the balance: although an *ad hoc* group of liberal church leaders including Davidson sought to support the miners, they did not convince Prime Minister Stanley Baldwin and the movement fizzled out. Meanwhile, conservative Christians had acted as volunteers to keep services running during the strike, Dean Inge was pleased to see the end of the strike, and the BBC played 'Jerusalem' in celebration of the miners' defeat. The range of religious views on the incident again demonstrates diversity of Christian culture at this time.

The story of Woolf's involvement with religion and politics in the 1920s reveals some unexpected allegiances; likewise, some instances of Woolf's personal engagement with the faith and religious practice of her contemporaries shows some complex and varied responses. Woolf explores questions of faith in her correspondence with the French painter Jacques Raverat from 1922 to 1925. Raverat was dying from a form of multiple sclerosis and he dictated his letters to his wife, Gwen, with whom Woolf continued a correspondence after his death. In a letter of July 1923 (*L3* 58–60), Woolf shares with Raverat her concern at what she sees as a 'religious revival', citing the conversions of J. M. Murry and Fredegond Shove. She starts rather teasingly by recounting gossip from Jane Harrison that Gwen and Jacques had become Catholics, on the strength of a rumour that a 'wave of Catholicism has invaded the young Frenchmen', and then her relief to have heard from Jacques that Gwen is 'a militant atheist'. But the humorous story has a more serious import, especially given Jacques's condition, for Woolf speaks of her 'sense of the transitoriness of existence' and then reiterates her critique of Christianity for failing to account for suffering:

> The spirit that inspires it, with its unction and hypocrisy, and God is love, which still leaves room for flea bites, pin pricks, and advertising astuteness, would enrage, were it not that there's something so mild and wobbly about that too that I can't waste good wrath.

Woolf was moved by Jacques's death on 7 March 1925, but as she had known him for many years through correspondence only, this led to a belief that he was still in many senses alive for her. As she wrote to Gwen: 'I have no difficulty in thinking him still alive. That is what I should like for myself, that there should be no breach, no submission to death, but merely a break in the talk' (*L3* 177). And in a speculation which clearly echoes her ideas about the posthumous connections between Clarissa Dalloway and Septimus, she tells Gwen that 'I become more mystical as I grow older and feel an alliance with you and Jacques which is eternal, not interrupted, or hurt by never meeting' (*L3* 171).

Woolf gives expression to a similar sense of connectedness in an account of a small but significant encounter with popular piety at the Adult School in Sutton, where Leonard gave a talk in May 1925. The School was a philanthropic venture endowed in 1910 by Thomas Wall, a man known throughout Britain for selling quality meat pies, sausages and the now very famous ice cream. He was a man of slight build, who wanted to give working-class people the educational opportunities that he had missed.[47] Woolf describes how Leonard's lecture was

> delivered in a semi-religious sanctuary, with hymns & prayers & a chapter from the Bible. The whole of Sutton was hymning something: soft intense strains of human [word omitted by VW] went warbling about, as I sat; & I was touched and moved by it: the world so beautiful, God's gift to us, said the Chairman, who looked poor man as if he had never had an ounce of pleasure in his life. (*D3* 22)

Woolf's vocabulary 'soft intense', 'touched', 'moved', 'beautiful', is positive rather than sceptical, only slightly qualified by the Chairman's doleful demeanour. She also shows a sympathy and sense of common humanity with working-class people that we might not expect and which perhaps took Woolf herself by surprise: 'Things become very familiar to me, so that I sometimes think humanity is a vast wave, undulating: the same, I mean: the same emotions here that were at Richmond.' Pressed to stay for refreshments, she finds that

> the same queer brew of human fellowship, is brewed; & people look the same; & joke in the same way, & come to these odd superficial agreements, wh. if you think of them persisting & wide spread – in jungles, storms, birth & death – are not superficial; but rather profound, I think.

Woolf's view of humanity as a 'vast wave' (an image likely to have been suggested to her by Wordsworth's 'Immortality Ode'), and sense of its commonality, can both be seen to feed into *The Waves*.

Woolf's ideas for *The Waves* were also stimulated by her reading Beatrice Webb's autobiography *My Apprenticeship* in 1926, in tandem with re-reading her own diary for 1923. She noted that 'Mrs Webb's book has made me think a little what I could say of my own life. . . . But then there were causes in her life: prayer; principle. None in mine.' This insight prompts Woolf to comment on her spiritual quest, in the same diary entry:

> I have some restless searcher in me. Why is there not a discovery in life? Something one can lay hands on & say 'This is it?' My depression is a harassed feeling – I'm looking; but that's not it – thats not it. What is it? (D3 62)

While, at this point, Woolf is made to feel an awareness of her own emptiness, she soon counters this by finding an image that sums up her own spirituality in contradistinction to Webb's when she notes seeing clouds piling up like mountains and feeling an 'astonishing sense of something there, which is "it"' (ibid.).

However, the relationship that provoked the most intense and complicated reaction from Woolf in the latter half of the 1920s was that with Vita Sackville-West. As we have seen, Woolf invoked Vita, along with Violet Dickinson, in her account of the 'religious' nature of love between women in the relationship between Sally Seton and Clarissa Dalloway. Woolf again evoked the sanctity of relationships between women in *To the Lighthouse* in Lily Briscoe's intimacy with Mrs Ramsay, which Lily sees in terms of having 'penetrated' into a 'sanctuary'. Both Vita and Violet can be seen to be reflected in this episode, alongside the well-attested representation of Julia Stephen in Mrs Ramsay, for Woolf regarded both of these women as maternal: Violet had been a 'mother-figure' to the Stephen siblings after Stella's death, and Virginia caricatured her teasingly in letters as being married but with many illegitimate children.[48] Woolf was particularly aware of Vita's motherhood, but significantly, she also described her as 'like a lighthouse, fitful, sudden, remote' (*L3* 215).

This remoteness became the keynote for Woolf's response to Sackville-West's religiosity. As Raitt has noted, Vita developed a 'growing preoccupation with religion and mysticism' over the years, making her more solitary and withdrawn as she entered the 1930s.[49] Vita retreated to Sissinghurst from 1930 onwards and went on to write a Life of St Joan of Arc (of which Woolf was highly critical) as well as studies of St Teresa of Avila and St Thérèse of Lisieux in the 1940s. Although Vita became more markedly introverted and religious after her intimacy with Woolf had declined, the first signs of unease are evident as early as April 1926, when their relationship was at its height. Vita wrote to Woolf that

> as I get older (I had a birthday only the other day,) I find I get more and more disagreeably solitary, in fact I foresee the day when I shall have gone so far into myself that there will no longer be anything to see of me at all. Will you, please, remember to pull away the coverings from time to time? or I shall get quite lost.[50]

Woolf did not respond directly to this letter, but she was both piqued and interested by Vita's desire to be alone for, two months later, she wrote and asked her: 'Are you so intensely, completely, happy that one drop more would make you spill? Is this solitude? I'm thinking of retiring to Rodmell too to try' (*L3* 272).

This interest spilled over into the germ of *The Waves* and four months later, on 30 October, Woolf noted in her diary that 'At intervals, I begin to think (I note this, as I am going to watch for the advent of a book) of a solitary woman musing . . . an endeavour at something mystic, spiritual' (*D3* 114), and a month later again, 'I am now & then haunted by some semi mystic very profound life of a woman which shall all be told on one occasion; & time shall be utterly obliterated; future shall somehow blossom out of the past' (*L3* 118). Woolf's interest in mysticism was inspired by many sources and not just Vita, of course, but these sketches suggest that Woolf was going in quest of her retreating lover as well as seeking to understand the mysticism that had come to preoccupy her. Woolf's plan that 'time shall be utterly obliterated' reflects her modernist interest in Messianic time, but also her tendency to see her female lovers in superhuman terms: her playing with time would more immediately turn Vita into the long-lived Orlando, and then spill over into a more radical playing with time in *The Waves* in which the lifespan of the individual is set in parallel with a narrative of the world from creation to apocalypse.

Significantly, Violet Dickinson had re-entered Woolf's life at this point: Violet had three major operations for cancer in 1926 and Woolf resumed a correspondence with her. Vita knew Violet too: they shared news of Violet's progress, and Woolf sends Violet greetings from Vita more than once. Just as both Violet and Vita are implicated in *Mrs Dalloway*, in *To the Lighthouse*, and in *Orlando*, so they can both be seen as part of *The Waves*: not in scenes of female intimacy but in images of a solitary female presence. In the childhood episode, Bernard and Susan make a secret visit to Elvedon, with the 'close-clipped hedge of the ladies' garden' and 'the ringed wood with the wall around it', in which they see a lady writing (*W* 11). This calls to mind both Dickinson's Edenic garden at Welwyn and Vita's garden at Sissinghurst. The lady is also both remote and god-like: echoing her earlier attributions of divinity to Violet, Woolf envisages a female deity in *The Waves*, not least when the opening passage reinterprets the creation story with female presence at sunrise, where the sky lights up 'as if the arm of a woman couched beneath the horizon had raised a lamp' (*W* 3). It is telling that the opening line of *The Waves*, 'The sun had not yet risen', echoes a line from *Friendship's Gallery* (*FG* 299); the Apocalyptic 'beast' that stamps throughout *The Waves* is also an echo of the monster defeated by the avatars of Violet and Katie in *Friendship's Gallery*. In *The Waves*, then, female intimacy feeds in to conceptions of female power and divinity, once more challenging Christian ideas of a male God.

In view of Woolf's relationships with her female companions, it is perhaps unsurprising to find that her attitude towards her contemporary male experimental writers was grudging and guarded.

Her view of the spirituality of Joyce and Eliot has none of the empathy she shows towards Violet Dickinson, Jacques Raverat or Beatrice Webb, and none of the piqued interest with which she treats Sackville-West's mysticism. In 'Modern Fiction' she tempers her praise of Joyce's spirituality with remarks on his obscenity, and her comments on Eliot's religion in her letters and diaries are frequently grudging and defensive. This is seen particularly in Woolf's attitude towards Eliot's conversion. She notes briefly to Clive Bell that she had been 'talking for two hours to Tom Eliot about God', and then more expansively in an oft-quoted letter to Vanessa:

> I have had a most shameful and distressing interview with poor dear Tom Eliot, who may be called dead to us all from this day forward. He has become an Anglo-Catholic, believes in God and immortality, and goes to church. I was really shocked. A corpse would seem to me more credible than he is. I mean, there's something obscene in a living person sitting by the fire and believing in God. (*L3* 457)

This statement can be seen as much as a comment on Eliot as on his faith. Earlier in the letter, Woolf had promised a 'few pieces of gossip' (*L3* 456), which partly explains the satirical tone of the anecdote. The tone also fits with Woolf's frequently patronising attitude towards Eliot, whom she often calls 'poor Tom', and her disdain for his nervous states, such as her diary account of his 'long gaslit emotional rather tremulous & excited visit' to tell her about leaving his job in the bank (*D3* 14). If Woolf finds Eliot's faith implausible, it is partly because it does not match the personality of someone she had described as 'sardonic, guarded, precise, & slightly malevolent' (*D2* 187), with a 'cadaverous' appearance (*D2* 171). She questions his credibility in a clever play on the Christian doctrine of life after death for, although Eliot professes to believe in immortality, he is no better than the 'corpse' he resembles. She further parodies religious language: being 'dead to us all', is a Jewish concept for someone who has left the faith, and 'from this day forward' parodies the marriage vows from *The Book of Common Prayer*.

It is significant also that Woolf stresses Eliot's denominational affiliation: Anglo-Catholicism is a particular branch of Anglicanism, one that places great emphasis on ritual and ceremony, sacraments, and the power and privilege of a male priesthood. Eliot's religiosity was therefore vastly different from the simplicity of the Quakerism that she found somewhat appealing in Caroline Emelia Stephen and

Violet Dickinson, from the Puritanism of her Clapham-Sect roots to which she admitted some affinity, and from the low-church candour of the act of worship at Sutton Adult School. Yet, it was Anglo-Catholicism that was steadily coming to the fore: there were major rallies in London in 1922, 1925 and 1927, and it would assume even greater prominence in the 1930s.[51] Woolf's disdain for Eliot's religiosity would become more of a hallmark of her attitude towards religion in the final decade of her life.

1930s: religion resurgent

While the 1920s was a quiet era in church history, Christianity came to prominence both culturally and politically in the 1930s. The conversions of prominent writers and intellectuals in the late 1920s and early 1930s seemed to give Christianity a credibility it had not enjoyed a decade earlier, through the production of distinctively Christian works: C. S. Lewis converted and began a career as a major and influential theologian and novelist; T. S. Eliot produced religious works such as *Choruses from the Rock* and *Murder in the Cathedral* after his conversion and went on to form The Moot with J. M. Murry, which, as Michael Lackey has argued, sought to re-establish the power and authority of Christianity as well as restoring Christian heritage and spiritually reinvigorating the church.[52] Graham Greene and Evelyn Waugh converted to Catholicism and created a particular genre of Catholic literature. As Adrian Hastings notes: 'The central tide of English thought and culture in the 1930s was flowing quite perceptibly in one direction: from irreligion to religion, from liberal or modernist religion to neo-orthodoxy, and from Protestantism towards Catholicism.'[53] While Woolf had responded with interest to the personal spirituality of many people she had known, she regarded these predominantly male intellectuals with suspicion. She also kept a close watch on the role of religion in current affairs: church-related business features heavily in the three scrapbooks of news-cuttings and notes she compiled in preparation for *Three Guineas*.

In national politics, the Church of England assumed a fairly conservative position: Cosmo Lang succeeded Davidson as Archbishop of Canterbury in 1928 and tried to steer a moderate, unchallenging line. So, although the Lambeth Conference of 1930 considered whether the church should seek a degree of autonomy from the State in order to have control over spiritual affairs, this was not pursued and the Commission appointed to review this in 1936 (chaired by Robert Cecil, husband of Woolf's friend Nelly) failed to bring about any changes. The Commission on the Ministry of Women, which Woolf discusses in depth in *Three Guineas,* also arose from this process: while the appointment of the Commission showed that the church recognised the need for change, its report nonetheless found in favour of maintaining the status quo by continuing to exclude women from ordained ministry. Significantly, too, the Church failed to speak out against Fascism, which was widely seen as a minority concern, and some churchmen even appeared to sympathise with it.[54] Many Church leaders, both clerical and lay, were actively seeking appeasement with Germany: Cosmo Lang and Lord Halifax the Foreign Secretary (an Anglo-Catholic) saw the Munich Treaty as divine intervention. As Lang wrote in *The Times:* 'More than one member of Parliament said to me today as we all trooped into the lobby: "This is the hand of God".'[55]

Nonetheless, views were still diverse, for many churchmen and theologians were exercised by the question of how religion might address the political crisis and, indeed, many clergy were pacifists.[56] In *Christianity and the Crisis,* a collection of essays that the Woolfs owned, a group of churchmen argued from various perspectives that the church could address world problems. As editor Percy Dearmer, a leading figure in Christian sociology and social criticism, commented, Christianity had 'partly solved' the 'enormously difficult problem' of combining liberty with commonwealth over nineteen centuries and 'there is no reason to despair we shall solve it, unless Christianity perishes.'[57] Dearmer concludes that 'There is an ideal of unity such as the world has not known before', and that such unity could provide the antidote to the world's problems (ibid.). E. M. Forster poured scorn on such attempts, arguing that 'no form of Christianity and no alternative to Christianity will bring peace to the world or integrity to the individual.'[58]

Woolf engages with these contemporary debates explicitly in *Three Guineas,* drawing especially on newspaper opinion pieces and letters pages to make a detailed comment on the state of religion and politics during the 1930s. While Woolf draws on examples from a wide range of historical periods and cultures for *Three Guineas,* as well as examining her own Evangelical heritage, the contemporary references in the essay engage specifically with the debates of the 1930s, and many of the conclusions that Woolf draws could only have been made at this time.

Early in the essay, Woolf acknowledges the wide diversity in the church, and the differences of opinion among churchmen about how to respond to the political crisis. From the one side, she quotes from Arthur Winnington-Ingram, Bishop of London (who had earlier famously declared the First World War a 'HOLY WAR'): 'the real danger to the peace of the world today were the pacifists. Bad as war was dishonour was for worse'. On the other, she quotes Ernest Barnes, Bishop of Birmingham, who 'described himself as an "extreme pacifist . . . I cannot see myself that war can be regarded as consonant with the spirit of Christ".'[59] Of the two, however, Woolf sees the warmongering attitude as most characteristic of Christianity in the 1930s and the Anglican Church in particular.

Three Guineas presents a close critique of the regime of Cosmo Lang and Woolf particularly attacks his liturgical style. Lang established a ceremonial dress for high-ranking churchmen that had not been seen for centuries: as his biographer notes, he 'had a strong sense of the value of the ceremonial' and he was the first Archbishop of York since the Reformation to wear a mitre and cope, a custom that he extended widely across the Church of England.[60] It is Lang who appears in the illustrations for *Three Guineas* anonymously as 'An Archbishop' wearing a mitre, a richly embroidered cope and a crucifix, and walking in procession with surpliced boys behind him. The liturgical dress Woolf describes in her text is distinctly high-church: 'Now you dress in violet; a jewelled crucifix swings on your breast; now your shoulders are covered with lace'. The ceremonies are similarly characteristic of high-church Anglicanism, 'here you appear to do homage to a piece of painted wood; here you abase yourselves before tables covered with richly worked tapestry'. Woolf links this English cultural movement with continental movements by pointing out that ceremonies are fascist practices designed to celebrate patriarchal power and assert hierarchy (*3G* 103).

While historians are divided as to whether the churches of the 1930s were pro-fascist, anti-fascist, or merely ignorant of the threat, Woolf's verdict is clear: in asserting hierarchy and celebrating patriarchal power, the Anglican Church is clearly in sympathy with fascism. She remarks on the place of church leaders within the political hierarchy, noting that in terms of prestige and financial remuneration, the 'Archbishop of Canterbury precedes the Lord High Chancellor; the Archbishop of York precedes the Prime Minister' (*3G* 196). She detects both in fascist leaders and church leaders a demand for unquestioning respect for authority, associating the words of the dictator Creon from

Sophocles' *The Antigone* with Hitler and Mussolini: 'whomsoever the city may appoint, that man must be obeyed, in little things and great, in just things and unjust' (*3G* 238, n39).

The specific hierarchy Woolf sees the church as enforcing is that of separate spheres: a legacy of the Victorian era, as we have seen, but one that had been reinforced by the 1936 Report on the Ministry of Women. As Woolf notes, the Report's argument that a male priest must have a wife to support him was also made by both Hitler and Mussolini: 'The emphasis which both priests and dictators place upon the necessity for two worlds is enough to prove that it is essential to the domination' (*3G* 247, n31). Excluding women from the priest-hood denies them a political voice, for unlike men, they cannot preach sermons or negotiate treaties (*3G* 97), but it also marginalises them financially: Woolf draws repeatedly on *Whitaker's Almanack* to show the lower earnings of women (notably, the annual salary of £150 for a deaconess compared with £1,500 for the Archbishop of Canterbury). And, if women's earnings are restricted and they are reliant upon their husbands, they are also kept in subjection by the marriage laws that are established by the state and implemented by the church: satirising the words of the marriage service, she notes that 'husband and wife are not only one flesh; they are also one purse' (*3G* 137), and that the husband is most likely to dictate how family finances are used.

Husbands, fathers, dictators – all claim a God-given right to assert control. Woolf questions this concept by referring to sceptical arguments that '"God" is now very generally held to be a concep-tion, of patriarchal origin, valid only for certain races, at certain stages and times' (*3G* 250, n42). This sceptical, politicised view of the concept of God as an ideological construct, based closely on the work of Jane Harrison, is distinctly contrasted with the more speculative, if hostile, views of God that Woolf expresses in other contexts. Woolf herself is not entirely consistent in her arguments about the nature of God and significantly, she does not dismiss all religions: she notes that dictators are attacking the Jews, implicitly noting that she might be classed as a Jew and accordingly disen-franchised when she noting that '"Our" country still ceases to be mine if I marry a foreigner' (*3G* 185). Indeed, Woolf makes a state-ment for religious freedom when she praises Barbara Bodichon for extending education to Roman Catholics, Jews and Freethinkers at a time when they were excluded (*3G* 209). And in her peroration to *Three Guineas,* she shows some empathy with the arguments of liberal Christians: in arguing that 'a common interest unites us: it is one world, one life', she endorses the 'dream of unity' voiced by Percy Dearmer, albeit by seeking a solution from outside the church (*3G* 215).

Although Woolf's views on religion in the 1930s were strongly influenced by contemporary politics, her thoughts on religious questions received particular impetus from her relationship with the composer Ethel Smyth. They met early in 1930 when Smyth began to pursue Woolf, who was finishing *The Waves*; Smyth was 72 and Woolf 48 (*L4* xvi) and they remained friends for the rest of Woolf's life, albeit with several major arguments. Smyth was a conservative in many ways: she had been brought up a High Church Anglican and that tradition, she wrote, 'never lost its grip on my imagination'.[61] As a result of Woolf's perceptions of Smyth's religiosity, she discussed religious topics at greater length with greater intensity with Ethel than she had done with anyone else. Woolf's letters to Ethel, like those to Violet, are profoundly dialogic, for her thoughts on religion were shaped in conversation, but also significantly marked by the vicissitudes of their relationship.

Woolf's letters to Smyth during the first year of their relationship are highly confessional. Nigel Nicolson notes that she 'opened up' to Smyth on matters she had not shared with anyone, including mental illness, sex, inspirations and suicide: he speculates that this was because she found Smyth 'exceptionally sympathetic'; Raitt agrees that Ethel could 'elicit conversational, and epistolary, autobiographies from Virginia, in a way that few others could', and that the two women sat by the fire comparing and testing their stories.[62] Like her letters to Violet, Woolf's letters to Smyth are peppered with religious terminology, frequently echoing her friend's mode of greetings ('blessings') and using the phrase 'O Lord'. Woolf remarks on this herself: 'O Lord – do all my letters to you begin O Lord? – O Lord again, that was a nice day with Ethel' (*L4* 187). But using this form of address, Woolf also subtly makes her friend an object of worship, as she did with Violet.

This positive early phase lasted less than a year, however, before Woolf began to see Ethel's religious background as increasingly threatening. She started to emphasise Ethel's otherness and to stake out her own spiritual ground as unorthodox but nonetheless valid: 'Irreligious as I am (to your eyes) I have a devout belief in the human soul – when I meet what can be called such emphatically; and your power of soul completely daunts me' (*L4* 208). This 'othering' of Smyth has many of the characteristics of narratives of alterity that are normally seen in cross-cultural encounters whereby the self is defined through contradistinction with an 'Other' that is exaggerated, 'imaginary, stereotypical and biased'.[63] Woolf therefore started to define her own religious position more clearly than ever by marking out perceived differences from that of Ethel.

One reason for this distancing was Woolf's suspicion that Smyth and her great-niece Elizabeth Williamson were trying to convert her. When Smyth accused her of not believing in causes, Woolf retorted that she resented proselytising, 'the whole doctrine of preaching, of causes; of converting; teaching etc.' (L4 329), adding a vitriolic attack on Hyde Park 'God inventor[s]' and Dorothea Stephen (D4 333). She accused Ethel and Elizabeth of self-righteousness in a riposte that makes fluent and satirical use of the Evangelical register: '"We" that is Ethel and Elizabeth, having saved our souls and purged our grossness, faintly and vaguely perceive in you, Virginia, signs of grace.' And she countered their accusation that Leonard's Jewishness had prevented her from having any religious feelings by retorting that 'my Jew has more religion in one toe nail – more human love, in one hair' than them (L5 321). Smyth therefore played an important role in helping Woolf critique her Clapham family background.

Woolf used her conversations with Ethel to explore her view of God as a vindictive power. She blames him for causing the crippling headaches that stopped her working: 'he smashed his fist on my head. Lord, I said, I will write. Then he altogether took from me the power of adding word to word . . . thats your God. What he likes is to take away, to destroy.' The grammar of this quotation demonstrates a significant change in Woolf's attitude towards God: Woolf starts by referring to him as a person '*he* smashed his fist . . . *he* altogether took from me . . . ', but intersperses this with a phase that clearly attributes such a belief to Ethel: 'thats *your* God' (emphasis added). Shortly after, Woolf describes Clive Bell's sight problems as having been inflicted by 'divine providence', again challenging Smyth to justify this doctrine: 'Its for you Christians to solve these little problems' (L4 372, 375).

Woolf's most vitriolic attack on Smyth's religious background, however, was personal and came from resentment of her friend's behaviour. She began to feel increasingly drained by Smyth's demands for support and sympathy and for advice on her writing and she resented what she saw as Smyth's unjustifiable egotism when her *Mass in D* was due to be performed at the Albert Hall in March 1934.[64] Woolf (almost literally) starts cat-calling, describing Ethel as 'a humbug and a hypocrite ... uncastrated Christian cat' and 'the most attitudinizing unreal woman I've ever known – living in a mid Victorian dentists waiting room of emotional falsity' (*L4* 275, 279). Woolf's escalating frustration resulted in her famous taunt at the post-performance celebration: '"I hate religion" I roared into her deaf ears' (*L5* 282). While Woolf clearly was angered by the religious climate of the 1930s, the statement, like her jibe at Eliot's conversion, is also highly charged personally and carries with it too much baggage to be read as a considered objection to organised religion.

When Woolf and Smyth were on more amicable terms, Woolf used her conversations with Smyth to discuss religious ideas. For example there is an ongoing exploration of the concept of Heaven: 'How I'd like to see what you see when I say Heaven' (*L4* 242) and 'I think heaven must be one unexhausted reading' (*L5* 319). Woolf blends Greek ideas with Christian ones: 'when we meet in Heaven – how does your religion envisage Heaven? – I shall pick a stem of asphodel and put it in your button hole by way of thanks' (*L6* 5–6). While Woolf alludes to classical consolations, as she did in 'On Not Knowing Greek', this image unifies them with Christian ideas, reconciling her differences with Ethel by imagining a hereafter spent together in a meld of two cultures. In these more productive discussions with Ethel, too, Woolf also attempted to open up serious discussions of religious texts that also made their way into *Three Guineas*: the Bible, biblical criticism, and the works of Bishop Charles Gore and George Herbert. Dialogue with Ethel therefore helped towards her theological perspective in that essay and Woolf drew on Ethel's personal experiences as a professional woman, citing her in *Three Guineas*, as a female composer in a world dominated by men.[65]

Much more powerfully, however, the confessional mode that Ethel opened up would feed in to 'A Sketch of the Past'. This memoir includes particular emphasis on the religious aspects of Woolf's background, including her memory of her mother reading the Bible, her maternal grandmother's faith, and the 'sacred spot' at the tea table at Hyde Park Gate. But the memoir also includes Woolf's statement that 'certainly and emphatically there is no God'; this statement (which we will explore in a moment) is consonant with the terse and antagonistic register that Woolf was comfortable using towards Ethel.

Woolf's relationship with Ethel also demonstrates her continued association between sexuality and spirituality, for it bore many similarities to that with both Violet and Vita. Woolf accorded superhuman powers to Ethel, as she had for her other female friends: where

Violet was a superheroine and Vita was immortalised as Orlando, Woolf saw Ethel's copious autobiographical writings as a form of immortality:

> you *do* continue, being, thank God, not a finished precious vase, but a porous receptacle that sags slightly, swells slightly, but goes on soaking up the dew, the rain, the shine, and whatever else falls upon the earth. Isn't that the point of being Ethel Smyth? (*L6* 406)

Conclusion: a question of God

This account of Woolf's shifting views, set against the changing religious climate of the twentieth century, has revealed not only a greater level of knowledge and understanding of Christianity on Woolf's part but also some surprising moments of sympathy or empathy with people of faith, especially women. This story significantly involves the narrative of her engagement with concepts of 'god'. In her correspondence with Violet and later with Ethel, she engages with their understanding that there is a God, but challenges them both that if such a being is omnipotent it must also be cruel. Woolf makes Clarissa Dalloway and Mrs Ramsay the focus of this debate too, and both characters come to a view that there cannot be a god for this very reason. Perhaps in contradistinction to this, she entertained the idea of female divinity: the female superpowers in *Friendship's Gallery*, the long-lived female character of Orlando, the creative and omniscient female presence in *The Waves*, and the indomitable Ethel.

However, we have also noted that Woolf becomes less sympathetic towards religion in the 1930s, giving voice to more explicitly critical and atheistic ideas in *Three Guineas* that 'God' may be a patriarchal construct, designed to celebrate male power and keep women under control, and in 'A Sketch of the Past' that 'certainly and emphatically there is no God' (*MB* 72). These statements, made in 1938 and 1939 respectively, can be seen as Woolf's reaction to the world of 'militant creeds' that Forster so resented, and as a reaction to Ethel Smyth's religiosity. While Woolf had frequently disputed the existence of God, these two comments preclude the spirit of debate and empathy seen in her earlier work. Rather than being position-statements expressing a thoroughgoing, lifelong atheism, therefore, we need to see them as reflecting her thoughts at a certain time, the conclusion to a lifelong argument with the final rejection of a cruel and distant God.

In the case of *Three Guineas,* Woolf's critique of organised religion needs to be read *both* as a culmination of her thinking on gender and society throughout her career, *and* as a specific response to the political context in the 1930s. For this reason, we will find that Woolf's argument in *Three Guineas* does not always accord with her representation of Christianity and its cultural manifestations in her other works.

The case of 'A Sketch of the Past' is different, for in it she defends the spiritual value of writing against those (like Ethel) who would seek to deny it, for Woolf's argument that 'there is no God' comes as part of her analysis of 'moments of being' in which she attests to receiving an 'intuition' that has come from outside the self, 'so instinctive that it seems given to me, not made by me.' Furthermore, the moments of being are revelatory, enabling her to see 'some order', a 'pattern' behind the 'cotton wool'. That pattern is a work of art of which we are all a part. Woolf's statement against the existence of God follows on from this:

> *Hamlet* or a Beethoven quartet is the truth about this vast mass that we call the world. But there is no Shakespeare, there is no Beethoven; certainly and emphatically there is no God; we are the words; we are the music; we are the thing itself. (*MB* 72)

Here, Woolf celebrates the power of great works of literature and music to embody truth without the agency of their creators: Shakespeare did not write *Hamlet*, Beethoven did not write his quartets. Equally, the world has truth and sanctity without the actions of a creator-God, for human beings can be centres of a truth unmediated by belief systems. The statement that 'there is no God' is therefore not a denial of divinity but its relocation: it is not external to the world but incarnational, within its life. It is an extension of Woolf's capacity of seeing eternity in the present moment and divinity in her friends. Rather than negativity and denial, therefore, these moments are positive: as Pericles Lewis notes, they express a 'broader religious vision' in which there is 'delight'.[66]

From this, Woolf recognises the cathartic value of writing: her capacity to have shocks and transmute them in her writing takes away from horrific experiences their 'power to hurt'. Here, Woolf explicitly and finally rejects the idea of the 'enemy' or the cruel force in life that seeks to harm: 'I feel that I have had a blow; but it is not, as I thought as a child, simply a blow from an enemy hidden behind the cotton wool of daily life.' Though she describes it here as a childish notion, she was still trying out these ideas with Ethel in the 1930s. In this analysis of her work as a writer, Woolf recognises that she has been involved in an ongoing process of using her art to deal with the painful experiences of loss and suffering. In the chapters that follow, we will explore this ongoing process by considering ways in which Woolf's experiences of Christian culture, both positive and critical, helped her develop this understanding of her art.

Notes

1. For a study of the influence of Greek ideas on Woolf's work, see Delgarno, *Virginia Woolf and the Visible World.*
2. Forster, *What I Believe,* p. 5.
3. See Lackey, review of *The Moot Papers,* p. 959; *The Modernist God-State.*
4. Jones, *Latter Periods of Quakerism,* vol. 2, p. 967.
5. Edwards, *Christian England,* p. 350.
6. Ibid., p. 351.
7. Hügel, *Reality of God,* p. 22.
8. Edwards, *Christian England,* pp. 364–6.
9. Harrison, *Epilegomena,* p. 5.
10. Mills, *Spirit of Modernist Classicism,* pp. 63, 65.
11. Braithwaite, *State of Religious Belief,* p. 60.
12. Ibid., p. 68.
13. Ibid., p. 39.
14. Hastings, *History of English Christianity,* p. 227.
15. Edwards, *Christian England,* p. 363. See also Rosman, *Evolution of the English Churches,* p. 271.
16. Masterman, *Condition of England,* p. 266.
17. McMahon, 'Mindfulness', pp. 218–19.
18. Ibid., 220, 232.
19. Ibid., 223, 221.
20. Ware, 'Dialectic of the Past', p. 103.
21. See, for example, Marwick, *Deluge,* pp. 298–9.
22. Hylson-Smith, *Churches in England,* pp. 145, 146.
23. Edwards, *Christian England,* pp. 347–8.
24. Thoby argues that while religious toleration had extended to different denominations within Christianity, with the lifting of university sanctions against Catholics and Nonconformists, the position of agnostics and atheists was the same as it had been a century earlier (*Compulsory Chapel,* n.p.).
25. Only the Anglican Church has kept detailed records of attendance, so there are no definitive statistics for Nonconformist churches. For the unreliability of statistics, see Masterman, *Condition of England,*

p. 264. Church growth is suggested by Hylson-Smith *Churches in England*, pp. 144–5; Wilkinson argues for a decline in *Church of England and the First World War*, p. 6.

26. Woolf's relationship with Violet cooled after 1911, when she moved into 38 Brunswick Square with Adrian, Leonard Woolf, Maynard Keynes and Duncan Grant (*MB* 201), though Woolf remained in touch with Violet throughout her life.

27. See Heininge, *Reflections*, p. 100 for the date of composition for the article 'Vision of Faith'.

28. Lewis, 'Caroline Emelia Stephen and Virginia Woolf', n.p.

29. Raitt, *Vita and Virginia*, p. 132.

30. Irigaray, *Ethics of Sexual Difference*, p. 46.

31. Edwards, *Christian England*, p. 358.

32. Hylson-Smith, *Churches in England*, p. 143; Marwick, *Deluge*, p. 298.

33. The statement was made in the published report on a series of Committees of Enquiry (Edwards, *Christian England*, p. 361).

34. Quoted in Hastings, *History of English Christianity*, p. 45.

35. Marwick, *Deluge*, p. 297.

36. *The Book of Common Prayer* provides a set prayer for rain (p. 38).

37. Edwards, *Christian England*, p. 362.

38. Rosman, *Evolution of the English Churches,* p. 271. Hylson-Smith, *Churches in England*, p. 157.

39. Rosman, *Evolution of the English Churches* p. 271.

40. Hylson-Smith, *Churches in England*, p. 158.

41. Hastings, *History of English Christianity*, p. 172.

42. Schwarz, *Theology in a Global Context*, p. 154.

43. Hastings, *History of English Christianity*, p. 179.

44. Masterman, *Condition of England*, p. 266.

45. See Hastings, *History of English Christianity*, pp. 186–92.

46. L3 260. See also Leonard's account in *Downhill All the Way*, pp. 217–18.

47. The Thomas Wall Centre, Our History, online.

48. Curtis, *Virginia Woolf's Women*, pp. 73, 71.

49. Raitt, *Vita and Virginia*, p. 117.

50. Sackville-West, *Letters to Virginia Woolf*, pp. 118–19.

51. Spurr, '*Anglo-Catholic in Religion*', pp. 82–9.

52. Lackey, *Modernist God State*. See also T. S. Eliot, *The Idea of a Christian Society* (1939).

53. Hastings, *History of English Christianity*, p. 289.

54. Ibid., p. 313.

55. *The Times*, 29 September 1938.

56. 'For the clergy as a whole, peace, to be pursued by all means and at almost any cost, was the overriding preoccupation of the thirties, whether or not they subscribed formally to Pacifism' (Hylson-Smith, *Churches in England*, p. 175).

57. Dearmer, *Christianity and the Crisis*, p. 12.
58. Forster, *What I Believe*, p. 13.
59. *3G* 95; Winnington-Ingram is quoted from *Daily Telegraph*, 5 February 1937.
60. Lockhart, *Cosmo Gordon Lang*, pp. 143,195; Hastings, *History of English Christianity*, p. 198.
61. Smyth, *Impressions that Remained*, p. 460.
62. *L4* xvii; Raitt, 'The Tide of Ethel', pp. 3, 10. See also Lee, *Virginia Woolf*, pp. 596–8.
63. Roberts, *Alterity and Narrative*, p. 4.
64. As Raitt notes, 'Virginia's difficulty is with Ethel's egotism' ('The Tide of Ethel', p. 9).
65. Curtis notes that *Three Guineas* 'owes much to Ethel's feminist militancy' (*Virginia Woolf's Women*, p. 183).
66. Lewis, *Religious Experience and the Modernist Novel*, p. 156.

Chapter 3

Reverend Gentlemen and Prophetesses

A reverend gentleman has written to the Times to record the first hawthorn flower – the earliest that has appeared in the parish since 1884. (*PA* 52)

Virginia Woolf was fascinated by clergymen and they surface in her writings with surprising frequency. Mary Datchet in *Night and Day* is a vicar's daughter, as is Susan in *The Waves*, but clergymen feature as characters in most of Woolf's novels: Mr Bax in *The Voyage Out*, Mr Floyd in *Jacob's Room*, Mr Whittaker in *Mrs Dalloway*, Mr Dupper in *Orlando*, Dr Crane in *The Waves*, Cousin James in *The Years* and, most famously, Rev. Streatfield in *Between the Acts*. Two of her stories, 'Miss Pryme' and 'The Widow and the Parrot', feature vicars based on the Rector of Rodmell, Rev. Hawkesford. Among her essays are sketches of James Woodforde, John Skinner, William Cole, Archbishop Thomson, and the 'mad clergyman' Richard Edgeworth who appears in 'Lives of the Obscure'. Woolf is keen to point out unexpected clerical connections, such as when she reminds us that Laurence Sterne was also a clergyman (*CE1* 100–1) or when she unearths 'my father's clergyman's collar' from a cupboard (*MB* 182), recalling the profession that Leslie Stephen had renounced long before she was born. She even imagines clerical beaux for her mother, Violet Dickinson and herself (*MB* 82; *FG* 276; *L1* 55).

The frequency of these references is partly attributable to the fact that clergy were integral to English culture and society, both historically and into the twentieth century. Historically, clergy or clerks had been the educated class of society, and dons at Oxford and Cambridge had traditionally been ordained, as had many headmasters of public schools. For many centuries, as Dinah Birch notes, ordination was 'seen as a mark of gentility';[1] such attitudes persisted during Woolf's lifetime, for Louis sees Susan's father's profession as a mark of respectability (*W* 13). University-educated men therefore often numbered clergy among their friends and peers: Leonard Woolf was a good friend of Leopold Campbell Douglas, the Rector of St Mary Magdalene, Great Elm in Somerset (he stayed with Leopold in 1911, attending church and accompanying him on parish visits).[2] Anglican parish clergy were prominent and influential figures within communities, expected to take a full and active part in local life and politics. To this day, Anglican clergy have the pastoral role of 'cure of souls' in their parish: anyone living in England has the right to have their child baptised, to be married, and to have their funeral conducted in their local church. Incumbents are also responsible for maintaining church buildings, and so have a particular role in preserving the heritage of the built environment.

The centrality of the clergy to English middle-class life meant that they were integral to Woolf's analysis of culture and society in *Three Guineas*. We have already seen how Woolf's analysis included a critique of the Clapham Sect and the ways in which clergy were closely involved in creating the middle-class establishment, along with lawyers, politicians and academics, as well as a specific attack on Archbishop Cosmo Lang and the Church of England in the 1930s when churchmen were making vocal contributions to national politics, and bishops sat in the House of Lords (as they still do). In this chapter, we will explore how some of Woolf's criticisms of the clergy in *Three Guineas* were formed through her fictional sketches of clergymen in her novels. These show that she knew and understood the range of duties and expectations that came with the clerical role and, in the tradition of Jane Austen and Charlotte and Anne Brontë,[3] she painted the clergy as ineffectual and, on occasions, as misusing their position.

Significantly, the Anglican clergy remained exclusively male throughout Woolf's lifetime (some other denominations, particularly the Nonconformist churches, admitted women as leaders much earlier). This point was reinforced for Woolf by the decision in 1936 to continue to exclude women from ordained ministry, a decision that is significant for *Three Guineas,* where she shows how all professional men had bought into a system that justified and promoted war, a society that 'like a gramophone whose needle has stuck, is grinding out, with intolerable unanimity "Three hundred millions spent upon arms"' (*3G* 183). This chapter will show how Woolf started critiquing the chauvinism of male clergy in her novels leading up to *Three Guineas* and how she explored the potential for women to be ministers, albeit of a very different kind from the clergy she knew.

Appraising parsons I: the cure of souls?

Woolf provides two accounts of clergymen attempting pastoral ministry, and in both cases, they exploit their position to exert power over women. Mr Floyd in *Jacob's Room*, the vicar of the large rural parish near Scarborough where Jacob grows up, initially appears to provide moral support for the widow Betty Flanders, acting as a father-figure to her sons. Betty appreciates his 'kindness' in agreeing to teach the boys Latin, going above and beyond the call of duty: 'it was more than most clergymen would have done, coming round after tea, or having them in his own room' (*JR* 21). However, Floyd has an ulterior motive, for he shocks Betty by proposing marriage, insensitive to the fact that she is still grieving the death of her husband (Seabrook Flanders comes 'vividly' before her as she reads Floyd's letter, which reduces her to tears and anger). The potted history of Floyd's life that Woolf inserts at this point suggests that he sees marriage as a career move, for he quickly asks for a parish in Sheffield, where he finds a wife. Floyd's marriage becomes the stepping-stone to advancement that sees him eventually becoming Principal of a theological college and editor of a 'well-known series of Ecclesiastical Biographies' (*JR* 24). Recalling both Sir James's *Essays in Ecclesiastical Biography* and Leslie Stephen's *Dictionary of National Biography*, this role places Floyd in the position of a middle-class man in the Clapham tradition. Woolf brings these ideas together in *Three Guineas* to show how a clerical career can be a form of self-aggandisement, when she satirises Thomas Gisborne, the Clapham Sect cleric much admired by Sir James, whose views on women expressed in *The Duties of the Female Sex* lead one to 'conclude that a biography of the Deity would resolve itself into a Dictionary of Clerical Biography' (*3G* 224 n20). Yet Woolf's summary of Floyd's career ends by drawing attention to his feet of clay: he keeps Betty Flanders' rejection letter for many years, deliberately hiding it from his wife, which suggests a hankering after another woman that, in gospel terms is tantamount to adultery (Matthew 5:27–8).

Mr Floyd can also be seen to play a part in inducting Jacob into the system that will lead to his death in the trenches. In teaching the boys Latin to prepare them for public school, he helps them make the transition from the female domain of home to the masculine world of school and university. This becomes explicit when Floyd discusses the boys' career choices in his parting conversation with them, talking to Jacob about Rugby School and to Archer about the Royal Navy. Floyd invites them to choose a present from his study, and Archer chooses a paper-knife (symbolically phallic and weapon-like), and Jacob chooses a volume of Byron's poems. The latter gift prefigures Jacob's death, for Byron died trying to support the cause for Greek independence. The connection is made explicit by the fact that Floyd spots Jacob passing in the street and recalls the gift of Byron just moments before a reference to gunfire over Greece, which in turn is followed by the scene of Jacob's room being cleared after his death.

Woolf continues to question the power that male clergy can hold over women in *Mrs Dalloway*, in Miss Kilman's relationship with Mr Edward Whittaker, the preacher who has converted her. Miss Kilman persistently recalls her conversion experience of entering a church feeling bitter and excluded from society and finding her feelings 'assuaged' by the preaching of Mr Whittaker, who invites her to his home. Whittaker declares that her conversion is 'the hand of God . . . The Lord had shown her the way': Whittaker's certainty that he has been the agent of God means that Miss Kilman struggles to distinguish between them, for when she needs to counter her negative feelings 'she thought of God. She thought of Mr. Whittaker' (*MD* 111). This act of act of self-aggrandisement keeps Miss Kilman in thrall: Whittaker's views feed her low self-esteem and prayer does nothing to improve her poor body-image as she finds herself

> struggling, as Mr Whittaker had told her, with that violent grudge against the world which had scorned her, sneered at her, cast her off, beginning with this indignity – the infliction of her unlovable body which people could not bear to see. (*MD* 115)

Whittaker's gospel of accepting suffering is oppressive and it is no coincidence that his name recalls *Whitaker's Almanac*, the official list of clergy hierarchy and salaries that Woolf had already satirised in 'The Mark on the Wall' (*CSF* 116) and would later use in

Three Guineas as proof of institutional inequalities in the Church of England.

Appraising parsons II: The conduct of worship

Woolf's novels include two examples of named clergymen leading services. The most detailed of these is in *The Voyage Out*, when Mr Bax, an English clergyman, takes Morning Prayer at the hotel chapel in Santa Monica with a small congregation of British guests (*VO* 261–9).[4] The service is a rare example of Woolf's use of social comedy, and she presents Bax humorously as 'a stout black figure . . . with a preoccupied expression', 'large and fat' and with a face that looks 'smooth and white like a very large egg.' The social realism of this novel enables Woolf to make a close critique of Bax, his sermon and his opinions; as Woolf would later encourage educated men's daughters to attend services and critique sermons in *Three Guineas*.

Woolf closely examines Bax's strategies for addressing his congregation, noting that he compensates for being much younger than them by delivering his text with 'weighty significance'. He makes no attempt to engage with members outside of the service, deliberately avoiding acknowledging anyone as he rushes into the chapel, but then becoming personable to draw people in once the service has started. Rachel perceives him as 'a man of the world with supple lips and an agreeable manner', who uses 'a certain innocent craftiness' to steer his congregation to see him as one of them: 'What we want them to say is, "He's a good fellow – in other words, "He is my brother."' And yet, for all this, he seems to become 'definitely clerical' as he talks, and then 'definitely priestly'. As he becomes more 'priestly', he addresses his female listeners in particular, 'for indeed Mr Bax's congregations were mainly composed of women and he was used to assigning them their duties in his innocent clerical campaigns.' Like Floyd and Whittaker, Bax seeks to dominate women by roping them in to do his bidding. Woolf therefore foreshadows *Three Guineas* by critiquing the priesthood for keeping women in subjection and excluding them from their ranks. Finally, Bax's sermon, which Woolf presents at length, first in summary and then in a long concluding quotation, demonstrates the subservience of the church to the establishment and endorses imperialism by emphasising the importance of making conversions in India. At this point, she comments, he hardly seems religious at all, for the sermon comes across like an opinion piece from a newspaper.

Bax's delivery shows a determination to reduce the congregation to a state of dependence. He reads the Lord's Prayer 'over' the congregation, and people gradually join in with 'a childlike babble of voices'. The recitation unites the congregation, making them 'pathetically united and well-disposed towards each other.' Woolf critiques the effectiveness of Bax as a minister by gauging the reactions of his congregation. While some of the men become 'more secular and critical' as they hear warmongering passages from the Old Testament, the dreamy and conventional Susan Warrington simply ignores the words and continues to be 'serene' and to praise God in her own mind. Woolf warns how religious practice can reduce people to complacency and compliance. The service is significant as the point in the novel where Rachel rejects Christianity. Rachel finds her fellow worshippers pretentious and ignorant, unable to grasp the 'beautiful idea, like a butterfly' they have come to contemplate: she criticises Bax, for as much as she tries to conceive something worth worshipping, she was 'always misled by the voice of Mr Bax saying things which misrepresented the idea'. As Heininge has shown, Rachel's reaction resembles Caroline Emelia Stephen's decision to turn away from Anglicanism.[5] As such Woolf does not denigrate the importance of spirituality, or the importance of grasping spiritual truths, but castigates the church and its clergy for failing to communicate these, not least by putting themselves between the congregation and God.

In Bax, Woolf presents a clergyman who is domineering, wedded to the establishment, spiritually impoverished, and perhaps even wilfully misleading; a laity that is often complacent and too willing to be led; and a liturgy that unquestioningly preserves primitive aggressive sentiments. Significantly, this is Bax's last appearance in the novel: where he might have offered pastoral support later when Rachel dies at the hotel, he is nowhere to be seen.

The only other named clergyman to lead a service is Dr Crane in *The Waves*: the headmaster of the school attended by Bernard, Neville and Louis, who like Mr Floyd initiates the boys into the male world (*W* 24–7). Dr Crane gives a speech of welcome to initiate the boys into public school on what Bernard notes is 'our first night at school, away from our sisters'. Woolf does not specify whether Dr Crane is ordained, but dressed in black with a crucifix on his waistcoat, it is clear that religion is a marker of his authority, and he fulfils the ministerial roles of taking a service in Chapel, reading lessons, leading prayers and preaching a sermon. Dr Crane could be a parody of Thomas Arnold, ordained headmaster of Rugby, whose sermons were famous for stirring up his charges, in which case he would represent a long tradition for headmasters of the public schools to be clergymen. Though that tradition had died out by the time *The Waves* was published in 1931, it would have been current in the late nineteenth century, when this passage is set.

As with Bax, Woolf assesses Crane's authority by noting the reaction of his listeners and, in this case, only one is persuaded: Louis, painfully conscious of his Australian origin, finds a sense of rootedness and 'continuity' as he hears the headmaster speak, senses his authority and feels reassured by his crucifix. If Louis is a parody of T. S. Eliot, as has often been suggested, then here is Woolf's cruel suggestion that Eliot had adopted Anglicanism as a coping strategy for his insecurity at being born in America: a further example of her denigrating Eliot's faith. By contrast, Bernard is a sceptical listener, finding Crane's words 'too hearty to be true' and in a direct echo of *The Voyage Out,* Bernard is angry with him, not for merely failing to grasp the 'beautiful butterfly' of faith, but for killing it off altogether: 'He has minced the dance of the white butterflies at the door to powder.' Neville is even more resistant: Crane's words 'fall cold' on his head, he sees the headmaster as too 'corrupt' to carry authority, reduces his crucifix to a cheap 'gilt cross', and sees him as the proponent of a 'sad religion'.

Woolf emphasises a resistant reading from a female perspective in the other church service to appear in her novels: a service at King's College Chapel, Cambridge in *Jacob's Room* (37–40). This time, there is no named officiant but an amorphous group of clergy and choir. Here, Woolf's criticism of the clergy is at its sharpest, for the service is described in a defamiliarised way, from the perspective of the sceptical outsider. Woolf abandons the liturgical vocabulary she incorporated into *The Voyage Out,* no longer guiding the reader through the contents of the service, instead describing a series of precise but to the uninitiated, meaningless manoeuvres whereby 'white-robed figures crossed from side to side; now mounted steps, now descended, all very orderly'. There is a militaristic feel to this, not least because the choristers 'pass into service' making their entry into the chapel synonymous with enlisting in military service, with their 'great boots' marching. The ghostly image of the gowns that seem to contain nothing, and the picture of the 'sculptured faces' reminiscent of tombs, hint that these men are destined to die and become ghosts, commemorated in stone statues. They thus prefigure Jacob's death, and those of many of his generation, in the First World War. Death seems both inevitable and an unavoidable consequence of their religious upbringing: the subservience that Woolf detected in some of the congregation in *The Voyage Out* is stronger and more sinister in this scene, for any 'authority and certainty' the young men possess are actually 'controlled by piety'. The 'orderly procession' of the choir and the 'orderly' choreography of choir and ministers, have the sinister connotations of an inevitable march towards war.

Women are unwelcome at this service, though not completely excluded. Jacob ponders why they are allowed to take part at all, and thinks that women are as inappropriate as a dog in church: his mind elaborates on the analogy with the scatalogical suggestion that a dog might end up cocking its leg against a pillar. This alludes to Samuel Johnson's objection to women preachers: 'a woman's preaching is like a dog's walking on its hinder legs. It is not done well; but you are surprised to find it done at all.'[6] The fact that Woolf places the thought in Jacob's mind shows that the sentiment is still alive in the mind of a young man in or around 1906. The scene therefore makes the association between warfare and the exclusion of women from ministry: a connection that would be made much more strongly in *Three Guineas*.

Woolf's defamiliarised representation of the chapel service in *Jacob's Room* anticipates her attack on ceremonies in *Three Guineas*, where she argues that institutions use symbolism to create an aura of reverence to support the patriarchal status quo and to enforce exclusion. Addressing educated men as a group, she remarks: 'Now you dress in violet; a jewelled crucifix swings on your breast; now your shoulders are covered with lace; now furred with ermine; now slung with many linked chains set with precious stones' (*3G* 103).

Her description deliberately refuses to name or accord any meaning to items of clothing, leaving it to the reader to identify the actors as bishop, judge and chancellor. The description of the bishop in frivolous 'violet' rather than stately purple, and with lavish jewellery rendering him cheap and pretentious rather than dignified, refuses to recognise his authority. Woolf treats religious, academic and civic ceremonies in the same manner:

> Here you kneel; there you bow; here you advance in procession behind a man carrying a silver poker; here you mount a carved chair; here you appear to do homage to a piece of painted wood; here you abase yourselves before tables covered with richly worked tapestry. (Ibid.)

Woolf's refusal to acknowledge the meaning of ceremonies, reducing the symbols to flimsy theatrical props, emphasises her outsider's perspective and renders these actions empty gestures.

As in *Jacob's Room* and *The Waves,* too, Woolf criticises the clergy for having a hold on education and for promoting an ideology that had sought to exclude women from learning. This is seen when she notes that the public schools and universities have a 'semi-monastic look' (*3G* 91), but it becomes more strident as she notes the difficulties that female benefactors faced in setting up women's colleges.

Appraising parsons III: The burial of the dead

Woolf did not consider clergy to be adept at taking funerals, though this is a role that many would consider to be essential to the vocation. Her fictional account of a funeral is that of Mrs Rose Pargiter in *The Years,* which is taken by a family member, Cousin James (*Y* 74–8). As Anna Snaith has pointed out, James was a significant family name within Woolf's family and in the Pargiters, she presented a well-connected middle-class family like her own whose members are to be found in the Church, the Bar and the House of Commons (*Y* 437–8n). As with her commentaries on Bax, Crane and the anonymous clergy at King's, Woolf uses the reactions of a congregation member, in this case Rose's daughter Delia, to gauge the effectiveness of leadership of the service.

The funeral liturgy is taken from *The Book of Common Prayer,* much of which is made up of biblical quotations, and Woolf ironically plays off the words against James's delivery. As the service begins in the church, Delia savours the opening sentence, 'I am the resurrection and the life' (John 11:25): 'the outspoken words filled her with glory. This she could feel genuinely.' These are the words of Christ, from the story of the raising of Lazarus, where he assures Martha that her brother will rise from the dead. The next lines that stir Delia speak of mortality, 'And fade away suddenly like the grass, in the morning it is green, and groweth up; but in the evening it is cut down, dried up, and withered' (Psalm 90:5–6). Although these words speak of death, they give a sense of a natural order and Delia experiences them as a 'burst of familiar beauty . . . like music'.

By contrast, James's delivery is a distraction: 'Cousin James went on reading, something slipped. The sense was blurred. She could not follow with her reason.' He speaks too fast, he 'seemed to hurry, as if he did not altogether believe what he was saying.' Significantly, Woolf passes over a lengthy passage of the liturgy that incorporates a theological explanation of eternal life from 1 Corinthians 15. Delia merely observes that James 'seemed to pass from the known to the unknown; from what he believed to what he did not believe.' The structure of this sentence echoes a central argument of the passage that works in binary oppositions:

> It is sown in corruption; it is raised in incorruption: it is sown in dishonour; it is raised in glory: it is sown in weakness; it is raised in power: it is sown a natural body; it is raised a spiritual body. (1 Corinthians 15:42–4)

The theological meaning asks one to accept what is unknown and cannot be proven, but Delia hears it as a marker of James's failure to communicate the message: 'what did he mean by what he was saying? She gave it up'. Delia objects to James's voice and he ceases to be a person: like the choristers in *Jacob's Room,* he dwindles to a set of empty vestments, for he 'looked clean, he looked starched and ironed like his robes.'

As the service moves to the graveside, Delia again hears words that she can savour: 'Man that is born of a woman' is a 'splendid gust of music' that helps unite the mourners. However, she finds the visual symbolism of the moment of interment more powerful than the words, and she has a revelatory moment on seeing earth being dropped on the coffin:

> a sense of something everlasting; of life mixing with death, of death becoming life. For as she looked she heard the sparrows chirp quicker and quicker; she heard wheels in the distance sound louder and louder; life came closer and closer.

These lines are deeply imbued with allusions. They echo lines from this stage of the funeral liturgy, 'in the midst of life we are in death'. Delia's thoughts echo those of Septimus in *Mrs Dalloway* who hears sparrows singing that 'there is no death' (*MD* 22): both sparrows and wheels could be background noise, but the wheels also echo Marvell's 'To his Coy Mistress', 'But at my back I always hear / Time's wingèd chariot hurrying near', here subverting the poem's argument that the passage of time hastens death by referring to the wheels bringing life closer.

However, this brief moment of consolation is broken by the words of the committal prayer and Delia blames Cousin James for them:

> 'We give thee hearty thanks,' said the voice, 'for that it has pleased thee to deliver this our sister out of the miseries of this sinful world – '
> What a lie! she cried to herself. What a damnable lie! He had robbed her of the one feeling that was genuine; he had spoilt her one moment of understanding.

Although James is reciting the liturgy as required, he has done so with complete insensitivity to those who are bereaved, for these words reinforce that idea of a God who causes people to die, a notion that Woolf resented consistently.

Woolf's account of this service partly draws on her experience of the funeral of Jane Harrison at Marylebone Cemetery in London in April 1928: 'We walked to the grave; the clergyman, a friend, waited for the dismal company to collect; then read some of the lovelier, more rational parts of the Bible; & said, by heart, Abide with me.' Like Delia, Woolf finds that the words had failed to make any connection with her: 'the usual obstacle of not believing dulled & bothered me. Who is "God" & what the Grace of Christ?' and, significantly, she could not see the relevance of the service to Harrison herself: 'what did they mean to Jane?' (*D3* 181). The services are also similar because of the poignant intervention of birdsong: Woolf recalls how a 'bird sang most opportunely; with a gay indifference; & if one liked, hope, that Jane would have enjoyed.' The sounds of the natural world pay a far more fitting tribute than all the words of the service.

Woolf particularly resented the verbosity of the Church of England funeral and its attempts to offer theological explanations for loss and death. By contrast, she was deeply moved by the wordless Quaker funeral of Roger Fry at Golders Green Crematorium in September 1934. Woolf noted that she was glad to have attended the service, which was 'all very simple & dignified. Music. Not a word spoken.' And unlike Jane Harrison's funeral, which seemed to have nothing to do with the person being commemorated, Roger Fry's service brought him back very powerfully for Woolf: 'I thought of him too, at intervals. Dignified & honest & large – "large sweet soul" – something ripe & musical about him – & then the fun & the fact that he had lived with such variety & generosity & curiosity' (*D4* 243).

'A piece of eternity': sacramental ministry

Significantly, Woolf does not show any of her clergymen presiding at Holy Communion, or indeed doing anything to provide spiritual guidance for their flocks: they mince the butterfly of faith and recite biblical lines without conviction. However, the character who comes closest to fulfilling such a role is, significantly, female, for Mrs Ramsay's dinner party has distinct overtones of a Catholic Mass at which she is president. Implications begin shortly before the meal, when Mrs Ramsay spends time in quiet reflection, as though she were preparing for a rite. She slips into a repetitive chant, 'Children don't forget, children don't forget . . . It will end, It will end, . . . It will come, it will come' (*TL* 86). Her reverie involves a stripping away of personality, for though she delights in the chance to 'be herself, by herself,' the self she uncovers is one that transcends the social, enabling her to experience peace, eternity, and unity with her surroundings: the precise qualities that she manages to communicate to her guests at the party.

Significantly, however, Mrs Ramsay rejects Christian ideas. Suddenly slipping into thinking that 'We are in the hands of the Lord', she dismisses the thought as a lie:

> How could any Lord have made this world? she asked. With her mind she had always seized the fact that there is no reason, order, justice: but suffering, death, the poor. There was no treachery too base for the world to commit; she knew that. No happiness lasted; she knew that. (*TL* 87)

This echoes Leslie Stephen's argument from David Hume that the existence of the universe is no proof that there is a God: an imperfect world cannot prove a perfect maker; a heterogeneous world cannot prove a unified maker.[7] Provocatively, then, Woolf presents Mrs Ramsay as a thinking, critical outsider who can access the infinite because of this. It is a position not unlike that of Caroline Emelia Stephen's 'agnosticism with mystery at the heart of it.'[8]

Woolf's description of the dinner party clearly evokes a church service which, unlike the routine acts of obligation of her clergymen, involves communion between the participants and a genuine experience of eternity. This can be seen when the guests gather, for even in a simple conversation about politics, the way they are 'bending themselves to listen' suggests an attitude of prayerfulness and a desire to enter into a common feeling. Indeed, Woolf specifically mentions prayer, as each of them thinks, 'Pray heaven that the inside of my mind may not be exposed' (*TL* 127). The lighting of candles helps draw the guests together and fosters an air of expectation. This increases the sense that the dining room is a church, for the flames create a ripple of lights on the windows that evokes stained glass. The babble of conversation sounds like 'men and boys crying out the Latin words of a service in some Roman Catholic cathedral' (*TL* 149). Mrs Ramsay becomes aware of emotion rising like incense, 'like a smoke, like a fume rising upwards' (*TL* 141). At the end of the meal, Augustus Carmichael becomes an acolyte, 'holding his table napkin so that it looked like a long white robe', chanting and then bowing to Mrs Ramsay as he leaves (*TL* 150). While the reference to a Roman Catholic cathedral is provocative because that church has never entertained women priests, Woolf uses these references to think beyond the Anglican tradition that she associated so closely with patriarchy and nationalism.

The sacramental element of the meal is enhanced with the arrival of Paul Rayley and Minta Doyle, and Mrs Ramsay's intimation that they have become engaged, whereupon the occasion becomes a celebration, indeed a kind of marriage ceremony with Mrs Ramsay as the celebrant, for Lily feels that Mrs Ramsay 'having brought it all about, somehow laughed, led her victims . . . to the altar' (*TL* 137). Peering into the dish of *Boeuf en Daube*, Mrs Ramsay reflects on how the meal is a celebration of love, a profound emotion greater than the love of matchmaking and romance. Lily imagines that Mrs Ramsay is worshipping love: 'Mrs Ramsay . . . exalted that, worshipped that; held her hands over it to warm them, to protect it' (*TL* 137). The language here suggests sacramental gestures: Mrs Ramsay exalting love – praising it, or in another meaning raising it up – evoking the moment in the prayer of consecration where the priest elevates the communion bread; the moment where she 'held her hands over it', suggests the moment when the priest holds his hands over the vessels of wine that are to be consecrated. At this point Mrs Ramsay is serving the *Boeuf en Daube*: in distributing meat to her guests, then, she has brought about transubstantiation.

This act of communion also provides an encounter with eternity. Mrs Ramsay thinks of this at the precise moment when she serves the meat to William Bankes: 'It partook, she felt, carefully helping Mr Bankes to a specially tender piece, of eternity.' This is a multivalent sentence. Mrs Ramsay is aware that they are touching eternity through the meal, but the structure of the sentence invites us to ignore the comma and run two phrases together to read that she is giving Mr Bankes a 'piece of eternity' (*TL* 142). Mrs Ramsay is aware that she is feeding her guests spiritually as well as physically, and therefore aware that she has recovered and shared the feelings she experienced in her private reverie. She experiences an 'element of joy' and a sense of 'profound stillness', emotions that seem to rise from all the assembled company (*TL* 141). This becomes even more powerful when we consider that this meal is, effectively, Mrs Ramsay's Last Supper, for this is the last day of narrative time in which she is alive and she dies 'rather suddenly' in the next section. Provocatively, then, since Mrs Ramsay's story replicates that of Christ, she is representing Christ at the Mass.

This image of a mother presiding over a ceremonial occasion has complex associations. It affirms the importance of the home as a place of worship that had been so important to the Clapham Sect, Caroline Emelia's home as her Quaker church, and also the emphasis on the home and on the mother as a site of religion that had arisen in response to the First World War. However it also looks back to a neglected history of women's involvement in sacramental religion. Jane Lilienfeld has made a convincing case for viewing Mrs Ramsay's meal as a bacchanalian celebration,[9] but this does not preclude a reading of the meal as Eucharistic. Deborah Sawyer has pointed out that Christianity grew out of a fusion of Greek, Roman and Jewish cultures. Sawyer has shown has women were active in cultic rites in the Graeco-Roman world, and that bacchanalian rites were performed by women. In the Roman and Jewish cultures, women had an important influence in the home, which was also a site of religious practice: they had parts to play in rituals and, crucially, they were charged with passing the culture on by educating their children.[10] Since the earliest Christian churches were based in homes – as Jerome Murphy-O'Connor points out, 'there was no question of a public meeting place, such as the Jewish synagogue . . . use had to be made of the only facilities available, namely the dwellings of families that had become Christian'[11] – these churches operated on territories where women were free to participate fully; Mrs Ramsay's meal therefore harks back to the earliest form of Christian practice, when women were empowered to perform sacred rites.

Through Mrs Ramsay, then, Woolf provocatively invites the reader to contemplate the possibility of a woman priest: something that leaders of both the Anglican and Catholic Churches deemed impossible at the time. Furthermore, when set against the other fictional clergymen considered so far, Mrs Ramsay seems more effective in engaging with sacred mysteries: she is the only one of these characters to preside at a ceremony that can be described as sacramental; the only one to engage in private contemplation rather than public prayer; and the only one to access a spiritual dimension. Yet in emphasising Mrs Ramsay's scepticism, Woolf implies that women's ministry would not fit comfortably with the Christian church of her time.

Women's ministry in *Three Guineas*

Woolf reaffirms her belief in women's ministry in *Three Guineas*, but by then her argument had the additional impetus of the Church Commissioners' report *The Ministry of Women* (1936) that had confirmed the longstanding position of the Church of England that women should be excluded from the Holy Orders of bishops, priests and deacons. The only position open to them was the ambiguous one of deaconess: although the role entailed an ordination ceremony, the Church made clear that this was an Order *sui generis* and distinct from the traditional orders; responsibilities of deaconesses remained unclear, and conflicting rulings alternately extended and limited their roles over the first decades of the twentieth century.[12] Woolf shows in *Three Guineas* that the exclusion of women from the priesthood stems from a deep-seated social resistance to professional women, especially in terms of remuneration, and the role that religious ideas had played in underpinning these ideologies. In challenging women's exclusion from ordained ministry, Woolf engages with sociopolitical questions and with spiritual and theological ones, showing that these were deeply interrelated.

Woolf draws on historical precedents to make the case that women have the gifts and insights to become spiritual leaders. In a move that parallels her invitation for women to 'rewrite history' in *A Room of One's Own*, she reclaimed the history of women in early Christianity through the figure of the 'prophetess whose message was voluntary and untaught', and who 'became extinct' with the establishment of the three orders, the domain of paid men (*3G* 198). Woolf traces a tradition from this ancient figure through to the female followers of Christ, and on to Emily Brontë as the 'spiritual descendent of some ancient prophetess, who prophesied when prophecy was a voluntary and unpaid occupation' (ibid.) and she quotes from 'No Coward Soul', in which Brontë affirms her visions of heaven and her sense of the presence of the deity within her.

It is important to note, however, that Woolf makes a specific case for women to exercise ministry within the Christian tradition, looking back to Christ and the New Testament. Here again, we see the influence of Caroline Emelia Stephen, including her desire to rescue Christ from the church, and her Quaker ministry of praying, writing, and nurturing new believers from her home, the convent of one. In defining what a Christian ministry might look like for women, Woolf distinguishes between the mind of Christ, the founder, and that of the church which has, she suggests, been far too ready to build its precepts on St Paul. She points out that Christ's followers were working-class men and that the early prophetesses were women, showing that 'the founder of Christianity believed that neither training nor sex was needed for this profession' (*3G* 197). In showing that the established church is no longer true to its roots, Woolf therefore accuses it of being anti-Christian in its misogyny.

However, although Woolf argues for the importance of the prophetess being 'untutored', she actually showcases her own biblical knowledge in order to undermine the Commissioners' arguments. Christine Froula has usefully described *Three Guineas* as Woolf's epistle in reply to St Paul, but through this Woolf also performs an exegesis in which she demonstrates that, *contra* Samuel Johnson, a woman could expound scriptures. Woolf shows that the church's decision against women priests is based on a selective reading of St Paul, as they have taken particular elements from his contradictory body of writings, choosing his writings on the subjugation of women in the letters to Titus and Timothy, dismissing his teaching in Galatians (3:28) that all are one in Christ Jesus and ignoring evidence that he had women ministers, such as Lydia and Chloe, in his churches. She also cleverly takes apart a passage that the Church Commissioners had used as an argument against ordination for women – St Paul's argument that women should only pray or prophesy if they are veiled (1 Corinthians 11:2–16) – demonstrating that the passage is anchored within a broader ideology about the subjugation of women to men, for it teaches that wives should be subject to their husbands because woman was created for the benefit of man, and because man is the image of God, but woman only the image of man.

Woolf continues to critique this passage in a lengthy footnote (*3G* 235–8) in which she relates it to an ideology prevailing even into the 1930s that women should be chaperoned, and that this leads to more general prohibitions against women's participation in public life. She shows how these attitudes are informed by St Paul's teachings on chastity, demolishing his argument over the veil by seeing it as an expression of his 'sexual and personal prejudices' as a bachelor whose notion of chastity is bound up with a desire for power and domination: 'If St Paul had said openly that he liked the look of women's long hair many of us would have agreed with him, and thought the better of him for saying so.' She notes that his decision to bring in both angels and nature to support his point is a sign of weak logic: 'he seems to have been doubtful of their [the angels'] support or he would not think it necessary to drag in the familiar accomplice nature.' She then deconstructs his attempt to invoke the authority of nature, pointing out that what is presented as 'natural' is in fact the result of economic forces: 'nature, when allied with financial advantage, is seldom of divine origin.'

Woolf tackles the passage from a different point of view in the body of the essay, to defend a private, conventual ministry. Here she uses the veil in a series of extended metaphors to create a critical distance between women and the patriarchal world, and to demonstrate the superiority of the private realm. She initially invokes the veil as a barrier through which the patriarchal establishment can be viewed from an ironic distance. She pictures the world 'as it appears to us who see it from the threshold of the private house; through the shadow of the veil that St Paul still lays upon our eyes' (*3G* 102). Once more describing patriarchal institutions in defamiliarised terms, Woolf uses the voice of the veiled woman to give her the moral high ground to criticise men for their finery and dismiss clothing that signifies rank as 'a ridiculous, a barbarous, a displeasing spectacle' (*3G* 105). A woman can exercise her ministry in private clothes, not clerical dress.

Woolf brings the issue of Pauline misogyny to bear on the question of women's ordination at the close of *Three Guineas* in a chain of allusions to the veil that pinpoint fear as the factor that has debarred women from public office in general and specifically from preaching, that is, from being empowered to speak with divine authority. Woolf takes St Paul's pronouncements that a woman must be veiled in order to preach literally, now interpreting it as giving women the licence to preach: 'The implication is that if veiled a woman might prophesy [i.e. preach] and lead in prayer' (*3G* 197). As Froula notes, Woolf adopts the veil in order to frame her own epistle in reply to that of St Paul.[13] The object Woolf uses as a veil at this point is the Commissioners' Report, including lengthy quotations from the Appendix by Professor L. W. Grensted on the psychological barriers to women becoming priests. In adopting this metaphorical veil, Woolf cleverly avoids speaking in her own words, confronting her opponents with the words of the report and of a male professor. The passages she quotes include Grensted's analysis that women have been excluded from the priesthood because of a 'non-rational sex-taboo' (*3G* 201), a deep-seated fear and anger against women, arising from the 'infantile fixation' of a father's obsession with his daughter. Woolf adds in a footnote that this fixation motivated both the patriarchal father in the Victorian home and contemporary dictators like Hitler and Mussolini. Woolf accuses the clergy of playing a key role in enforcing this for, she argues, the 'emphasis which both priests and dictators place upon the necessity for two worlds' – separate spheres – 'is enough to prove that it is essential to the domination' (*3G* 247).

When Woolf finally rejects the veil, she raises it to address her male interlocutors 'face to face' (*3G* 202) by voicing home-truths about the anger and fear that colour relationships between men and women, no longer hiding behind academic psychology but discussing three historical examples of jealous fathers: those of Elizabeth Barrett, Charlotte Brontë and Sophia Jex-Blake. The phrase 'face to face' echoes another passage from Corinthians, this time from St Paul's famous rhapsodic hymn to love, when he looks forward to the Second Coming when there will be no need for prophecies or speaking in tongues: 'now we see through a glass, darkly: but then face to face' (1 Corinthians 13:12a). The allusion gives Woolf's rhetoric revelatory power: when fear and misogyny are brought to light, they will be easier to eliminate. Woolf thus writes prophetically, expressing the hope that such a resolution will be achieved in time, rather after the end of all time.

It is no coincidence that the most famous of the possessive Victorian fathers Woolf discusses is a clergyman: Patrick Brontë. Woolf comments that the fact that he was not defrocked for the misery he caused Charlotte by blocking her marriage shows that his actions were condoned by both society and the church. Woolf extends the argument by showing that what is practised in the private house is mirrored in society at large: the father's jealousy over his daughter is mapped out onto the professional man's jealousy over his own territory: 'The infantile fixation develops, directly the priest's right to practise his profession is challenged, to an aggravated and exacerbated emotion to which the name sex-taboo is scientifically supplied' (*3G* 211–12). At this point, Woolf's use of the word 'priest' broadens from the specifically religious to include other professional groups ('priests of medicine' and 'priests of science', and she hears the 'priests and professors') wishing to preserve the exclusivity of their territories.

Having identified the pathological psychology of the professional man, Woolf concludes that women are better off conducting their vocation outside the church, for this frees them from obligations. Women do not have to swear an oath to a monarch or a bishop,[14] and their unpaid status gives them freedom. Woolf urges women to practise their professions in their own ways and significantly, she encourages them to follow a way of life that revises religious commitment: instead of poverty, chastity and obedience, she advocates poverty, chastity, derision and – crucially – freedom from unreal loyalties; in other words, freedom from the demands of the church as a profession.

Here we see how Woolf argues that women are better equipped for ministry than men. Many of the inadequate clergymen that Woolf depicts in her novels have been ground down by their obligations, reciting services meaninglessly because that is required of them and sacrificing spiritual leadership for career advancement like Mr Floyd. Parallels can be seen in Woolf's brief sketches of real-life clergy in *Three Guineas,* where she notes that high-ranking clergy, like other successful professional men, gain their positions by sacrificing home, family and personality. She quotes from the biography of Bishop Charles Gore: 'This is an awful mind- and soul-destroying life. I really do not know how to live it. The arrears of important work accumulate and crush'. Woolf notes that this 'bears out what so many people are saying now about the Church and the nation. Our bishops and deans seem to have no soul with which to preach and no mind with which to write', and she cites the journalism (significantly not the preaching) of Dean Inge as a further example (*3G* 152–3). Her sketch of William Thomson, Archbishop of York, in her essay 'Outlines' depicts someone whose piety was suppressed by the administrative demands of the role, so that, although a person of 'simple faith' might believe that 'a vicar is a good man, a canon a better man, and an archdeacon the best man of all', this is questionable: 'is it easy, is it possible, for a good man to be an Archbishop?' (*CE4* 116, 119). So she concludes that women, by abstaining from professionalised religion and learning, and by exercising an unpaid vocation in private, can best protect culture and intellectual liberty and prevent war.

Appraising parsons IV: custodians of the 'dear old Church'

However, not all of Woolf's depictions of clergymen fall into this category, for a competing strain of her writing shows clerics who are thoroughly human, and are often depicted in humorous or endearing ways. Significantly, this usually happens when they have nothing to do with church ceremonies. In 'Two Parsons', in *The Second Common Reader,* Woolf reproduces reviews, from 1927 and 1932 respectively, of the diary of eighteenth-century parson James Woodforde, where she is intrigued by one line in which he regrets being too shy to propose marriage; and depressed nineteenth-century vicar John Skinner, whose bad temper alienated his parishioners and estranged him from his family, and whose life ended in suicide. In the same year as her original review of Skinner's diary, Woolf wrote a review of the latest instalment of the diary of eighteenth-century vicar, Rev. William Cole, in the form of a letter, demanding that he reveal more about himself: 'I beg you, William, now that you are about to begin a fresh volume, at Cambridge too, with men of character and learning, that you will pull yourself together. Speak out' (*E2* 121). Here, we see Woolf's alternative to the Clerical Biographies she satirised in *Jacob's Room* and *Three Guineas:* the life of the intriguing human subject who happened to be a clergyman.

Woolf wrote about Cole a second time in December 1938, when she was inspired to write an unsolicited review of his correspondence with Horace Walpole for the *Yale Review.* Her cover-note reveals that she was fascination with their letters, reading them with 'great interest' that prompted her to 'write a sketch of the characters of Cole and Walpole'. She adds that she has turned to this 'by way of a respite' from the mounting political crisis (*L6* 306). In this collection, Cole writes as an antiquarian – a passion he shared with Walpole. Woolf pictures him in seclusion, 'wrapped up from the least draught, for he was terribly subject to sore throats; sometimes issuing forth to conduct a service, for he was, *incidentally, a clergyman;*

driving occasionally to Cambridge to hobnob with his cronies; but always returning with delight to his study, where he copied maps, filled in coats of arms, and pored assiduously over those budgets of old manuscripts which were, as he said, "wife and children" to him' (*E2* 112, emphasis added).

Woolf's final and most famous clergyman, the Rev. G. W. Streatfield, can be placed in this strand of her work. Streatfield is markedly different from Woolf's portraits of clergy in her earlier novels and he is spared the scathing criticism of *Three Guineas*. There is no description of Streatfield leading a service, no summary of his clerical career, and his only connection with the educational establishment is the slight and dubious one of 'calling himself . . . MA' (*BA* 137). Streatfield is not powerful and domineering, but uncomprehending and ineffectual. His stature actually diminishes over the course of the novel. We are first introduced to him as 'a clergyman, a strapping clergyman, carrying a hurdle, a leafy hurdle' who is seen 'striding through the cars with the air of a person of authority, who is awaited, expected, and now comes' (*BA* 54). The sense of anticipation in this last phrase suggests that Streatfield has a Messiah complex, but by the final part of the novel, he is reduced to a halting, uncertain speaker, many of whose words are carried away by the wind.

Woolf's earlier satire of the powerful union between the church and the state with its war machine is almost absent from *Between the Acts*. The link is made only by Mrs Mayhew (a colonel's wife) as she envisages what she would like to see: 'a Grand Ensemble. Army; Navy; Union Jack; and behind them perhaps – Mrs Mayhew sketched what she would have done had it been her pageant – the Church. In cardboard' (*BA* 128). Miss La Trobe's play deliberately eschews such a scene and avoids all jingoistic sentiment. The symbolic link between nation, the armed forces and the church is relegated to the nostalgic dream of an army wife and even then, the church is flimsy (a cardboard cut-out) and it may only 'perhaps' be represented in the scene.

With Streatfield, Woolf shows a completely different aspect of the clerical role: the vicar as a figure in the local community. This ties in with a very different understanding, still current, of the church as a focal point for community, especially in rural areas or small towns, where locals have a particular sense of affection for and ownership of their local church, even if they do not worship there.[15] The church in *Between the Acts* is a focal point for local history and a concomitant sense of belonging: many of the families in the village have lived there for centuries, and the 'green mounds in the churchyard had been cast up by their molings.' The role of the church as a place of worship is in decline, however, for 'there were absentees when Mr. Streatfield called his roll call in the church. The motor bike, the motor bus, and the movies – when Mr. Streatfield called his roll call, he laid the blame on them' (*BA* 55). Unlike his predecessors in the other novels, Streatfield does not have a captive audience and though there is a suggestion of military life in his 'roll call', fewer people are there to answer. Woolf's representation of the tobacco-stained Streatfield owes something to her impressions of Rev. Hawkesford, a chain-smoker whom she saw 'an old decaying man, run to seed. His cynicism, & the pleasant turn it gives his simple worn out sayings, amuses me.' Streatfield's affinity with the village reflects Woolf's sense of Hawkesford's representing an ancient way of life as 'he tumbles into an armchair; & tells over his stock of old village stories' (*D3* 159). Leonard, similarly, had felt that Hawkesford belonged 'to the ancient English village way of life which in Sussex has completely disappeared . . . I never heard him say a word about religion or his work as a clergyman.'[16]

This is not to say that Streatfield is presented entirely without satire. His initial appearance after the play is regarded as offensively incongruent. After the *avant-garde* scene with the flashing reflective objects, he appears like a throwback to a lost age: 'they saw, as waters withdrawing leave visible a tramp's old boot, a man in a clergyman's collar surreptitiously mounting a soap-box' (*BA* 136). The collar (like Leslie Stephen's) seems a piece of a detritus from an age long past, and until the vicar is identified in the next line, we might even expect this to be another costume in the play. The audience at first resent his arrival: he is seen as 'an intolerable constriction, contraction and reduction to simplified absurdity', someone who is likely to try to reduce the complex production to a simplistic message, because wearing 'the livery of his servitude' (ibid.), his mind is not his own. As he opens his mouth to speak, the words that follow are not his own but a parody prayer of the audience wishing him to desist, 'Oh Lord, protect and preserve us from words the defilers, from words the impure!' (ibid.). Rather than an appeal for protection against the wicked 'the words *of* the defilers', the audience pray for protection against all words: speech of any kind at this time feels wrong.

Alongside this critical reception, however, we find a set of more positive views from observers who accept him as a member of the community. The sight of his tobacco-stained finger actually helps the audience warm to him, for they recognise his humanity: 'He wasn't such a bad fellow; the Rev. G. W. Streatfield; a piece of traditional church furniture; a corner cupboard; or the top beam of a gate, fashioned by generations of village carpenters after some lost-in-the-mists-of-antiquity model' (ibid.).

The comic image of Streatfield as a piece of furniture demonstrates his integral role in the village; the phrase 'fashioned by generations of village carpenters' from ancient times is a hint that he is shaped by Christ, whose earthly work was carpentry. A later description of his clerical collar as a 'white gate' echoes Christ's description of himself as the good shepherd and 'the gate for the sheep' (John 10:7); again suggesting that Streatfield follows Christ as his model of priestly calling. Of all Woolf's clerics, then, Streatfield comes closest to shaping his life on New Testament models.

The audience recognise in Streatfield a human being like them-selves. He is 'their representative spokesman; their symbol; themselves' (*BA* 137). As such, he is almost a sacrificial model of priesthood, becoming a scapegoat for their embarrassment at the play and their uncertainty as to its meaning.

While a cursory reading of the passage would suggest that Rev. Streatfield is wrong-footed by the situation, a closer reading shows a level of humility. Though the audience expects him to have the answers and suddenly turn into a congregation, as '[t]hey folded their hands in the traditional manner as if they were seated in church' (*BA* 137), but in fact he points to his collar as a sign of his *lack* of qualifications to interpret the play:

> 'As one of the audience,' he continued (words now put on meaning)
> 'I will offer, very humbly, for I am not a critic' – and he touched
> the white gate that enclosed his neck with a yellow forefinger – 'my
> interpretation.' (*BA* 137)

The brief comment he offers on the play is not so much an inter-pretation as a theological reflection, for he sees biblical themes reflected in the play. First, the notion that 'A few were chosen; the many passed in the background' (ibid.), echoing Christ's words that 'many are called, but few are chosen' (Matthew 22:14). But then he counterbalances the theme of the few important ones by also see-ing an emphasis on community in the play: 'we are members of one another. Each is part of the whole . . . We act different parts; but are the same,' (*BA* 137–8), a suggestion that carries another biblical message that 'as the body is one, and hath many members, and all the members of that one body, being many, are one body, so also is Christ' (1. Corinthians 12:12). Of all Woolf's clergymen, then, it is Streatfield who comes closest to delivering a speech that applies biblical ideas to the world around him.

Moreover, he puts his words into practice, when Mrs Parker takes offence at Albert, the man with learning disabilities. She seems to appeal to Streatfield 'to exorcise this evil, to extend the protection of his cloth'; and in this, too, Woolf seems to recognise the expectations that parishioners can have of their clergy – which, in Mrs Parker's case, entails a superstitious belief that the vicar can cure or exterminate the mentally handicapped as manifestations of evil. Yet Streatfield refuses to rise to the bait, and instead he honours Albert as a member of the community: 'The good man contemplated the idiot benignly. His faith had room, he indicated, for him too. He too, Mr. Streatfield appeared to be saying, is part of ourselves' (*BA* 139).

Lest Streatfield be seen as too much of a 'good man', however, Woolf introduces the jarring note of the collection for church funds. Yet, this is true to life, for being a steward of funds and custodian of an ancient building, are parts of the vicar's role, and the criticism implied here is mitigated by the fact that fundraising is destined to be ineffectual for just as he announces that they shall be collecting money for 'the illumination of our dear old Church' (*BA* 138), his speech is cut off by the sound of aeroplanes overhead. In June 1939 these would have been on a practice exercise but for Woolf writing the scene in 1940 and for the first readers of *Between the Acts* in 1941, the planes are a portent of the war which would necessitate blackout rather than illumination. This village church is no longer aligned with the warmongers, for the social and communal values it now represents are at risk of destruction in the coming conflict.

Streatfield's attempts to generate unity and community represent a different aspect to the church in the 1930s than the one Woolf satirised in *Three Guineas*: the move on the part of some churchmen to support peace, as a counterbalance to those who wanted to build a Christian state. Besides her awareness of Percy Dearmer and churchmen who were engaging with socialist arguments and pacifism,[17] Woolf had also by this point received sympathetic responses to *Three Guineas* from clergymen. These included William J. Piggott, who described himself as pro-feminist and another, J. E. Callister, who asked for an autographed copy of the book for his daughter. Callister and another vicar, Leonard J. Holson, qualified Woolf's representation of the links between church and state by pointing out that clergy stipends are not paid through taxes.[18] We do not know Woolf's reaction to these letters or, indeed, whether she entered into any correspondence with these readers, as she did with some of the others, but perhaps their contributions, received from late 1938 to early 1939, made Woolf a little more sympathetic towards the ordinary cleric as she developed the character of her final fictional clergyman.

Conclusion

The examples discussed in this chapter have shown the complexity and subtlety of Woolf's understanding of clergy and their roles in society. Woolf engaged with political questions in powerful rhetoric about the clergy's implication in the establishment, but she also demonstrated a more nuanced understanding of the clergy as men with feet of clay. However, as Woolf shows in her depiction of Mrs Ramsay, Emily Brontë and the ancient figure of the prophetess, it is women who have the greatest potential for administering the sacraments and experiencing the sacred, and the home has great potential as a space for spiritual experience. The next two chapters will explore these questions by examining women's relationship to public places of worship and to the domestic realm as a sacred space.

Notes

1. Birch, *Our Victorian Education*, p. 52.
2. Leonard Woolf, *Beginning Again*, pp. 52–3.
3. Consider, for example, Mr Collins in *Pride and Prejudice*, the 'shower of curates' in *Shirley*, and the contrasting examples of the Evangelical Mr Weston and High Church Mr Hatfield in *Agnes Grey*.
4. Morning Prayer can clearly be identified from the sequence (taken from *The Book of Common Prayer*): The Lord's Prayer, recitation of psalms, readings from the Old and New Testaments, a litany and a sermon. Woolf owned a copy of *The Book of Common Prayer*, but she may also have drawn on the Stephen family's visit to St Mary Abbots to hear the reading of Banns of Marriage for Stella Duckworth and Jack Hills.
5. Heininge, *Reflections*, p. 126.
6. Boswell, *Life of Johnson*, p. 327.
7. Leslie Stephen, *History of English Thought*, 1, 324–6.

8. C. E. Stephen, *Vision of Faith*, p. cxi.
9. Lilienfeld, '"The Deceptiveness of Beauty"'.
10. Sawyer, *Women and Religion.*
11. Murphy-O'Connor, 'House-Churches and the Eucharist', p. 129.
12. Gill, *Women and the Church of England,* pp. 236–9.
13. Froula, 'St. Virginia's Epistle', p. 29.
14. Woolf's Library in Washington State University shows that she owned a copy of the 1683 *Book of Common Prayer,* but also an edition from around 1936 that included ordination services, suggesting that she may have bought the latter copy to research ordination specifically.
15. See for example, Carr, *Priestlike Task*, pp. 5–7.
16. Leonard Woolf, *Beginning Again*, p. 64.
17. Dearmer, *Christianity and the Crisis.*
18. Snaith (transcribed and annotated), *'Three Guineas* Letters', pp. 95–7, 110–11 and 91.

Sacred Spaces: Churches and Cathedrals

In 'A Sketch of the Past', Virginia Woolf recalls that Leslie Stephen's study looked out 'over the roofs of Kensington, to the presiding church of St Mary Abbots, the church where our conventional marriages were celebrated' (*MB* 119). This observation demonstrates how the prominence of church buildings in the cityscape reflected the significance of the church as an institution during her youth, for St Mary's 'presides' over the outlook of this agnostic scholar and the church continued to fulfil a social function even for an unchurched family.

Church buildings had a much greater significance than this for Woolf, however, for she visited places of worship with surprising frequency, as her diaries, letters and travel writings attest. Cathedrals and major churches feature prominently. During her walks around London, she often visited St Paul's Cathedral and Westminster Abbey (the Stephens regularly visited the latter when Adrian was at school there). Elsewhere within Britain, Woolf spent two weeks on holiday in the precincts of Wells Cathedral in 1908, and visited the cathedrals of Gloucester, St Alban's, Salisbury and Canterbury. Her travels abroad included trips to cathedrals at Notre Dame, Seville, Le Mans, Florence, Chartres and Najac and, crucially, Hagia Sophia in Constantinople. As one might expect, Woolf was interested in these buildings for their architectural and historical value (for example, she remarked on the completion of the restoration project at St Alban's (*PA* 60) and her 1903 diary includes a plan for a detailed study of Salisbury Cathedral), but she was also interested in them as places of worship. There are sporadic examples of her attending services, including the Palm Sunday service at St Paul's Cathedral in 1937, but more importantly, she was profoundly interested in how they operated as sacred spaces.

The word 'sacred', in its primary meaning, refers to what is holy, set apart and dedicated to a religious purpose, but it also has broader implications of something that is especially valued or reserved exclusively for a particular person or purpose. Woolf was particularly exercised by this broader conception, for it implies control and privilege, raising questions as to who determines what is of value and how the lines of inclusion and exclusion are drawn. As a feminist, Woolf was powerfully aware of patriarchal constructions of the sacred that were enforced literally by the built environment and metaphorically by ideology.

Woolf's writings on sacred spaces are part of a wider concern with the occupation of space within her work: she was constantly exploring the themes of containment (the Victorian home); exclusion (the beadle shooing the narrator of *A Room of One's Own* from the Cambridge lawns); refuge (the room of one's own); and liberation (*flânerie* on the London streets). As Anna Snaith and Michael Whitworth note, her writing is 'consistently concerned with the politics of space', and as Tracy Seeley adds, her work is 'rife with awareness of spatial practices, and of women's relation to privilege in terms of space'.[1] Woolf had a keen sense of how the built environment structures our lives, physically and conceptually, along gender lines so that the organisation of physical space has a deep impact upon our thinking and our behaviour. She was aware of a concept, now well established within architectural theory that, in the words of Jane Rendell, Barbara Penner and Iain Border, 'space is at once real and metaphoric: space exists as a material entity, a form of representation and a conceptual and political construct.'[2] However, in writing imaginatively about space, Woolf was able to re-conceptualise it: to flag up its metaphoric element and articulate ways in which could be used differently. The physical and the metaphorical are especially closely entwined in the concept of sacred space.

Woolf's writings on gender and space foreshadow more recent analyses of gender and architecture. She displayed a keen sense of the gendering of space, as analysed by Helen Hills:

> Space, the fundamental aspect of material culture, is . . . of central importance in constituting gender. It determines how men and women are brought together or kept apart; it participates in defining a sexual division of labour; its organization produces, reproduces and represents notions about sexuality and the body. Space determines and affects behaviour, just as the organization of space is produced by and in relation to behaviour.[3]

Woolf's approach accords with recent gender–space theory, which suggests that we do not have to let our built environment shape us, for the balance of power can be affected by the ways in which we use space. As Rendell, Penner and Border note, 'different activities reproduce different architectures over time and space.'[4] Elizabeth Wilson has shown that women in particular represent a disorder that challenges attempts to structure and control the use of space in cities.[5] As this chapter will show, Woolf was interested in exploring how women can reproduce different kinds of sacred space within public buildings.

Woolf was, however, also concerned with the sacred in the sense of the spiritual, special or holy. Space was important to her in this respect as part of an aesthetic challenge to represent the sacred in fiction. In 'Modern Fiction', she uses religious language to describe the novelist's task as one of capturing 'life or spirit, truth or reality, this, the essential thing', which 'refuses to be contained any longer in such ill-fitting vestments' as those provided by conventional plot devices (*CE2* 105). The ecclesiastical overtones of the word 'vestments' suggest that her quest is spiritual as much as it is aesthetic. Woolf's spiritual quest involved a concern to find metaphorical and physical spaces in which 'life or spirit, truth or reality' could be experienced. The word 'sanctuary' occurs frequently in Woolf's lexicon, often with more positive implications than 'sacred'. 'Sanctuary' is an ecclesiastical term for the holiest part of a church or temple, but it also refers more generally to a special place including one of safety and refuge particularly for political refugees: in the medieval church, it had the particular meaning of the provision of a space where felons and debtors were immune from arrest. So, in parallel with her criticism of society's persistent exclusion of women, Woolf was concerned with finding sacred space or sanctuary for women and social outcasts of many kinds.

The early journals

Woolf's observations on places of worship in her early journals are useful indications of how they helped her develop her aesthetic. Her early travels were family holidays, taken with her siblings and often led by George Duckworth, so the destinations were not entirely her choice, as can be seen in her disengaged and sometimes scathing treatment of English churches: a photograph of a church in Bognor Regis is 'too uninteresting to keep', the churchyard of St Mary Magdalene in Warboys is 'sombre', and Woolf finds Stonehenge more spiritual and a worthier destination for 'pilgrimage' than Salisbury Cathedral (*PA* 36, 138, 200, 204). Nearby Romsey Abbey was deemed 'too thoroughly scrubbed & scoured to be entirely satisfactory', and recent attempts to refurbish it for the tourist trade had not only robbed it of atmosphere but made it sinister: Woolf writes that the restorers 'have laid their cloven hoof upon it . . . the atmosphere of the place is curiously profane' (*PA* 202). The tone of these remarks conveys a sense of emptiness, as though she felt that these churches failed to fulfil their spiritual function as sacred spaces.

Woolf preferred to avoid acts of worship. In a comic sketch ironically entitled 'An Evening Service', she describes how she and George planned to attend a service at Salisbury Cathedral and, wanting to avoid something 'drawn out by a sermon &c.', supposed there would be an Evensong at 7pm. They were proved wrong, so tourism called instead: 'Our only way of worship therefore – & a thoroughly happy one – was to drive slowly round the close' (*PA* 194).

Paradoxically, Woolf becomes more sympathetic towards English sites when writing about continental Europe. In England, she found churches uninteresting and even slightly 'other', with words like 'queer', 'curious' and 'bewildering' featuring prominently. Conversely, descriptions of sites in Western Europe called out an English identity, as she saw those cultures as 'foreign' against English ones: 'English cathedrals have certainly one inestimable advantage over the only foreign ones that I have seen; they stand in a perfect garden of their own, whereas the great French churches open on to the street' (*PA* 194).

It is an unfair generalisation, as while the 'perfect garden' does apply to Salisbury Cathedral, which inspired the comment, it does not work for the great London churches like Westminster Abbey or St Paul's. Travelling through France in April 1905, she dismisses Notre Dame in a brief remark that 'we saw three great churches, a funeral & a burial ground' (*PA* 260).

She also, at this time, implicitly adopted the prevailingly Protestant character of England in taking a critical tone towards the Catholic culture of the continent, perhaps unwittingly influenced by her Clapham roots, by the conventional George Duckworth or by Violet Dickinson, who came on some of the holidays. Woolf was sometimes uncomfortable with the level of decoration in the European Churches, remarking of Seville Cathedral that, 'I dont very much care for such elephantine beauty', and describing Grenada Cathedral as 'a dull florid building, very ornate' (*PA* 262, 264). Statues commemorating the martyrdom of Joan of Arc are deemed 'worthless & insignificant' (*PA* 260).

Hagia Sophia

A turning-point occurred on Woolf's visit to Constantinople with Vanessa and Violet Dickinson in 1906, for in contrast to her perceptions that English buildings were dull and that continental churches were too elaborate, she was enraptured by her first sighting of the Cathedral of Hagia Sophia:

> [S]uddenly we found ourselves confronted with the whole of Constantinople; there was St Sophia, like a treble globe of bubbles frozen solid, floating out to meet us. For it is fashioned in the shape of some fine substance, thin as glass, blown in plump curves; save that it is also as substantial as a pyramid. Perhaps that may be its beauty. But then beautiful & evanescent & enduring, to pluck adjectives like black berries – as it is, it is but the fruit of a great garden of flowers. (*PA* 347–8)

This was a seminal moment and there can be no doubt that the visit to Constantinople, and this view of Hagia Sophia in particular, were hugely significant to the growth of her vision and imagination. As Lyndall Gordon, Julia Briggs and others have noted, the combination of delicacy and strength – seen in the paradoxes of 'fine' and 'thin' against 'plump' and 'substantial' and of 'evanescent' against 'enduring' – became essential to her aesthetic. Woolf later praised similar qualities in Proust, whose work she saw as combining 'the utmost sensibility with the utmost tenacity . . . He is as tough as catgut & evanescent as a butterfly's bloom' (*D3* 7). Lily Briscoe aims for the same combination in her picture: 'the light of a butterfly's wing lying upon the arches of a cathedral' (*TL* 67). As Gordon notes, these instances 'repeat exactly her own idea of art as she gazed at St. Sophia in 1906'.[6]

Woolf's intense friendship with Violet was at its height at this time and possibly as a result of this, Hagia Sophia and Constantinople more generally became associated in Woolf's work with same-sex desire between women. In *Mrs Dalloway,* Constantinople is the place where Clarissa 'failed' her husband; in *To the Lighthouse,* Hagia Sophia comes to the mind of Minta Doyle as she clasps Nancy's hand. Constantinople also features in Woolf's first sketch for *Orlando,* as the Sapphic Ladies of Llangollen gaze on the city and its 'dreams of golden domes'.[7] Consequently, it became the site for Orlando's sex-change, and Woolf hypothesises how this city and its surroundings were sufficiently free of the constraints of both west and east to allow the performance of alternative gender roles and sexualities. While the aesthetic and sexual implications of the sighting of Hagia Sophia have both been well attested within Woolf scholarship, these sit in a powerful nexus with the spiritual or religious, which has attracted less attention, and Violet was a significant influence here too.

Hagia Sophia had a rich significance for Virginia, for it represented a palimpsest of competing religious cultures. It had been built on the site of a former church as a Christian cathedral in the Orthodox tradition by the Roman emperor Justinian in the sixth century and later, briefly, converted to a Catholic cathedral. It became a mosque when the Turks captured Constantinople in 1453 and, gradually, the Christian symbolism was occluded: by the nineteenth century, the ninth-century mosaics were painted over and boards bearing Arabic inscriptions were added to the piers. This would have been the condition in which the Stephen party saw it when, as Rowland Maidstone notes, 'the richest colour must have been that of the prayer rugs which covered the whole floor.'[8] Constantinople too had a rich cultural heritage, as it had originally been settled by the Greeks as the city of Byzantium, and the remains of its flagship building, the Hippodrome, are still to be found next to Hagia Sophia. Although this sedimentation of cultures was the result of war and conquest, the Balkans having a strategic importance that makes the area volatile politically to this day,[9] it also gave the city immense imaginative appeal, as W. B. Yeats would later demonstrate in his poems 'Byzantium' (1927) and 'Sailing to Byzantium' (1932). Cam reflects this fascination when she thinks of 'Greece, Rome, Constantinople' as 'sparks of light' when she experiences a 'fountain of joy' while sailing to the lighthouse (*TL* 255).

Justinian built Hagia Sophia, the Church of Holy Wisdom, as a symbol of his power, a celebration of his triumph over a rebellion that nearly brought his reign to an end. But it also became the most influential building within Orthodox Christianity: as Diarmaid MacCulloch notes, the architecture of Hagia Sophia took the dome, 'which previously had rarely been more than a subsidiary theme in a Christian building', and made it the key feature; this then became the established design for both for Orthodox Christian churches and for mosques.[10] The central dome 'seemed to float on two half-domes to east and west', and a further dome topped the apse at the east end.[11] The building was a feat of architectural ingenuity, achieving stability against all odds: a combination that Virginia Stephen recognised when she described the building as both 'thin as glass' and 'substantial as a pyramid'. Her use of the simile of the pyramid is significant as it acknowledges the palimpsestic nature of the city by alluding to the enduring legacy of a much older civilisation, albeit the Egyptians rather than the Greek founders of Byzantium. Her use of the mixed metaphor 'fruit of a great garden of flowers' for Hagia Sophia similarly acknowledges the hybrid nature of the building.

An important factor in this cross-cultural experience was that the visit to Constantinople was her first significant encounter with Islam. From the demographics of the Britain of her youth, she would not have seen Muslims in any great number: Britain's Muslim population was only 10,000 at the end of the nineteenth century and largely concentrated in the ports.[12] There was no mosque in London: the first one opened in 1910 in inconspicuous rented premises and the first purpose-built mosque would not open until 1941.[13] Constantinople therefore presented her with an opportunity of gaining a sense of alterity and thus of learning to understand her own affinities for, as Kathleen Roberts notes,

> narratives about alterity for any given culture are highly significant to identity because alterity construction is typically much more pertinent to *Self* than Other. The Other that is created through narratives of alterity is imaginary, stereotypical, and biased. But the details of the narratives lend crucial insight into the identity formation of the *Self* as differentiated from the exaggerated Other.[14]

Woolf's account of her first brush with Islamic worship, on taking a guided tour inside Hagia Sophia, initially bears this out: it shows a further development in her formation of an English identity, for it calls out in her a strong sense of Englishness and even a nominal allegiance to Christianity in her resistance to Islam. She is discomfited at having to remove her shoes, seeing the requirement to wear slippers as an 'oriental superstition'. She initially finds the building 'fragmentary & inconsequent', and she brings to bear the

expectations learned from visiting churches in England and Western Europe and struggles to read Hagia Sophia from this perspective: it is not a church, she notes, but 'a great hall of business, or
learning or law.' She notes that its status as a cathedral-turned-
mosque makes it hard to read, as the absence of features such as
stained glass and a rood-screen makes it 'not very sympathetic to
the stranger' (*PA* 349–50).

However, her account of her second visit, when she observed worship from the gallery, betrays a conflicted response that reveals that
her English, Christian identity is provisional and not fully inhabited.
Although her description of the bowing figures as 'puppets of an
unseen power' (*PA* 356) has a derogatory tone, with its implications
that the worshippers are submissive and unthinking, the mention of
an 'unseen power' also implies a recognition that they may be worshipping a force that she cannot experience; a fleeting perception
akin to Thomas Hardy's sensation in 'The Darkling Thrush' that the
bird perceives 'a blessed hope whereof he knew / And I was unaware.'
The otherness of Islamic worship, the 'mystery of the sight', the
'strangeness of the voice', the use of a foreign language, and the lack
of visual symbolism, all serve to enhance a sense that the reverence
is genuine. Woolf is attracted to the worship, finding it 'wonderfully
beautiful' and, surprisingly, rather than wanting to remain aloof she
expresses frustration at being shut out: the people 'would not suffer
us to worship with them' and were 'quite determined' to leave the
tourists outside (*PA* 356).

Woolf's description of the Suleiman Mosque in Constantinople
(a building closely modelled on Hagia Sophia)[15] evinces a similar
sense of awe, alongside a feeling of being privileged to glimpse something from which she would normally be excluded: 'You raise a great
leather curtain, & so admit yourself to a sight that is as strange as
it is beautiful' (*PA* 352). Her description of Islamic prayers conjures
up a sense of unfamiliarity similar to what she felt at Hagia Sophia:
'nor did it seem in any way strange that men should say their prayer
to rare carpets & painted tiles, without the figure of a saint or the
symbol of a cross to inspire them' (*PA* 353). The absurdist description of men venerating furnishings nonetheless acknowledges that
the worship has its own purpose and sincerity, and draws attention
to the contrast between Islamic religious art, which bans representation, and Christian religious art, to which representation is central.

Woolf reflects on religious differences in one of the last diary
entries of the visit, noting that maybe she should have discussed these

earlier, and once more she appears to be entrenched in an English point of view:

> [T]he only remark I can make with any confidence is that no Christian, or even European, can hope to understand the Turkish point of view; you are born Christians or Mahommedans [*sic*] as surely as you are born black or white. (*PA* 355–6)

But again, this retreat into Englishness or even nominal Christianity is only superficial; what is more powerful is her deep fascination with the 'beautiful' mosque and the 'beautiful' and 'mysterious' Hagia Sophia. She leaves Constantinople transfixed with Hagia Sophia, asking, 'why is she the most cryptic church in Europe?' (*PA* 357). Its appeal comes precisely from the otherness of the building, for it gives her a sense of awe and mystery without calling upon her to assent to dogmas or pin anything down.

To complicate the picture further, Hagia Sophia also introduced Woolf to the architecture of the Orthodox Church, and this sits in tension with the Islamic lack of representation. Hagia Sophia is an iconic building in the original sense of the word, for in Eastern Christianity, an *ikon* is an object that allows direct access to what it represents. So, as MacCulloch notes, the dome was nothing less than 'a recreation of the canopy of Heaven'.[16] Its appeal was such that Procopius wrote twenty years after its dedication: 'whenever one enters the church to pray, one understands immediately that it has been fashioned not by any human power or skill but by the influence of God', and that as a result, 'the mind is lifted up to God and exalted, feeling that He cannot be far away but must love to dwell in this place which he has chosen.'[17] The architecture of the building therefore seeks to house the divine. In visiting Constantinople and engaging with this conundrum of representation, the quest to capture the spirit, Woolf laid the foundations of the key concept of her aesthetic: the quest to capture 'life or spirit' in something other than the 'ill-fitting vestments' can now be seen not just as a metaphor for dispensing with conventional fiction, but of seeking to go beyond the conventions of western Protestant Christianity.

Woolf's encounters with different dimensions of otherness in Constantinople, with Islam and with Orthodox Christianity, gave impetus to her later aesthetic. Hagia Sophia in particular would continue to haunt Woolf's imagination, and it reappears in several works (including *To the Lighthouse*, *Orlando*, *A Room of One's Own* and 'A Sketch of the Past'), often in connection with an exploration of questions of expression and representation. Woolf represents literary endeavour as a craft akin to cathedral-building. In 'How Should One Read a Book?' she notes that writing a novel 'is an attempt to make something as formed and controlled as a building' and that a book may take the shape of a cathedral (*CE2* 2, 8). In *A Room of One's Own* she uses Hagia Sophia as an example of how the structure of a novel should, like the structure of a building, reflect life and inspire a certain emotion in the reader so that it leaves a 'shape on the mind's eye, built now in squares, now pagoda shaped, now throwing out wings and arcades, now solidly compact and domed like the Cathedral of Santa Sofia at Constantinople' (*Room* 54).

The spiritual dimensions of the problem of form and representation surface intensively in Lily Briscoe's attempts to paint Mrs Ramsay in *To the Lighthouse*, for Lily wishes not only to represent Mrs Ramsay in art, but also to gain intimacy with her. As Lily struggles with her painting, under the curious, though not entirely critical, gaze of William Bankes, she resists the subtle coloration and hazy shapes that are in vogue and instead aspires to an aesthetic that replicates the paradox of Hagia Sophia: 'She saw the colour burning on a framework of steel; the light of a butterfly's wing lying upon the arches of a cathedral' (*TL* 67). Lily therefore considers the structural problem of how to provide the architectural infrastructure of a steel framework and arches, alongside a spiritual quest to capture Mrs Ramsay. Lily thinks of this in terms that recall 'Modern Fiction', for she seeks 'the spirit' and 'the essential thing' of Mrs Ramsay. Significantly she identifies this spirit with the English translation of Sophia: 'Was it wisdom? Was it knowledge? Was it, once more, the deceptiveness of beauty, so that all one's perceptions, half-way to truth, were tangled in a golden mesh?' (*TL* 69–70). The 'golden mesh' evokes the inside of the dome of Hagia Sophia, pierced with forty windows. Hagia Sophia, that attempt to represent the holy in architecture, becomes Lily's model for her art.

The reverie that Lily slips into as she ponders her structural conundrum reaches an intense pitch that is spiritually questing and speaks of same-sex desire. She recalls Mrs Ramsay visiting her bedroom at night, cradling her head in her lap and urging her to marry. The relationship is a fusion of the maternal (Lily is a generation younger than Mrs Ramsay) and the lesbian (after all, Lily is not one of the Ramsay daughters) and, as we saw in Chapter 2, it carries shades of Violet Dickinson and Vita Sackville-West, along with the better-known allusions to Julia Stephen.

Lily sees her intimacy with Mrs Ramsay in terms of entering sacred space, for she has a feeling of having 'penetrated' into a 'sanctuary'. This echoes Woolf's visits to the two mosques in Constantinople, with desire and exclusion working in tension: the experiences of being an outsider to Islam and of being unable to explicitly voice same-sex desire are intermingled. Touching Mrs Ramsay, Lily slips into an image reminiscent of Carter's 1922 expedition to uncover the tomb of Tutankhamun, another act of trespass, and one that echoes Woolf's earlier use of a pyramid as a simile for Hagia Sophia:

> [I]n the chambers of the mind and heart of the woman who was, physically, touching her, were stood, like the treasures in the tombs of kings, tablets bearing sacred inscriptions, which if one could spell them out would teach one everything, but they would never be offered openly, never made public. (*TL* 70)

The intensity of the scene breaks as Lily realises she cannot attain what she wants ('Nothing happened. Nothing! Nothing!' (*TL* 71)), but her imagination compensates her with another metaphor: she is a bee visiting the 'dome-shaped hives' of other people (ibid.). The image of Mrs Ramsay that lingers is that of a 'dome', so again, Woolf takes an analogy from the sacred space of Hagia Sophia. This image once again brings sexual desire, spirituality and aesthetics into a powerful combination.

Allusions to Hagia Sophia surface again when Lily tries to complete her painting after Mrs Ramsay's death. Lily struggles with the attempt to paint Mrs Ramsay and to convey 'reality': it is something of profound spiritual significance, a 'worshipful object' more demanding than other objects of reverence, such as 'men, women, God' (*TL* 214). Lily achieves this by means that reflect Woolf's aesthetic precisely: the quest to produce something that is at once delicate, 'feathery and evanescent . . . like the colours on a butterfly's wing', and firmly structured, 'clamped together with bolts of iron'. This again replicates the structure of Hagia Sophia, and, when Lily regains a sense of Mrs Ramsay's presence, she feels as though she has entered a cathedral: 'as if a door had opened, and one went in and stood gazing silently about in a high cathedral-like place, very dark, very solemn' (*TL* 231). Inhabiting this structure, she comes closer to solving the problem of the shape of her painting, but significantly, this goes alongside the achievement of finally entering that sanctuary and come into contact with something holy.

Woolf returned to this image years later, when she alluded to Hagia Sophia as an analogy for her childhood: a 'vast place . . . a great hall I could liken it to; with windows letting in strange lights; and murmurs and spaces of deep silence' (*MB* 79). These windows evoke the forty windows piercing the dome of Hagia Sophia, a connection that is reinforced in her description of her mother as being 'in the very centre of that great Cathedral space which was childhood' (*MB* 81). Woolf evokes Hagia Sophia again when she describes the genesis of *To the Lighthouse* as 'blowing bubbles out of a pipe' (ibid.). This indicates that this novel, which she identifies as a turning-point in coming to terms with the memory of her mother, was simultaneously conceived along the pattern of Hagia Sophia.

For Woolf, as for Lily Briscoe, the attempts at representation are impelled by an elegiac desire to recuperate loss. As Roessel notes, Woolf associated Constantinople with disease and death: Vanessa and Violet became seriously ill on the trip, and Thoby (who had been with them on the first part of their holiday) fell ill at the same time and died shortly after his return to England. This adds a further dimension to Woolf's response to Hagia Sophia as an attempt to engage with the unattainable: besides same-sex desire and her attraction to Islamic worship, there is a longing to experience again the presence of lost loved ones.

A further image of Constantinople and Hagia Sophia that persists in Woolf's writing is a scene she watched several times on her visit: dawn breaking over a cityscape shrouded in mist 'like a veil that muffles treasures across all the houses & all the mosques.' The mist gradually lifts with the sunset, first offering 'hints of the heaped mass within; then a pinnacle of gold pierces the soft mesh, & you see shapes of precious stuff lumped together', before the mist rises completely and the city is seen 'clear on the solid earth' (*PA* 351). Orlando witnesses a similar scene each morning, watching 'apparently entranced' as the mist rises over Constantinople (*O* 116), but more significantly, the image recurs in Woolf's discussions of her aesthetic, for it informs her concept of 'moments of being': the sudden revelation of life from behind the 'cotton-wool' of everyday existence. This life, like the buildings of Constantinople, has a shape and pattern; the city therefore gave early impetus to her concepts of the revelation of the truth behind appearances.

Woolf was haunted by the image of Hagia Sophia as a representation of otherness and mystery. Although, as is the case with alterity, Hagia Sophia helped her understand and express herself and her own aesthetic rather than build bridges of understanding with another culture, it is by her questing and her acceptance of the mystery of the Cathedral, her refusal to be reductive, that she made it a powerful symbol for articulating emotions and ideas that could not be voiced directly.

Trespass and tourism

However, 'nothing was simply one thing' (*TL* 251) as Woolf attests, and while her visit to Hagia Sophia was revelatory in terms of her spirituality and aesthetic, it also provided impetus for her lifelong interrogation of difference and exclusion. Woolf continued to analyse the feelings of exclusion arising from the experience of being admitted on strict conditions (the removal of shoes) and in a limited capacity (confined to the gallery) and she came to see that her position in British society was akin to being a tourist in Turkey, for women's involvement in public life was both limited and conditional. This gives rise to a very different metaphorical use of sacred space in Woolf's work: an ironic one that denotes the exclusion of women. In 1935 when E. M. Forster hinted that she was to be invited to join the committee of the London Library, as an exception to their traditional exclusion of women, she commented: 'The veil of the temple – which, whether university or cathedral, was academic or ecclesiastical I forget – was to be raised, & as an exception she [woman] was to be allowed to enter in' (*D4* 298). The physical partitioning of sacred space in a place of worship is replicated psychologically and politically in the exclusion of women from positions of influence in any sphere. This incident fed in to the development of *Three Guineas*, in which Woolf again uses sacred space as a metaphor for exclusion: the professions are 'temples', and the first generation of professional women were 'cautiously pushing aside the swing doors of one of these temples' (*3G* 102). The universities too are sacred, exclusive spaces, for educated men's daughters have acquired culture 'outside the sacred gates' of Oxford and Cambridge (*3G* 112). *Three Guineas* was Woolf's fullest articulation of her awareness that religion reified social and political exclusion.

The solution that Woolf adopted was for women to embrace their position as aliens in their own country: 'the outsider will say, "in fact, as a woman I have no country"' (*3G* 185). This enabled women to be dispassionate observers of British culture, visiting sites in their own country as tourists or trespassers. In 'The Leaning Tower', she quoted Leslie Stephen's aphorism 'Whenever you see a board up with "Trespassers will be Prosecuted", trespass at once' (*CE2* 181), to urge women to read as widely as possible and evade the ideological barriers that patriarchy had constructed to control interpretation. In envisaging women as trespassers and tourists, Woolf anticipates what Elizabeth Wilson has described as a woman's capacity to be both a *flâneur* or 'detached observer' and a force of disorder that challenges attempts to structure and control the use of space.[18] Although Woolf formulated these arguments relatively late in her career, her practice of *flânerie* and her representation of it in her work start much earlier;[19] we can therefore fruitfully apply these formulations to her visits to places of worship and her representations of them in fiction from earlier in her career.

Tourism is an important way of challenging discourses of exclusivity. As Roland Recht notes in his analysis of the medieval cathedrals, the celebration of power is built in to the architecture of public places of worship, especially cathedrals: '[w]hen art is dependent to that extent on the person or institution commissioning the work and on the function assigned to it, it becomes, at least partly, an expression of power.'[20] On the other hand, he notes, these buildings are 'also entered and traversed by the people of the time in which they were built.'[21] Churches, and especially the cathedrals, are on the one hand spaces where access to the sacred is carefully controlled but are also open to the public (as tourist attractions and places of prayer).

The layout of many English churches as Woolf would have seen them in the early twentieth century was determined by the Gothic revival. During the late nineteenth century, with the influence of the Oxford Movement and Cambridge's Camden Society, there had been a renewed emphasis on the ordering of space within a church to control access to the holiest parts. The latter part of the nineteenth century had seen extensive building of churches to this design, while existing churches were reordered to a similar plan.[22] This reordering was effected on gender lines. There was renewed emphasis on the altar within the sanctuary: this space was reserved for the exclusively male clergy. In front of this was the chancel, the domain of the surpliced choir, traditionally boys and men, along with the clergy. In front of this was the chancel step, which demarcated the nave, the domain of the congregation. In reordering churches, there was a trend towards pulling down the chancel screen (as happened at

St Paul's Cathedral), which served both to make the altar more prominent and to emphasise the distance between it and the congregation. George Addleshaw, looking back on these developments in 1948, wrote that

> their aim is not so much that the services should be a corporate offering of priest and people but that they should be offered by clergy and a choir in such a way as to call out from the people an attitude of awe and adoration.[23]

This was a decisive staging of power.

However, a contrasting movement was taking place simultaneously: during the early part of Woolf's lifetime, city churches began to be opened to the public to a greater extent than had been seen for centuries. As T. Francis Bumpus noted in 1908:

> Within the last quarter of a century an extraordinary change has come over City church life. Churches which, thirty years ago, were barred and bolted from one Sunday to another are now open for the best part of every day for prayer, meditation, rest and short services.[24]

While the architecture of English churches was turning congregation members into mere onlookers, weekday opening made these holy spaces available for members of the public to use for personal interest and spirituality outside of set acts of worship.

The effect of these two developments is seen in Augustus Hare's account of St Paul's Cathedral in his *Walks in London* (which Woolf owned):

> Week-day services are well attended now (1894), though when this book was published, it seemed, from the nave, as if the knot of worshippers near the choir was lost in the immensity, and the peals of the organ and the voices of the choristers were vibrating through an arcaded solitude.[25]

The small congregation, located near the choir but nonetheless distinct from it, seems overpowered, 'lost in the immensity', but Hare, the tourist, is at liberty to wander around the cathedral during the service, hearing the music clearly but having no involvement in the worship. Woolf experienced both these dynamics: while she was deeply aware of the politics of the architecture of exclusion she also experienced churches as a visitor.

Woolf's most detailed study of exclusivity in worship comes in her depiction of King's College Chapel, Cambridge in *Jacob's Room*. The Chapel is particularly significant as a symbol of gender segregation within the British establishment, as it links academia, church and state in a predominantly male environment, for Cambridge University refused to allow women to take degrees. Cambridge University is one of the major scholarly institutions of the nation and its link with the church comes from its ecclesiastical foundations in the thirteenth century, when most of the scholars would have been in holy orders.[26] Sowon Park notes that Woolf frequently returned to 'the idea of Cambridge as a sanctuary or a cloistral refuge' (ibid.); this theme suggests that Woolf saw it as preserving a kind of ritual purity by excluding women. The particular connection of King's College with the establishment comes from Henry VI, who founded it along with Eton; the building work was continued by his descendants over subsequent centuries as a shrine to him. The organ screen was the gift of Henry VIII, who commissioned it as a model of a triumphal arch from the Roman Empire. This screen divides the insiders from the public: the all-male group of choir and college members sits in graduated stalls in the chancel, while the mixed group of visitors sits in the nave. The Chapel in Woolf's time was therefore a place of worship that was open to visitors on limited terms, much like the mosques of Constantinople.

Woolf's description of the chapel suggests that it has been designed to control: the stained glass lets in light 'accurately', ensuring that it only lets in particular colours: blue, yellow and red, the predominant colours in the stained glass. She does not comment on the pictures in the windows (which are in reality a detailed set of illustrations of biblical scenes), but rather on how they evoke a mood within the building. The walls of the chapel likewise provide containment, ensuring that all within is 'orderly'. The precision with which the building is designed therefore not only constrains those gathered for worship, but is an attempt to lay claim to what the institution sees as holy.

Woolf describes the actual service impressionistically from an outsider's point of view, emphasising choreography and the staging of power, and deliberately ignoring the content of the liturgy. There is a clear division between the choir and clergy on the one hand and the congregation on the other: in the front are the young men in white gowns and the 'white-robed' figures who climb and descend steps, orderly but meaninglessly. By contrast, the congregation is a riot of colour, for Jacob is distracted by the clothes and hats of the women who are gathered there. So, although women are excluded from the conduct of worship, they are present nonetheless (much as Jacob wishes this were not so) and their presence subverts the seriousness of the occasion.

Yet Woolf undercuts the power displayed by the building for she suggests that, unlike Hagia Sophia, the Chapel fails to embody the spiritual matters it purports to explain. Her narrator castigates the College and its Chapel for attempting to lay claim to some spiritual truth, reasoning with heavy irony that, *if* the sky is a source of 'consolation, and even explanation' for those of a 'mystical tendency', then the sky above King's College Chapel, being 'lighter, thinner, more sparkling' than it is elsewhere, must be an even greater source of insight. As the University attempts to preserve the sacred character of knowledge and its buildings, in the sense of keeping them reserved and exclusive, it has failed to create a space that is sacred in the sense of being holy.(*JR* 37–8).

St Paul's Cathedral and Westminster Abbey each provided Woolf with ample opportunity to criticise the celebration of establishment power. The conventional view of both these buildings, one still presented to the twenty-first-century visitor, is summed up by P. H. Ditchfield's guide to cathedrals (which went into five editions between 1902 and 1932). Of St Paul's, Ditchfield writes:

> The great Cathedral of St Paul has abundant claims to the love and veneration of every Englishman. Situated in the heart of the city of London, it has ever been associated with the religious, social and civic life of the people, and as the great national Cathedral of England all the principal events of our country's annals have been connected with St Paul's.[27]

As well as its links with historical events, St Paul's is also the place where the nation's heroes are commemorated and Ditchfield remarks that this 'endears it to us'. He likewise praises Westminster Abbey, 'the church of the king and the government', for its part in the national story, 'the pageants and coronation festivals which have taken place therein' and its commemoration of the powerful, the 'monarchs and great men, poets, sages, and generals who sleep within the hallowed precincts'.[28]

When Woolf noted that she had collected 'enough powder to blow up St Pauls' [*sic*] (*D4* 77) in researching *Three Guineas*, she was casting herself as a modern-day female Guy Fawkes seeking to demolish the centre of civilisation which she placed not in the Houses of Parliament but in its national church. As Charles Andrews notes, St Paul's

Cathedral 'becomes for Woolf the architectural center of the city, an emblem of Anglican Christianity and British authority . . . a sign of the tyrannical Church and a reassurance of Englishness.'[29] Woolf makes this connection in the essay itself by analysing the symbolic configuration of the cityscape, in which St Paul's Cathedral stands in close proximity to the Bank of England, the Mansion House, and the Law Courts; and Westminster Abbey stands alongside the Houses of Parliament. The flagship buildings of the nation's religious institutions sit alongside those of its legal, political and financial ones in order to reinforce patriarchal power (*3G* 102). She highlights the physical and symbolic proximity between St Paul's and the financial quarter again in the 1891 section of *The Years*, in which 'clerks posed with their pens on the ruled page' near St Paul's (*Y* 79).

However, Woolf also associates both buildings with literary history and here we start to see a more complex picture. Orlando on her return to London blurs her memory of Shakespeare's bald head with the dome of St Paul's, and she hears the poetry of Shakespeare, Marlowe, Ben Jonson and Milton beating like the clapper of a bell 'in the cathedral tower that was her mind' (*O* 157). In *Night and Day*, Mrs Hilbery asks Ralph Denham if he will marry Katharine in 'Westminster Abbey if the worst came to the worst'. And he replies, 'I would marry her in St Paul's Cathedral' (*ND* 514). Mrs Hilbery's sentimental reaction, which seems to confuse the two churches, mingles a love of poetry and liturgy, family pride and middle-class respectability, so that Woolf makes a comic mockery of the involvement of the church in all of these things:

> 'Thank God!' exclaimed Mrs Hilbery. She thanked Him for a variety of blessings . . . not least the prospect that on her daughter's wedding-day the noble cadences, the stately periods, the ancient eloquence of the marriage service would resound over the heads of a distinguished congregation gathered together near the very spot where her father lay quiescent with the other poets of England. (*ND* 515)

This episode presents a far more light-hearted commentary on the involvement of the church in the life and culture of the nation than is found in *Three Guineas*.

A wider set of examples shows that Woolf saw St Paul's and Westminster Abbey as integral to the London scene: they are prominent and attract attention, and not simply as bastions of patriarchal power. Many of Woolf's references to London's cityscape are less schematic than the account in *Three Guineas*. St Paul's is mentioned in

Mrs Dalloway when the aeroplane goes 'soaring' over the city, 'over the little island of grey churches, St Paul's and the rest' (*MD* 25); Orlando too sees St Paul's as part of a panorama, 'the dome of a vast cathedral rising among a fretwork of white spires' (*O* 158). Both these descriptions offer a painterly, picturesque view of the city rather than a political interpretation, and the lines in *Orlando* describe St Paul's in terms that are remarkably similar to those used for Hagia Sophia. In *The Waves,* Bernard admits to the charm of cathedrals as he wonders at 'many-domed London', including them in a more varied sketch of London life along with factories, institutions and theatres (*W* 87).

Many of Woolf's cityscapes suggest a tourist's view of London, providing a way back in to her own culture but with a critical sense of detachment. Woolf's essay 'Abbeys and Cathedrals' (1932) best illustrates her visitor's-eye view of St Paul's Cathedral and Westminster Abbey. Here Woolf provides an alternative visitors' guide that subtly and cleverly undercuts the power and significance of Westminster Abbey and St Paul's Cathedral in a way that is satirical while making the buildings accessible to the uninitiated. She describes St Paul's as '[v]ery large, very square, hollow-sounding . . . august in the extreme' but, she adds, 'not in the least mysterious' (*LS* 52). She thus encourages the reader not to be over-awed by the building but to enter the space with confidence.

While Woolf, like Ditchfield, finds the monuments the most compelling sight at St Paul's, she rejects the power and grandeur they represent by presenting them quirkily as 'majestic beds' that 'lie between the pillars.' Where Ditchfield venerates the 'national heroes' who 'sleep' as though possessed of that mythical ability to wake up should the nation be threatened, Woolf presents them comically as still living, 'robed in all their splendour' and ready 'to accept the thanks and applause of their fellow-citizens'. She describes Nelson as 'smug', inviting the viewer to see his grand bearing in a comic light. Woolf suggests that such a show of civic pride has robbed the cathedral of its religious meaning. The posthumous pride of these national figures undercuts the Christian message (from the collect for Easter Eve) carved on a false doorway that 'through the gate of death we pass to our joyful resurrection.' For them, the afterlife is just another stately chamber where they continue their civic duties; there is no 'joyful resurrection' but the secular immortality of earthly fame. Civic pride has replaced the Christian message in the cathedral: 'Effort and agony and ecstasy have no place in this majestic building' (*LS* 52–3).

Woolf finds the tombs and monuments in Westminster Abbey equally fascinating, and again she sees the great and the powerful continuing to command attention and demand respect: 'Kings and queens, poets and statesmen still act their parts and are not suffered to turn quietly to dust' (*LS* 56). They seem to stand alert, listening to what is going on. Again, Woolf points to the disjuncture between these memorials and the ostensibly Christian function of the Abbey, noting that many of the royals buried here are commemorated only for their 'greatness of birth' because they were too 'violent' or 'vicious' to be remembered for their virtue. Woolf imagines dead politicians challenging biblical precepts. As a clergyman reads the Ten Commandments 'for the millionth time', she imagines that Gladstone and Disraeli are 'about to put the statement just propounded – that children should honour their parents – to the vote' (*LS* 55–6). Here she invites the visitor to look at the statues in a comic light: we notice that they are in line with the pulpit from which hourly readings are delivered but that they stand sideways to the pulpit, chests thrust out and clutching lapels in gestures of pride and defiance. In showing Gladstone and Disraeli's disregard for the Ten Commandments, Woolf drives a wedge through the union of church and state that the building appears to represent, dividing the two forces against one another. Woolf as *flâneuse* visits these spaces with indifference: resisting the display of national pride, refusing to be awe-struck by the building, and hearing a service with a temptation to be 'irreverent'.

Conversely – and precisely *because* she has drawn the sting of civic and national pride – Woolf finds refreshment in these buildings too. St. Paul's provides peace and stasis in the midst of the busy city: 'directly we enter we undergo that pause and expansion and release from hurry and effort which it is in the power of St Paul's, more than any other building in the world, to bestow.' She experiences 'serenity' as 'mind and body seem both to widen in this enclosure, to expand under this huge canopy' (*LS* 51–2). The paradox of 'widening' within 'enclosure' presents a very different dynamic from the constraints of King's College Chapel and draws attention to the fact that the cathedral is both a vast space and set apart from the world. So, between the lines of her critique of nation and patriarchy, she shows how St Paul's can nevertheless be experienced as a spiritual space.

In challenge to the rhetoric of exclusion, then, Woolf identifies a position from which church buildings can be experienced spiritually, but not in the way their architects and patrons had intended.

This dynamic is seen in instances from Woolf's novels, where social outsiders visit the major London churches for the purposes of prayer and reflection: rather than feeling excluded, these are the characters who get the most out of places of worship. In *Jacob's Room*, Mrs Lidgett, a cleaner, goes for a rest in St Paul's Cathedral (*JR* 86–7). She is not bothered by authority, for she is undaunted by the verger and his rod, and blissfully ignorant about the Duke of Wellington beside whose tomb she sits. She reads the building in her own way, for she 'never fails to greet the little angels' on the Duke's tomb. The two faces of *putti* on the west side of the tomb are a minor detail: they are a level below the Duke's effigy, which is the main focus, and indeed they can only be seen from the narrow gap between the tomb and a pillar. Mrs Lidgett therefore resists the conventional reading of the tomb, and indeed the building, but in doing so she experiences it for herself. With her folded hands and 'half-closed' eyes, she is resting as much as praying, and the cathedral feeds her spiritually for she feels that the 'leathern curtain of the heart has flapped wide'. This is a direct echo of Virginia Stephen's description of entering the Suleiman Mosque, and it conveys a very similar effect of having gained entry to something awesome and holy despite the barriers that are in place. (Woolf repeats this image again when she describes Mrs Ramsay's feeling of 'pushing aside the thick leather curtain of a church in Rome' in a reverie where she sheds her identity as wife and mother to touch a deeper reality (*TL* 86).)

In *Mrs Dalloway*, another outsider figure, 'a seedy nondescript man' thinks of entering St Paul's and placing his bag before a cross or altar, 'the symbol of something which has soared beyond seeking and questing and knocking of words together and become all spirit' (*MD* 25–6). Contemplating (though significantly not carrying out) a gesture that many would see as a violation of sacred space, he makes his own meaning that ignores the wealth of symbolism within the building and, in the spirit of Quakerism, dismisses the verbosity of liturgy to touch the 'spirit'.

Miss Kilman is another outsider who uses one of the great London churches for prayer. She is reminded of the consolations of faith on passing the Catholic Westminster Cathedral as she wallows in self-pity after Elizabeth leaves her to attend Clarissa's party. She reflects that '[i]n the midst of the traffic, there was the habitation of God' (*MD* 119). It is a reminder that the cathedral is not secluded but is part of the cityscape: a symbol of faith in the midst of commerce and secular life. Not wishing to enter a Catholic building, Miss Kilman sets off to the Anglican Westminster Abbey, ten minutes' walk away, and joins a group of others who have gathered there for private prayer. Woolf's narrator offers a study of why people might wish to do this, for among the sightseers are some who seek 'sanctuary' and 'shelter'. In prayer, these people temporarily lose their social roles ('divested of social rank, almost of sex'), for the social and sexual divisions so evident in King's College Chapel and so crucial to the government buildings that surround the Abbey do not pertain here, although social markers reassert themselves once their prayers are over, revealing the contrast between the dishevelled Miss Kilman and the dapper Mr Fletcher 'retired of the Treasury'. Visiting the Abbey for private prayer is very much an individual experience, not a corporate one, and Woolf's sketch indicates that the experience is very different, even for people sitting near one another: Miss Kilman struggles, twitching her hands and shifting her knees. She feels that the object of her devotions is very distant: 'it was so rough the approach to her God – so tough her desires', while others (it seems to her) find that 'God was accessible and the path to Him smooth' (*MD* 120). Woolf's description, which tellingly draws a contrast between 'God' and '*her* God', shows how Miss Kilman's private prayer in this public space does not lead to enforced orthodoxy: the petitioners come with their own needs and their own conceptions of the object of their worship that are not subjected to challenge or correction by anyone else.

Sara in *The Years* is a close counterpart to Miss Kilman, as an outsider taking refuge in a cathedral. Seen by her cousin Martin crossing the square outside St Paul's, she is talking to herself and looking like a 'dishevelled fowl' in her unfashionable cloak (*Y* 205). She too has been a *flâneuse*, 'listening to the service', that is, not taking part in one, even though she is carrying a prayer book. (Woolf likewise 'listened to a full service' at Canterbury Cathedral in January 1936 (*D5* 11).)

Whereas Woolf had satirised King's College Chapel for its exclusion of women, this scene does precisely the opposite, for it is Martin who is on the outside. He does not enter St Paul's and Sara declines to share her experiences with him: she ignores his opening gambit 'I didn't know you went to services' and when he asks her view of the Prayer Book, she embarrasses him by reading aloud an obscure line from the Athanasian Creed. She then rebuffs his question about what she made of the service by asking a question of her own, 'What do *they* think of it Martin?', going on to describe the 'woman praying and the man with a long white beard' (*Y* 207), who could be fellow visitors or could even be her enigmatic sketch of her relationship with God. Sara's disconcerting manner reverses the power imbalance between poor spinster and wealthy retired army officer. When Martin jokes that the old family servant Crosby sees him as a god, Sara ridicules him by raising her glass to toast 'Crosby's God! Almighty, all-powerful Mr Martin' (*Y* 208). Here Woolf satirises the mindset that she also attacked in *Three Guineas*, by which men create a version of God to aggrandise male power (*3G* 250, n42).

This scene also echoes Miss Kilman's experience of Westminster Cathedral as the 'habitation of God' in the 'midst of the traffic', for something of the atmosphere of the cathedral spills out of the door into the crowds: as Sara and Martin stand on the steps of St Paul's, a 'gust of organ music came out from the Cathedral behind them as the doors opened and shut. The faint ecclesiastical murmur was vaguely impressive, and the dark space of the Cathedral was seen through the door' (*Y* 206). This cathedral, situated among shops and within the financial quarter of the city, is not an exclusion zone but a permeable space where sacred and quotidian interpenetrate.

Finding sanctuary

Mrs Lidgett, the seedy man, Miss Kilman and Sara Pargiter all reconfigure ecclesiastical space by bypassing the sacred-as-exclusive to embrace the sacred-as-holy, thus exemplifying the process described by Rendall, Penner and Border, whereby 'different activities reproduce different architectures over time and space'.[30] However, it is in metaphor that Woolf presents her most radical reconfiguration of church architecture, for it is here that she interrogates what constitutes the built environment in the first place. This is found in a cluster of images, from across Woolf's work, in which she shows the interpenetration between the built environment and the natural world.

In one such image, Woolf compares the cathedral to a snail. In *Jacob's Room,* she speculates that 'if there is such a thing as a shell secreted by man to fit man himself' it is on the banks of the Thames, where the 'great streets join and St Paul's Cathedral, like the volute on the top of the snail shell, finishes it off' (*JR* 86). This is a clever but telling pun, for a 'volute' is both a mollusc and an architectural feature (the swirling capital of Ionic and Corinthian columns). It suggests an organic process of architectural design: rather than seeing the built environment as one commissioned by those in power to constrain those who use the space, the city streets with the cathedral as their crowning glory have been shaped by human activity over time. Woolf's perception of cathedral-building as an organic process is confirmed in *The Waves* where she makes the same comparison from the opposite direction: a snail is described as being 'like a grey cathedral, a swelling building burnt with dark rings and shadowed green by the grass' (W 57). The image of the snail also informs Woolf's understanding of her own creative process, for shortly after comparing St Paul's to a snail in *Jacob's Room*, she describes her plans for writing *Mrs Dalloway* using the simile 'as the oyster starts or the snail to secrete a house for itself' (D4 550). As we have seen, Woolf speculated that the novel might take the shape of a cathedral; this conflation of novel with mollusc with cathedral goes further to suggest that novel-writing is a specifically organic process by which a textual space may be created for expressing spiritual truths.

Even more pervasive is Woolf's comparison between the cathedral and trees. In her *London Scene* essay, she notes how one of the windows at St Paul's (which in Woolf's lifetime were of clear glass) 'shakes down a broad green shaft' (LS 52). At Westminster Abbey, the play of light through the windows makes the solid structure appear shifting: 'Lights and shadows are changing and conflicting every moment.' In contrast to the stained glass of King's College Chapel, which for Woolf contributed to a rigid and constrictive built environment, the stonework in the Abbey is 'beautifully softened' by the light and 'changes like a live thing under the incessant ripple of changing light'. Describing the Abbey's fan-vaulted ceiling, she remarks on how the 'fine fans of stone that spread themselves to make a ceiling seem like bare boughs withered of all their leaves and about to toss in the wintry gale' (LS 54–5). Both buildings therefore become living organisms; furthermore, the Abbey appears to be roofless for, rather than having a ceiling that reproduces the canopy of a forest, the spectator feels exposed to the wind.

The importance of this association is confirmed by her use of the complementary image by which trees are compared to cathedrals. The children in *The Waves* roam among 'leaves as high as the domes of vast cathedrals' (W 16) (an image Woolf later conflates with Lily Briscoe's 'high cathedral-like space' to produce the 'cathedral space that was childhood' in 'A Sketch of the Past'). In *Between the Acts*, Miss La Trobe looks at her outdoor performance space and sees an avenue of trees that are 'regular enough to suggest columns in a church; in a church without a roof; in an open-air cathedral' (BA 47).

Miss La Trobe's is the creative mind that can make a cathedral of her
own, eschewing establishment attempts to confine the sacred within
walls. There is a delicious double irony that the proceeds of her play
will contribute to a fund for 'the illumination of our dear old Church'
(*BA* 138) when the impending war will necessitate blackout rather
than lighting. In this particular example, the natural world of the outdoor cathedral will survive where buildings might not (the roofless
church evoking images of aerial bombing).

Both these analogies contain echoes of Ruskin, who argued that
buildings should follow 'the spirit which rounds the *pillars of the
forest, and arches the vault of the avenue* – which gives veining to
the leaf, and *polish to the shell,* and grace to every pulse that agi-
tates animal organization.'[31] Ruskin also noted the specific similar-
ity between Gothic architecture and trees,[32] and argued that true
or 'living' architecture should model itself on the forms of nature,
admiring as examples the slightly irregular spacing of pillars, arches
or columns in St John the Evangelist in Pistoja, St Mark's in Ven-
ice, and Bayeux Cathedral because they reflect 'variations as subtle
as those of nature.'[33] Woolf's impression that natural features are
like buildings also has a counterpart in Ruskin: 'the pinnacles of the
rocky promontory arrange themselves, undegraded into fantastic
semblances of fortress towers.'[34] Reading Woolf's analogies in the
light of these echoes enables us to see a sympathetic view of church
architecture within her work as something which can, in imagination
at least, be made both to replicate the forms of nature and to convey
the spiritual.

An antecedent to both Woolf and Ruskin, is the much-contested
view that the Gothic cathedral was modelled on a grove of trees
(it is a characteristic Woolfian slippage that she sees sylvan proper-
ties in St Paul's, which exhibits a mixture of styles, as well as the
conventionally Gothic Westminster Abbey). The theory is generally attributed to Bishop Warburton, who argued that the Goths,
on adopting Christianity after invading Spain, had sought to replicate in architecture the sacred groves in which they had worshipped
as Pagans, so that the columns represented trunks, window tracery
branches and the arches overlapping branches.[35] It is particularly
instructive to read Miss La Trobe's vision in the light of this theory,
for it encompasses the past (the Pagan making a sacred site out of
trees and the Goths devising Christian architecture modelled on
woodland) and the future (a time when the sacred can continue,
even after the destruction of a building).

This metaphor has a counterpart in Woolf's experience as a tourist. She hints at it in *Mrs Dalloway*, where Lady Bradshaw enjoys photographing ruined churches, but she expresses it more clearly in the conclusion to her *London Scene* essay on 'Abbeys and Cathedrals', where she argues that 'the only peaceful places in the whole city' and 'the most peaceful of our London sanctuaries' (*LS* 58, 59) were the former graveyards that had been landscaped and reclaimed as gardens and playgrounds. This was a trend in landscaping, as Augustus Hare notes disparagingly (in a comment highlighted in pencil in Woolf's copy of *Walks in London*):

> a time-honoured burial ground is turned into a recreation-ground
> . . . levelling them, and overlaying them with yellow gravel and imi-
> tation rockwork, ruthlessly tearing up tombstones from the graves
> to which they belong, and planting paltry flowers and stunted ever-
> greens in their place, as in the historic though now utterly ruined
> burial-grounds of South Audley Street and St Pancras.[36]

Woolf disagrees, for she sees this as a positive development in that these spaces are occupied and domesticated by women and children: 'Here, mothers and nursemaids gossip; children play.' They also offer sanctuary to the outsider: 'Here . . . the old beggar, after eating his dinner from a paper bag, scatters crumbs to the sparrows' (*LS* 58–9). Here Woolf's *flâneuse* takes up the position described by Wilson, whereby she is a 'rootless outsider' who 'identified with all the marginal that urban society produced . . . not so much with the organized working class as with the down and outs: the ragpickers, the semi-criminal and the deviant.'[37] Both these examples show Woolf's concern to find spaces that were conducive for women and outsiders: a concern to find sanctuary and the sacred, peace and stability, in places where designated places of worship had once stood.

Woolf's concept of sacred space therefore takes in a wider perspective than Christianity. Bonnie Kime Scott has argued that Woolf's persistent references to the natural world throughout her works (encompassing animals, molluscs, insects, trees, flowers and even the primordial swamp) form part of a holistic view of the world by which the human is part of a vast network of being.[38] This view exposes the insignificance of patriarchy, Christianity and man-made buildings and offers alternative approaches to spirituality and consolation: 'In reordering things of the earth, Woolf may disperse the self into them, enter a collective of creatures, deconstruct patriarchal ideas of power and domination, and at least briefly defy spiritual defeat and death.'[39]

However, while a logical extension of this argument would make nature the true site of the sacred and of sanctuary over and above church buildings, Woolf does not make these distinctions, neither is her response to nature simply one of pastoral retreat. The cityscape was also a 'significant space' for Woolf, as Scott acknowledges, and buildings, or sites where buildings had stood, remain important.[40] Woolf reflects an attitude described by Elizabeth Wilson, whereby women can find the 'second city': 'instead of setting nature against the city, they find nature in the city.'[41] The images of the snail and of woodland do not present nature and church buildings as mutually exclusive, but they present church buildings as spaces in which it is still possible to be in touch with the natural world. She not therefore making a simple distinction whereby Paganism is preferable to Christianity, but she allows both to stand: a sacred wood is also a cathedral, and a cathedral is also a sacred wood.

Conclusion

In her accounts of places of worship, Woolf frequently breaks down the metaphorical walls that have been constructed to restrict access to the sacred. She shows how visitors to churches and cathedrals can challenge discourses of political, academic or clerical power, by subverting or even simply ignoring them. In doing so, she does not dismiss the concept of the sacred-as-holy, but values it as something that is greater than the powers of the establishment and that can be encountered in places of worship even when structures are in place to control and restrict the visitor and the outsider. Architecture rises above establishment values when it becomes an expression of the infinite: be it the dome of Hagia Sophia recreating the vault of heaven, or the Gothic arch putting the viewer in mind of the natural world, with all its hopes for renewal and survival. Places of worship also represent sanctuary, offering peace, rest and refreshment, even for the marginalised in society.

As a result, Woolf's accounts of sacred space do not make an indictment of faith: after all, she holds out the 'joyful resurrection' of the Easter liturgy and the Ten Commandments as yardsticks against which to judge the statues at St Paul's and Westminster Abbey. Instead, many of her accounts retain the possibility that there may be a valid object of worship in the form of a mystery that will be lost or diminished if one tries to pin it down. King's College Chapel and the tourist exhibition at Romsey Abbey fail on this count, precisely because they purport to explain and define. Hagia Sophia, on the other hand, succeeds through its otherness: the strangeness of the worship gave the young Virginia Stephen a sense of awe and beauty that endured because she could not understand its language or read its actions, and the building remained a frequent point of reference for Woolf. Miss Kilman's difficulty in experiencing God and Sara Pargiter's statement that God is 'incomprehensible' are not judgements against the characters so much as statements that divinity resists definition. Similarly, the most conducive sacred spaces were ones that resisted attempts to make them exclusive and reserved and instead offered genuine access to something special and holy.

Notes

1. Snaith and Whitworth, Introduction to *Locating Woolf*, p. 1; Seeley, 'Flights of Fancy', p. 33.
2. Rendell *et al.*, *Gender Space Architecture*, pp. 9–10.
3. Hills, 'Architecture as Metaphor for the Body', p. 67.
4. Rendell *et al.*, *Gender Space Architecture*, pp. 9–10.
5. Wilson, *Sphinx in the City*, p. 6.
6. Gordon, *A Writer's Life*, p. 194.
7. Roessel, 'The Significance of Constantinople', pp. 401–2; Briggs, *Reading Virginia Woolf*, pp. 153–4.
8. Maidstone, *Hagia Sophia*, p. 12.
9. Roessel, 'The Significance of Constantinople', pp. 409–15; Briggs, *Reading Virginia Woolf*, pp. 158–9.
10. MacCulloch, *History of Christianity*, pp. 430–1. See also Maidstone, *Hagia Sophia*, p. 9.
11. MacCulloch, *History of Christianity*, p. 431.
12. Gilliat-Ray, *Muslims in Britain*, p. 32; Ansari, *The Infidel Within*, p. 40, n43.
13. East London Mosque, 'History', online.
14. Roberts, *Alterity and Narrative*, p. 4.
15. Maidstone, *Hagia Sophia*, p. 253.
16. MacCulloch, *History of Christianity*, p. 430.
17. Qtd in Maidstone, *Hagia Sophia*, p. 10.
18. Wilson, *Sphinx in the City*, p. 6.
19. See, for example, Hindrichs, 'Feminist Optics and Avant-Garde Cinema'.
20. Recht, *Believing and Seeing*, p. 2.
21. Ibid., p. 1.
22. Bumpus, *London Churches*, p. 270.

23. Addleshaw and Etchells, *Architectural Setting of Anglican Worship*, p. 209.
24. Bumpus, *London Churches*, p. 10.
25. Hare, *Walks in London*, 1, p. 114.
26. Park, 'Apostolic Minds and the Spinning House', p. 70.
27. Ditchfield, *Cathedrals of Great Britain*, p. 8.
28. Ibid., p. 30, 8, 39.
29. Andrews, 'Under the Volute', p. 64.
30. Rendell *et al.*, pp. 9–10.
31. Ruskin, *Seven Lamps of Architecture,* pp. 73–4, emphasis added.
32. Ibid., p. 64.
33. Ibid., pp. 167–74, p. 174.
34. Ibid., p. 74.
35. Quoted by Captain Grose in Warton, *Essays on Gothic Architecture*, pp. 120–2. The theory is contested even within this volume: Grose cites it approvingly but Milner dismisses it as historically inaccurate (p. 128).
36. Hare, *Walks in London*, 1, p. 16.
37. Wilson, *Sphinx in the City*, p. 54.
38. Scott, 'Ecofeminism, Holism, and the Search for Natural Order in Woolf'.
39. Ibid., p. 5.
40. Ibid., p. 2.
41. Wilson, *Sphinx in the City*, p. 8.

Chapter 5

Domestic Sacred Spaces

In the autumn of 1928, after she had finished *Orlando* and while she was slowly feeling her way towards writing *The Waves,* Woolf reflected somewhat wistfully on the importance of Monk's House as a place of retreat:

> This has been a very animated summer: a summer lived almost too much in public. Often down here I have entered into a sanctuary; a nunnery; had a religious retreat; of great agony once; & always some terror: so afraid one is of loneliness: of seeing to the bottom of the vessel. That is one of the experiences I have had here in some Augusts; & got then to a consciousness of what I call 'reality': a thing I see before me; something abstract; but residing in the downs or sky; beside which nothing matters; in which I shall rest & continue to exist. Reality I call it. (D3 196)

Woolf uses religious language to describe the ideal function of Monk's House. It is a 'sanctuary', a holy, safe, and reserved place. It is a 'nunnery', a term that feminises the name of her home and suggests a specifically female space associated with celibacy as psychological and sexual freedom from men. Woolf sees it as a place of specifically 'religious' disengagement from the world, and the rest of the passage expands upon that suggestion by evoking experiences she has had at Rodmell, including the terrifying sensation of being alone with no one and nothing to spare her from facing a profound and frightening 'reality'.

Such a retreat homewards paradoxically also involves a movement outwards, a shift from domestic space to the natural world and a sense of 'something abstract' found in the landscape. It is an imaginative relocation of self away from the confines of the home to

become part of the natural world. This is an imaginative and medi-
tative moment of peace and stillness, of resting and existing in a
space outside of the self; but also a feeling or a wish for continuing
existence beyond the confines of the body and beyond death akin to
Clarissa Dalloway's feeling that something of us survives in the natural world of trees, mists and branches (*MD* 8).

This passage encapsulates much of what characterises Virginia
Woolf's conception of the home as a sacred space. It reflects two
key definitions of the word 'sacred': the home is both a holy place fit
for religious experience that she explicitly compares with an ecclesiastical building, and also a space set apart for a specific purpose
(at least in principle, for this passage laments the interruptions she
has been experiencing). It also suggests that the home has permeable boundaries: it is a space from which one can move outwards, at
least in the imagination. Just as the previous chapter showed that she
was concerned with reconfiguring space in public places of worship
so that women could access the sacred, so Woolf was interested in
reconfiguring private spaces to free women to reflect, write and have
spiritual experiences.

Separate spheres and 'The Angel in the House'

The reconfiguration of space is integral both to Woolf's modernism
and to her negotiation of the values of her Victorian past. As Victoria
Rosner has argued, modernist writers

> sought to bring the spirit of the avant-garde into the staid environs of
> the home, to erode the physical and social divisions that structured
> the Victorian domestic sphere, and to find new artistic forms for rep-
> resenting intimacy and daily life.[1]

Modernist writers and artists championed alternative lifestyles and
family structures, through the design and decoration of their homes
as well as in their relationships. As Christopher Reed notes, Bloomsbury artists in particular 'dedicated themselves, individually and
collectively, to creating the conditions of domesticity outside mainstream definitions of home and family', and they developed a 'group
identity in a shared sense of exclusion from traditional domesticity.'[2]
In a related move, modernists sought out new artistic forms, new
ways of configuring textual or artistic space: what Woolf described

in 'Modern Fiction' as finding an alternative to the 'ill-fitting vestments' of the conventional novel.

However, the importance of challenging the Victorian household was an ongoing concern for Woolf. As Rosner adds, '[n]o other major novelist of the period was so preoccupied with the critique of Victorian domesticity or so explicit about the relationship of literary modernism to the changing nature of private life.'[3] The two elements go side-by-side: Woolf saw the persistence of Victorian values and their effects as an ongoing problem and so, in conceptualising domestic sacred space, she continually had to challenge powerful patriarchal ideologies that had for generations used religion to enforce gender roles within the family and to define the nature of home. So, although Reed sees domesticity as Bloomsbury's antidote to the values both of the mechanical modern age and the oppressive past – an 'ideal' he identifies in Forster's *Howards End,* where home is invested with 'the power to connote and even to create – new ways of life'[4] – Woolf did not see the concept of 'home' in such simple or idealistic terms.

Throughout her career, Woolf was exercised by separate spheres ideology: the mindset that had seen home as a sacred space created and maintained by the wife, who must retain her purity and distance from public life, so that her husband could retreat from the world and renew his moral focus. As we have seen, these were prominent ideas within the Clapham Sect, starting with Henry Venn's delineation of the well-regulated home in which the husband should preside and the wife provide support; an ideology which was reiterated by Sir James in his *Letters;* and by Leslie Stephen, who endorsed the ideal in 'Social Rights and Duties' and made Julia Stephen its prime exemplar in *The Mausoleum Book.* The ideology was embedded by generations who had made the home a church through the custom of family prayers. This system enabled the Stephen men to have careers in the public spheres of law, Parliament, academia and the church, supported by the sacrifices of women who, as Woolf pointed out in *Three Guineas,* were denied education so that family finances could be concentrated on their brothers' education.

The ideology had also taken hold in popular thought through influential conduct books, notably Sarah Stickney Ellis's manual *The Women of England* (n.d. [1843?]), which argued that the masculine world of work was a sinful and irreligious place, and that women needed to remind men of providence and divine love by exerting influence in the home through 'the minor morals of domestic life.'[5]

Similarly, John Ruskin wrote in 'Of Queen's Gardens' (1864) that man was 'in peril' in the world of work and so the home was a place where he could shield his wife from dangers and find sanctuary from them himself: 'within his house, as ruled by her . . . need enter no danger, no temptation, no cause of error or offence. This is the true nature of home – it is the place of Peace.' In a markedly religious register Ruskin wrote that home is 'a sacred place, a vestal temple, a temple with the hearth watched over by Household Gods.'[6] These ideologies went on to influence architectural theories: as Ernest Newton stated in his address to the Architectural Association in 1891, '[b]elief in the sacredness of home-life is still left to us, and is itself a religion.'[7] The attitude persisted into the early twentieth century: as German diplomat Hermann Muthesius noted around 1904–5, the Englishman 'sees the whole of life embodied in his house. Here, in the heart of his family, self-sufficient and feeling no urge for sociability, he finds his happiness and his real spiritual comfort.'[8] This meant that domestic space continued to be organised by ideas that had initially been religious in character.

Paradoxically, the ideologies that emphasised women's spiritual influence on others also tended to restrict their right to personal religious experience. Thus, for Ellis, a woman must lay aside her 'very self – assuming a new nature, which nothing less than watchfulness and prayer can enable her constantly to maintain to spend her mental and moral capabilities in devising means for promoting the happiness of others.'[9] Ruskin likewise argued that a woman should be 'wise not for self-development but for self-renunciation.'[10]

Furthermore, the ideology sought control over women's bodies. For Ruskin in particular, the home was analogous to the woman's body: 'wherever a true wife comes, this home is always round her.'[11] Woman is therefore inextricably tied to the domestic sphere, and her body is not hers but constitutes a diffuse sense of home. Ironically, too, although Victorian writings such as these sought to identify women with 'higher' thoughts, the effect was to tie them to domestic chores for, as Emily Blair notes, 'domestic labor . . . creates the male house of retreat.'[12] So, although Ellis advised women to make themselves available to their families rather than busying themselves with chores, in practice women's domestic occupations prevented them from having time and space for reflection.

The crushing effects of this ideology can be seen in a novel, which Woolf owned, written by Sarah Stephen, one of Woolf's female Clapham ancestors: *Passages from a Life of a Daughter at Home*

(1846). Sarah was first cousin to Caroline Emelia, and the two were close friends. Woolf owned this book and, although she never refers to it directly, it raises concerns that make it a significant part of Woolf's intellectual heritage in her thinking on roles for women. The novel has a lengthy introduction, in which Sarah critiques the impact of the Protestant work ethic on women: although they were taught that they needed to exercise a vocation as a means of demonstrating grace and salvation, they were also denied vocation by being taught to accept the roles that life gave them.[13] This was frustrating for women who felt called towards greater projects than domestic tasks: in the case of the novel's protagonist Anne, this project was to improve the lot of the poor, as both Sarah and Caroline Emelia sought to do. The early part of the novel sees Anne searching for her vocation, with the guidance of her cousin Margaret who advises her to look beyond herself, looking outwards to God not inwards to her own aspirations.[14] Accepting this, she learns to exercise will to choose her vocation and adopts a rule of life of reading and prayer. Significantly, Anne sets aside a room in the family house for this purpose, but her mother and sisters throw her off course, demanding that she engage with their social life of visiting the sick, looking after children and entertaining guests. They interrupt her reading, pluck her from her study, and then take away her room altogether to make it into a drawing-room, cruelly failing to recognise its significance: '"You may be sure," said Mary, laughing, "that Anne has had good reason for appropriating that room to herself".'[15] This key passage foreshadows Woolf's argument for a woman's right to a room of her own, for the loss of the room is a sacrifice for Anne: 'she had given up her room, and with it, she fondly thought, all individual choice and personal wishes for ever!'[16] The novel continues rather bitterly with Anne's attempts to live out this sacrifice by accommodating herself to a life of trivial tasks rather than a great work.

Woolf's most satirical portrait of the Victorian domestic ideology was in 'Professions for Women' (1931). Here, she picks Coventry Patmore's poem *The Angel in the House* (1854) as an epitome of the spiritual enslavement of women in the home and their exclusion from the public sphere. Patmore wrote that

Man must be pleased; but him to please
Is woman's pleasure; down the gulf
Of his condoled necessities
She casts herself, she flings her best. (l. 111)

The values that Woolf satirises in her essay reflect wider concerns than those of Patmore's poem, for she famously attacked the Angel in the House for all that it represented in terms of pandering to the male ego, running a home and living sacrificially:

> She was intensely sympathetic. She was immensely charming. She was utterly unselfish. She excelled in the difficult arts of family life. She sacrificed herself daily . . . she was so constituted that she never had a mind or wish of her own but preferred to sympathize always with the minds and wishes of others. (*CE2* 285)

This final point has a distinct echo of Sarah Stephen's protagonist losing 'all individual choice and personal wishes for ever'. In Woolf's essay, as in Stephen's novel, this ideology mitigates powerfully against a woman having a vocation outside the home. It also excludes her from personal experience of the sacred, for her spirituality was defined as self-denial including, significantly, making her a stranger to her own body and her sexuality: 'Above all – I need not say it – she was pure.'

Woolf consistently critiqued the mindset that prevented women from reading, thinking and imagining by forcing them to support and protect their husbands, fathers and brothers, often through domestic labour. In a pointed allusion to the middle-class occupations of men in the Stephen family, Woolf notes in *A Room of One's Own* that women are mirrors to magnify male self-esteem: 'How is he to go on giving judgement, civilizing natives, making laws, writing books, dressing up and speechifying at banquets, unless he can see himself at breakfast, and at dinner at least twice the size he really is?' (*Room* 28).

Here, the home is a space for men to be nurtured, particularly at the table at mealtimes. Similarly, in her fiction, Woolf depicts female characters who create safe and nurturing spaces for their academic husbands in Helen Ambrose in *The Voyage Out* and Mrs Ramsay. Similarly, Mrs Hilbery in *Night and Day* hosts tea-parties for elderly gentlemen and devotes herself to the characteristically Clapham task of family biography, trying to honour the memory of her father, the poet Richard Alardyce, including seeking to airbrush his image by glossing over marital infidelities.

Woolf presents her most detailed analysis of how this ideology impacted on domestic architecture in 'A Sketch of the Past'. Here, as Blair notes, she shows how the architecture of the Victorian home organised the household socially and sexually into distinct zones: the servants' quarters, the bedroom 'the sexual centre; the birth centre, the death centre' of the home, and her father's study, 'the brain of the house'.[17] Woolf identifies the tea-table as the 'centre of Victorian family life' and analyses it anthropologically as a 'focal' or 'sacred spot in our house,' a phrase that shows how religious prescriptions had survived the loss of faith. In a distinct echo of Ruskin's image of the sacred hearth at the centre of the home, Woolf describes the tea-table as 'the centre to which the sons returned from their work in the evening; the hearth whose fire was tended by mother pouring out tea' (*MB* 118–19). Furthermore, by locating the 'sacred spot' in the mother's presence at the tea-table, Woolf echoes Ruskin's notion that 'the home is always round' the true wife, so that the woman's body is synonymous with the home; the idea appears also when Woolf describes how 22 Hyde Park Gate and Talland House were 'full of' her mother (*MB* 83). And Woolf shows the problems that these values and ideals presented for a younger generation when she describes how 'Victorian society exert[ed] its pressure' on herself and Vanessa when they had to perform tea-table duties after the death of their mother (*MB* 148).

As well as critiquing these ideologies, however, Woolf challenges them by subversively reconfiguring space in each of these works. At its simplest, this is found in moments when female characters create alternative mental spaces for themselves even while being confined to the physical places assigned to them. So, in both *Night and Day* and *To the Lighthouse,* she uses younger women to counteract the expectations of the older generation: Katharine Hilbery only attends to serving tea with 'a fifth part' or the 'surface skin of her mind' (*ND* 3, 7), saving her true intellectual energies for mathematics, while Lily Briscoe spends the dinner party resisting pressure from Mrs Ramsay to sympathise with men by keeping her mind focused on her painting and symbolically reordering the space of her painting, repositioning a tree as an expression of her resistance both to marriage and pandering to men (*TL* 115).

In both 'Professions for Women' and 'A Sketch of the Past', Woolf tames separate-spheres ideology by containing it within the locus of the drawing-room. In 'Professions for Women', when Woolf notes how Victorian ideologies of female sympathy and purity impinge upon her ability to write honest reviews of books by men, she describes the Angel's advice in terms of an etiquette lesson for hosting a tea party:

> My dear, you are a young woman. You are writing about a book that has been written by a man. Be sympathetic; be tender; flatter; deceive; use all the arts and wiles of your sex. Never let anybody guess that you have a mind of your own. Above all, be pure. (*CE2* 285)

Woolf suggests that the Angel, although purporting to offer moralistic advice, was actually encouraging dishonesty, prevarication and flattery, and excluding women from spiritual experience by denying them imagination and sexuality. In this talk, for which Woolf shared a platform with Ethel Smyth[18] (who enabled her to reflect on her Puritan background and to speak more frankly about sex), Woolf offers as an alternative the attractive scenario of the woman writer getting carried away with the work of the imagination, entering a 'dream' or a 'trance', sinking into 'pools' and 'dark places' not unlike the 'bottom of the vessel' that she recalls encountering at Monk's House. The trance is both spiritual and sexual for 'she had thought of something, something about the body'; it founders because this was unreadable to male understandings of spirituality and counteracted Puritan ideas about sexuality, as it involves 'passions which it was unfitting for her as a woman to say' (*CE2* 287–8). It is therefore appropriate that the space that frees her to write and send off her work (and to be paid for it) is not the drawing room but the bedroom (*CE2* 284): a space where a woman can exist in relation to her own body and spirit, unimpeded by the wider social setting. The 'bed-sitting room' (*MB* 122) similarly functions as a liberating space in 'Sketch' when Virginia and Vanessa free themselves from the Victorian norms of the drawing-room to unlock their creativity in alternative spaces. While Vanessa spends the rest of the day outside the home at art school, Virginia reads in her room (*MB* 148–9). Woolf therefore shows how creative spirituality can find its expression once the expectations imposed by domestic architecture have been disrupted.

Reclaiming the study

Woolf's strongest challenge to domestic architecture and its enforcement of the gendered separate spheres is in her representation of the study. Historically, the study was the architectural marker of male privilege: a man's right to a spiritual life and freedom from domestic duties. While the ideology dictated that the whole home be set up for the benefit of the man, the study was an area set apart for man's exclusive use: as Blair argues from Mark Wigley, 'the development of architecture' from the Renaissance onwards 'contains the woman in the house at the same time that it gradually creates a space for the private male self.'[19] The man therefore enjoyed a double retreat: having already withdrawn from the world to the home, he could further withdraw to his study in order to escape the demands of family and domestic life. Woolf's description of her father's study in 'A Sketch of the Past' clearly shows this: situated at the top of the house, this 'big fine room' seems not to be part of the house at all, having been 'added on', and its 'three long windows' provide further escape from the home, by giving a view over the city (*MB* 119).

The study was a space in which the two implications of the sacred were intertwined: it was both reserved and set apart, and holy and clerical. As Rosner has shown, the study originated as a monastic cell, and the Victorians and Edwardians clearly continued to think of it as a sacred space: she cites *Daniel Deronda*, where the study is 'odorous as a private chapel'; R. A. Briggs's *The Essentials of a Country House* (1911) which notes that the study is for 'clergy and writers'; and Sarah Grand's *The Heavenly Twins*, where the library is a 'private sanctum'.[20] Woolf satirises the religious ideology of male exclusivity in her essay on Ruskin, where she remarks that Victorians liked great men to be isolated from society; 'the great man of that age had much temptation to withdraw to his pinnacle and become a prophet, denouncing a generation from whose normal activities he was secluded' (*CE1* 205). In *Night and Day,* the shrine devoted to Richard Alardyce is an extreme version of the study:

> The smaller room was something like a chapel in a cathedral, or a grotto in a cave . . . but the comparison to a religious temple of some kind was the more apt of the two, for the little room was crowded with relics. (*ND* 9)

Ruskin's withdrawal renders him out of touch; Alardyce is shown to be outdated and irrelevant.

Woolf also satirises the doubly sacred conception of the study in her description of Ridley Ambrose's scholarly life in *The Voyage Out*. His room is reserved and exclusive: the door is 'always shut'; it is a place of secrets, for the other inhabitants of the house are 'vaguely conscious' that something went on inside it 'without in the least knowing what it was'. Ambrose is freed to do his research by the ministrations of others, including their cooking and other domestic duties. Woolf invokes but takes a highly satirical view of the sacred nature of the study when she compares Ambrose to 'an idol in an empty church' (*VO* 191). Ambrose uses the mystique of the study to separate himself from others, but it is doubtful whether he is achieving anything significant by doing so.

However, the episode also depicts a female challenge to exclusive male space, for Rachel Vinrace disregards the household rules by brazenly entering the study, shouting for Ambrose's attention and demanding a book. Such an intrusion is bolder than the *flâneur's* ironic view of a church building, for Rachel's entry changes the mood of the room entirely. This episode foreshadows the move in *A Room of One's Own* that Rosner has described as an 'act of usurpation' of the study which 'is a founding moment for the modern woman writer.'[21] In storming the study in *The Voyage Out* and making the case for a private room for women in *A Room of One's Own*, Woolf was appealing for them to share a privilege that had once belonged exclusively to men, but she is also explicitly arguing for them to have a space that as Blair has suggested, is both private and spiritual: a space where women are free to retreat, reflect and find renewal.[22]

In championing a woman's right to a room of her own, Woolf was readjusting women's position in relation to public and private life and thereby contesting the ideology of separate spheres, for this room was not a place of withdrawal, exile or imprisonment in the private sphere as Elaine Showalter has suggested.[23] First the Victorian man's study was a haven from domestic life, and Woolf makes a case for women to share this facility to escape from domestic chores. Second, the Victorian man went to his study in order to prepare himself afresh for the public world and to engage vicariously with others through writing (especially letter-writing), and reading. As Charles Rice notes, the house did not cut off private from public for 'in the nineteenth century, the development of rooms such as the study and the library became the context for the bourgeoisie to engage with the media in the form of books, newspapers and magazines.'[24] Woolf therefore envisaged the private room as a space through which women could enter into public life. As Anna Snaith has argued, Woolf saw the 'conceptual dichotomy between public and private spaces' as one 'to be reworked and questioned, rather than accepted wholesale in any particular form,' so that she saw the study as a 'liberating private space, an active choice, and, importantly, it is from the room that the woman will gain access to the public sphere through writing.'[25]

Woolf presents this dynamic markedly in *A Room of One's Own*, for she constantly elides the difference between interior and exterior space. This is seen in the very format of the essay, for it was originally written to be delivered in a space that was both communal (a meeting-room in a women's college) and private (she was addressing an invited audience and she jokes about watching out for eavesdroppers). Sold as an essay, it preserves the tone of oral public delivery but is now packaged for a wider readership who will nevertheless consume it in private. Woolf's account of the study in *Room* is therefore more transformative than Rosner appreciates when she argues that Woolf does not 'debunk the mystique of the study' and does not seek to change the space but its ownership.[26]

A Room of One's Own, surprisingly, rarely envisages exclusively private spaces, for it persistently delineates a movement out of doors, similar to the one described in Woolf's diary entry on Rodmell. This is seen in the earlier chapters of the essay, when Woolf presents the (internal) creative process metaphorically as a series of (external) journeys, drawing an 'analogy between physical movement and meandering thought', as Tracy Seeley notes.[27] Woolf's narrator develops her thoughts as she makes a *flânerie* around public spaces, strolling along a river bank, attempting to cross college lawns, touring Oxbridge colleges, taking meals at two colleges and visiting rooms around the university, visiting the British Museum, and eating at a restaurant. All these visits are punctuated by walks on the street. The *flânerie* takes her to places where she is free to roam, and so she does not need to storm the bastions of the chapel and the college library, although she remarks upon their exclusivity.

When the narrator goes indoors and we follow her perusal of her bookshelves, we discover that what appeared to be a cosy private space (the wish to 'draw the curtains; to shut out distractions; to light the lamp' (*Room* 32)) is revealed to be the shared space of a drawing-room full of people: 'people's noses and bare shoulders showed naked against a starry sky, for someone had twitched the curtain in the drawing-room' (*Room* 71). This revelation again delineates a movement out of doors, for the twitching of the curtain reveals the night sky; this movement is replicated shortly afterwards in a significant moment where the narrator looks out of the window on to a London street. The room of one's own is therefore not a confined space, but one that (like Leslie Stephen's study) had windows giving a view outside. Woolf is therefore championing the right to a view on the world as much as she is championing the right to a room.

Caroline Emelia Stephen and domestic sacred space

A Room of One's Own is deeply concerned with achieving the spiritual freedom of a peaceful state of mind conducive to writing. This can be seen more clearly when we recognise the significance of Caroline Emelia Stephen to the essay. Woolf alludes to her inheritance of £2,500 from Caroline Emelia when the narrator speaks of the liberating effects of a legacy from her aunt (*Room* 29–30), but this is more than a passing acknowledgement, for the passage engages ideas and images that are central to the essay as a whole. The narrator says that the legacy is even more important than getting the vote, because it has freed her to be vocational: before inheriting the money, the narrator had to be content with menial tasks like local journalism, reading to old ladies, and teaching infants: the 'chief occupations that were open to women before 1918.' Such work was done unwillingly with the kind of dishonest 'flattering and fawning' that Woolf would blame on the influence of the Angel in the House. Significantly, like Sarah Stephen, Woolf sees such work as spiritually damaging, for it frustrates her narrator's true vocation of being a writer:

> the thought of that one gift which it was death to hide – a small one but dear to the possessor – perishing and with it my self, my soul – all this became like a rust eating away the bloom of the spring, destroying the tree at its heart.

This quotation uses a compound allusion to emphasise the need for meaningful work. The phrasing echoes Milton's lament on being unable to fulfil his writerly vocation in 'On his Blindness': 'that one talent which it is death to hide / Lodg'd with me useless, though my soul more bent / To serve therewith my Master.' This, in turn, alludes to the Parable of the Talents (Matthew. 25:14–30) where a servant who has buried rather than invested the coin entrusted to him by his master is condemned to a place of utter darkness, wailing, and the gnashing of teeth. Woolf is therefore engaging precisely with the Protestant work ethic and its implications for women by showing that the ideology is not merely frustrating but cuts women off from the very means of demonstrating their salvation. Woolf elaborates on this by showing how restrictions on women breed hatred and bitterness towards men, leading women into the evil 'red light of emotion' rather than the 'white light of truth', evoking the image of light that pervades Caroline Emelia's work.

The aunt's legacy provides an antidote to this by bringing spiritual redemption as well as financial benefits, for the money helps to 'rub off' some of the rust and corruption in the narrator's soul, and it leads her to a new attitude towards men in general, a realisation that it 'was absurd to blame any class or any sex as a whole.' The passage ends by describing the aunt's legacy as the catalyst for a conversion experience: 'Indeed my aunt's legacy unveiled the sky to me, and substituted for the large and imposing figure of a gentleman, which Milton recommended for my perpetual adoration, a view of the open sky' (*Room* 30).

This is another compound allusion. It rejects the notion – so central to separate spheres ideology – that a woman must look up to a man as a representation of God by serving and worshipping her husband. Milton endorses this in his description of the ideal relationship between Adam and Eve in *Paradise Lost:* 'He for God only, she for God in him' (4 299); this in turn alludes to St Paul's injunctions on household organisation: 'But I would have you know, that the head of every man is Christ; and the head of the woman is the man; and the head of Christ is God' (1 Corinthians 11:3). The fictional aunt in *Room* has enabled the narrator to reject the social order that patriarchy had used Christianity to defend, as Caroline Emelia had done for Woolf.

Released from these social and spiritual restrictions, the narrator experiences truth and freedom; her perception that the legacy has 'unveiled the sky to me' alludes to Caroline Emelia's account of her own conversion experience: 'It is as if my painted roof has been smashed and, instead of the darkness I had dreaded, I had found the stars shining.'[28] Caroline Emelia sees her spiritual freedom as a reconfiguration of space: she had broken from the confines of the home and of the established church with its painted ceilings in order to experience God without the intervention of men or the church. Woolf therefore draws on an image from Caroline Emelia when she depicts spiritual freedom and fulfilment in terms of seeing the open sky both here and in the speaker's glimpse of the 'starry sky' through a gap in the curtains.

The concept of androgyny, which Woolf introduces later in the essay, can be seen as a further development of the idea of spiritual freedom for it denotes a movement beyond the confines of sex and the self. This is seen in Woolf's elaboration of Coleridge's idea of the androgynous mind, describing it as one that is 'resonant and porous . . . transmits emotion without impediment . . . is naturally creative, incandescent and undivided' (*Room* 74). This moving out of the self rejects the self-denial and constraint of Protestant ideology and embraces what Val Gough has described as the route to radical alterity characteristic of a mysticism that resists patriarchal ideas of God.[29]

Caroline Emelia was an important influence on Woolf's mysticism, in terms of spiritual practice and the domestic arrangements that supported it. Caroline Emelia had pioneered an alternative lifestyle choice of living alone, enabling her to be deeply religious and socially useful outside of a family structure: as Jane Marcus has shown, she evaded the patriarchal family without causing controversy.[30] Her home at The Porch was a sacred space for prayer, privacy and introspection, as she wrote: 'all the ups and downs of one's own inner life must be part of a process of which we don't see enough to under-stand them – if we did, I suppose they would not have their present intensity.'[31] Woolf likewise valued introspection: the contemplation of 'an ordinary mind on an ordinary day' and the investigation of 'little apprehended . . . states of soul in creating' (*CE2* 106; *D3* 253). And although Woolf was ambivalent about her aunt and nicknamed her 'the Nun', she also found her lifestyle appealing. The Porch was clearly a sanctuary for Woolf, particularly when recovering from her breakdown of 1904.

The Porch was also significant to the start of Woolf's public career as a writer, for Caroline Emelia encouraged her and helped her with her article for Maitland. The Porch was not a place of confinement, for it was also a space in which guests were received and meetings held: for example, Caroline Emelia provided hospitality for male and female Quaker students from the university. Home for Caroline Emelia was a space for engaging with the world through writing let-ters and books, and a space that energised her to re-engage with the wider world: Stephen had a life outside the home, for she attended Quaker meetings, she worked to build houses for the poor alongside Octavia Hill, and she helped Sarah Stephen break the deadlock of being a daughter in the house when they worked together to found a society to help working women.[32] Caroline Emelia engaged with Cambridge University, giving guest lectures, such as her paper to Newnham Sunday Society on the beauty of living alone.[33] When Woolf began *A Room of One's Own* by giving papers on 'Women and Fiction' at Girton and Newnham in October 1928, then, she was following in her aunts' footsteps. Caroline Emelia therefore mod-elled a way of respecting the sanctity of the home and using it as a place for spiritual reflection and mystic experience and a space from which she could engage with the wider public world.

Home as ecclesiastical space

A Room of One's Own therefore reconfigures space in order to blur the boundaries between public and private and envisage domestic sacred spaces for women that resisted the restrictions that had been associated with the concept of home. A further manifestation of this reconfiguration of space is when Woolf explores the interpenetration of home and public places of worship. We saw in the previous chap-ter how the sacred could spill out of churches and cathedrals like the 'gust of organ music' from St Paul's (*Y* 206). This is an example of what Elicia Clements has identified as Woolf's use of sonic effects to achieve the 'disruption of typical borders',[34] and Woolf repeatedly uses soundscapes as a way of showing how the ecclesiastical could penetrate into the domestic. She frequently remarks on hearing the sound of church bells in her living space, sometimes with annoyance but nearly always with a sense of being reminded that worship was taking place.[35] She also described Caroline Emelia's voice as being like a church bell: 'I feel as though I were living in a Cathedral Close, with the big bell of the Quakers voice tolling at intervals' (*L*1 144). It is an annoyance, but it also replaces the traditional association between woman and (private) home with an association between woman and (public) church. The interpenetration of church and home can be seen in *Mrs Dalloway* in the chimes of St Margaret's Westminster as an antidote to the slightly earlier sound of Big Ben:

Ah, said St. Margaret's, like a hostess who comes into her drawing-room on the very stroke of the hour and finds her guests there already. I am not late. No, it is precisely half-past eleven, she says ... the sound of St. Margaret's glides into the recesses of the heart and buries itself in ring after ring of sound, like something alive which wants to confide itself, to disperse itself, to be, with a tremor of delight, at rest. (*MD* 44–5)

Here, the sound of a public place of worship enters not only the home but the physical space of the body itself.

Woolf envisages this further reconfiguration of space – the interpenetration between the domestic, the physical and the ecclesiastical – most fully in significant moments in *Mrs Dalloway* and *To the Lighthouse*, when female characters have spiritual experiences through which Woolf demonstrates the sanctity of the home as a place of refreshment and inspiration, but also plays with space to resist the confines of the domestic.

Clarissa Dalloway has three significant spiritual experiences in moments of retreat. The first is when she returns home from shopping and views her house as a convent: 'she felt like a nun who has left the world and feels fold round her the familiar veils and the response to old devotions' (*MD* 26). The phrase recalls the ideology of home as a sacred place away from the world and there are suggestions that Clarissa is the 'household nun' of Ruskin's imagination, for she sees her husband Richard as the 'foundation' of the joy she feels. However rather than feeling constrained, Clarissa finds the veils 'familiar' and they 'fold round' her gently. Furthermore, alongside the dynamics of entering an enclosed and comforting space, there are implications of entering a larger public building, for Clarissa's hallway is 'as cool as a vault', and she enters her house as one would a church, performing an act of obeisance that Woolf would have witnessed in cathedrals on the continent: 'bending her head over the hall table, she bowed beneath the influence, felt blessed and purified.' She also experiences a movement outwards into the natural world (as with many examples discussed in this chapter), for Clarissa thinks that 'moments like this are buds on the tree of life, flowers of darkness' like 'some lovely rose'. Though Woolf chooses this moment to pointedly remind us of Clarissa's atheism – 'not for a moment did she believe in God' – she also invokes the ancient mystic symbol of the rose.

Clarissa's second retreat is into her bedroom: the inner sanctum where a woman can be creative and at home in her own body. Clarissa is driven into this space when the joy of her homecoming is almost immediately shattered by the news that Richard has gone to a lunch party without her. Woolf explains that Clarissa is not feeling 'vulgar jealousy', but an awareness of her own mortality, the fear that Richard will socialise without her when she is dead: a feeling reinforced by her recalling of the dirge for Imogen from *Cymbeline*, 'fear no more'. She experiences a dreadful fear of solitude, much like Woolf's fear of loneliness at Monk's House, as though she is leaving a party as a 'single figure against the appalling night.' Darkness had had mystic potential a moment earlier, but now it is frightening (*MD* 27–8).

However, Woolf repeats the image of retreat as entering a convent, for Clarissa goes upstairs 'like a nun withdrawing'; as with her homecoming, this is intermixed with suggestions of a visit to a church or cathedral, for she is like a 'child exploring a tower'. Significantly, then, the episode involves a movement from a private to a public space and a perspective beyond the house, for Clarissa pauses to look out of the window (*MD* 28). Private space therefore points outwards rather than inwards, and Clarissa is not enclosed but liberated in this inner sanctum, for here she can read without being interrupted and, more importantly, she can sleep alone having renounced or, more accurately, revoked sexual relations with her husband: 'she could not dispel a virginity preserved through childbirth.' Here, Woolf reinterprets patriarchal ideologies of purity and chastity. In such discourses, sex was morally acceptable for purposes of reproduction and so by having a child, Clarissa has fulfilled this criterion. However, Woolf resists these heterosexual notions, for Clarissa goes on to reflect that she does not have sexual feelings for men, even to the extent of being unable to have sex with her husband on occasions, but that she has had moments of attraction to women which are profoundly spiritual: 'a sudden revelation, a tinge like a blush . . . an illumination; a match burning in a crocus; an inner meaning almost expressed' (*MD* 29). She therefore escapes her domestic role by remembering 'the revelation, the religious feeling' of her love affair with Sally Seton (*MD* 32). Furthermore, she eludes religious discourses of self-abnegation, for she realises an image of herself as 'pointed; dart-like; definite', a self quite unlike the one she puts on for others, which is characterised by her role of hostess and her attempts to do good deeds (*MD* 33–4).

Clarissa's third retreat is at the party when she goes to a private room on hearing the news of Septimus's suicide. In this passage, the things that Clarissa had feared earlier come to pass: she *is* leaving a party alone; the news of Septimus's death bears out her intimations of mortality; and the 'appalling night' she feared earlier is echoed in the 'suffocation of blackness' she imagines for Septimus's last moments (*MD* 164). However, Clarissa's withdrawal helps her come to terms with the news for this experience is again characterised by a movement outwards, as she thinks of the sky: at Bourton, in London, and (like the narrator of *A Room of One's Own*) seeing it 'over people's shoulders at dinner'. Read against other instances of Woolf's references to the sky, we can see this both as liberating and as a sign of a reality beyond the self. Clarissa once more looks out of the window, but this time she sees another woman in her inner sanctum of the bedroom: an elderly lady 'going to bed alone.' The sight of the lady reassures Clarissa of the presence of other people and, when the lady puts out her bedroom light it is not frightening but affirming. Clarissa now recalls the dirge for Imogen less as a *memento mori* than as an instruction not to be afraid: 'fear no more the heat of the sun'; sunlight is not to be feared because she has embraced darkness and understood Septimus's desire to die (*MD* 166).

Woolf testifies more fully to female spiritual power and an escape from the traditional confines of the home in her account of experiences of the sacred in *To the Lighthouse*. Mrs Ramsay's nocturnal visit to Lily Briscoe's bedroom (*TL* 68–70) is a moment of female intimacy in a space that is set apart and reserved for women. Lily, resting her head in Mrs Ramsay's lap and laughing uncontrollably at the thought of Mrs Ramsay's futile attempts to persuade her to marry, is suddenly struck by her mentor's mood of calmness, seriousness and simplicity. Lily views this as a moment of entry into sacred space: 'Into what sanctuary had one penetrated?' The word 'sanctuary' is laden with meaning. It means safe space, the kind of retreat that Ruskin had envisaged for the Victorian man, but Woolf's use of the word here detaches it from the sexual ideology of marriage and rewrites it with lesbian overtones. The word 'sanctuary' also denotes the holiest area of a church or cathedral, the domain of male clergy, but figures it as a female-only space, and one that is contained within a female body. This radically rewrites the Ruskinian trope of the home as the woman's body; the woman's body and mind are now part of a church: the domestic and the ecclesiastical interpenetrate once again. As in earlier examples, the focus shifts outwards to the sky, which becomes the locus of the sacred, as Lily sees in Mrs Ramsay 'something clear as the space which the clouds at last uncover – the little space of sky which sleeps beside the moon.'

The second episode is Mrs Ramsay's reverie in her brief moment of solitude after James has been put to bed (*TL* 85–7). Unlike Clarissa, Mrs Ramsay does not retreat into a room of her own: rather, like the narrator in *A Room of One's Own*, she is in the liminal space of the drawing-room window. However, like Clarissa, she gains a sense of a self that is hers alone, invisible to others, and immune from the demands to sympathise and sacrifice herself to others. The episode speaks of the spiritual potential of darkness, with Mrs Ramsay's perception that she is 'a wedge-shaped core of darkness', bringing an awareness of fathomless depths: 'Beneath it is all dark, it is all spreading, it is unfathomably deep', leading to a feeling of 'peace' and 'eternity'.

In this scene, darkness is not counteracted by stars but by the beam of the lighthouse, the 'long steady stroke, the last of the three, which was her stroke'. The lighthouse image has a parallel in Caroline Emelia's writing, from a meditation on how God is always present even if people are only intermittently aware of him:

> Have you ever seen a revolving lighthouse at night from across the sea with its steadfast light alternately hidden and displayed? Have you watched the faint spark as it slows into splendour for a few seconds and then fades away again into darkness? And have you considered how the very fact of its intermittency is the means by which it is recognized and its message is conveyed? It is a light given not to read by, but to steer our course by. Its appearances and disappearances

are a language by which the human-care that devised it can speak to the watchers and strugglers at sea. That care does not wax and wane with the light; but in its unchanging vigilance it provides a means of communication which no unfaltering beam could afford.[36]

The echoes here may not be entirely intertextual, for Caroline Emelia and Woolf had both been captivated by the Godrevy lighthouse during summers at St Ives. However, the fact that Mrs Ramsay's train of thought takes her briefly to a similar insight to Caroline Emelia's ('We are in the hands of the Lord') suggests that Woolf was working through her aunt's ideas. Mrs Ramsay's rejection of the idea marks out Woolf's refusal to accept her aunt's faith in a caring God.

Like Clarissa Dalloway and like the narrator of *A Room of One's Own,* Mrs Ramsay's momentary experience of privacy takes her away from the home: 'this self having shed its attachments was free for the strangest adventures' (*TL* 85). Significantly one of the places she travels to is a public place of worship, 'she felt herself pushing aside the thick leather curtain of a church in Rome.' She has a reprieve of this reverie later, when she is carried away by the power of the dinner party and pictures herself at a service in 'a Roman Catholic Cathedral' (*TL* 148–9). Here again public and private interpenetrate one another: Mrs Ramsay's imagination takes her from the domestic spaces of the drawing room and the dining room to a public place of worship, the Catholic cathedral taking her explicitly away from Evangelical Protestant domestic ideology, from Clapham and its family prayers, and its connections with England and Empire.

Woolf therefore radically reconfigures private sacred space in both these novels. Private space (whether it be in a dedicated room, like Clarissa Dalloway or a temporarily empty family room like Mrs Ramsay) becomes a springboard for imaginative explorations of the public sphere, including spaces where women might not ordinarily venture, and by referring to Mrs Ramsay's body as a sanctuary Woolf rewrites the association between the female body and the home, instead associating the female body with large public sacred spaces.

Monk's House

This chapter has revealed close analogies between Woolf's argument for the importance of a room of one's own, her representation of female characters' spiritual experiences in relation to space, and her reflections on the spiritual importance of Monk's House in her diary entry from the autumn of 1928. These parallels suggest that Woolf saw her own writing as a spiritual activity and show that space was important to her personally. Woolf's reconfiguring of domestic space in her works had a practical counterpart in her living-space at Monk's House: the Woolfs redesigned the house almost immediately after buying it in 1919, removing internal partitions from the ground floor to give their house a more spacious feel and in doing so they broke down the configurations of the traditional home. They also blurred boundaries between indoors and outdoors because they saw the garden and surrounding land as an extension of their living-space: as Frances Spalding notes, 'a major attraction of this small house was the large stretch of land and small orchard that lay behind it, opening on to a view across water-meadows and fields to Mount Caburn.'[37] Virginia Woolf also saw overlaps between her domestic space and ecclesiastical space. Historically, Monk's House appealed to her because of a legend that it was once owned by Lewes Priory and used by the monks for retreats: 'I said to myself; you must discount the value of that old chimney piece & the niches for holy water. Monks are nothing out of the way' (*D1* 286).[38] Woolf's writing lodge, where she worked for three hours a day, abuts the churchyard wall of Rodmell Church, so she could see the church and hear the sound of bells and even singing from the house.

Monk's House was the Woolfs' country retreat, but Virginia Woolf created further retreats for herself and her writing. Her writing cottage was one such sanctuary, but in 1929 she used her earnings from *A Room of One's Own* to create an additional private space. As Anna Snaith notes, 'the proceeds from *A Room* literally turned into space' (*Room* xxiii) for, while completing the essay, she noted in her Diary, 'I am summoning Philcox next week to plan a room – I have money to build it, money to furnish it' (*D3* 219–20). The planned room became two rooms, one of which was Virginia's own bedroom with its narrow bed tucked beneath a bookcase and next to a window. It was entered from the outside and Woolf watched the stars at night when she could not sleep. Hermione Lee writes, the 'new room at Monk's House and the "room of one's own" of her essay are connected' and she suggests that the essay is Woolf's 'disguised economic autobiography'.[39] Given the importance that Woolf accords to being in a spiritual frame of mind for writing, the essay can also be read as Woolf's disguised spiritual autobiography.

Woolf rehearsed her ideals for a female domestic sacred space in *Mrs Dalloway* and *To the Lighthouse*; she theorised them as recommendations for writing in *A Room of One's Own,* in which she demonstrated the importance of engaging with transcendent realities in private meditation and looking outwards to the world as prerequisites for writing. As we have seen, this method derives from Christian practice, traceable in many ways to the customs of the Clapham Sect, but rewritten from a feminist point of view, displacing the concept of self-surrender to a man by affirming the importance of androgynous freedom of thought. Woolf pushes beyond Evangelical attempts to reify the deity by talking in more mystical terms about the more abstract 'something' in the universe, in the sky, among the stars (*D3* 196). Woolf's creation of her own domestic space after publishing *A Room of One's Own* helped break her deadlock of 1928 and go on to finish *The Waves:* that 'mystic, spiritual' book that would envisage 'a world without self', no longer in the Victorian sense of female self-abnegation but with a mystic insight that it is 'not oneself but something in the universe that one's left with' (*D3* 113). As we will see in the next two chapters, *The Waves* was significant for Woolf's engagement with particular expressions of Christian culture and for the development of her own spirituality and aesthetic.

Notes

1. Rosner, *Modernism and the Architecture of Private Life,* p. 13.
2. Reed, *Bloomsbury Rooms,* p. 7.
3. Rosner, *Modernism and the Architecture of Private Life,* p. 15.
4. Reed, *Bloomsbury Rooms,* p. 6.
5. Ellis, *Women of England,* pp. 500–1, 496.
6. Ruskin, *Sesame and Lilies, p.* 72.
7. Quoted in Stamp and Goulancourt, *The English House,* p. 14.
8. Muthesius, *The English House,* p. 7.
9. Ellis, *Women of England,* p. 498.
10. Ruskin, *Sesame and Lilies,* p. 73.
11. Ibid., p. 72.
12. Blair, *Woolf and the Nineteenth-Century Domestic Novel,* p. 31.
13. Sarah Stephen, *Passages from a Life,* pp. xviii-xx.
14. Ibid., p. 64.
15. Ibid., p. 107.
16. Ibid., p. 112.
17. *MB* 118. Blair, *Woolf and the Nineteenth-Century Domestic Novel,* p. 29.
18. Raitt, 'The Tide of Ethel', p. 8.
19. Blair, *Woolf and the Nineteenth-Century Domestic Novel,* p. 24.
20. Rosner, *Modernism and the Architecture of Private Life,* pp. 97, 108.

21. Ibid., p. 92.
22. Blair, *Woolf and the Nineteenth-Century Domestic Novel*, pp. 30–1.
23. Showalter, *Literature of Their Own*, p. 285.
24. Rice, *Emergence of the Interior*, p. 113.
25. Snaith, *Public and Private Negotiations*, pp. 1, 2–3.
26. Rosner, *Modernism and the Architecture of Private Life*, pp. 123, 93.
27. Seeley, 'Flights of Fancy', p. 32.
28. C. E. Stephen, letter to Miss Wedgewood, December 1872, *Vision of Faith*, p. lxii. Marcus, *Languages of Patriarchy*, pp. 124–5.
29. Gough, '"That Razor Edge of Balance"', pp. 70–1.
30. Marcus, *Languages of Patriarchy*, p. 116.
31. C. E. Stephen, *Vision of Faith*, p. cxxvi.
32. Ibid., pp. xvi–xvii.
33. Around 1904. C. E. Stephen, *Vision of Faith*, p. cxviii.
34. Clements, 'Reconfigured Terrain', p. 72.
35. Lee, *Virginia Woolf*, p. 248.
36. C. E. Stephen, *Vision of Faith*, p. 49.
37. Spalding, *Art, Life and Vision*, p. 118.
38. See *Downhill All the Way*, p. 12, for Leonard Woolf's account of the legend and how it was disproved.
39. Lee, *Virginia Woolf*, p. 556.

Chapter 6

The Purple Triangle and Blue Madonnas: The Virgin Mary

One wanted, she thought, dipping her brush deliberately, to be on a level with ordinary experience, to feel simply that's a chair, that's a table, and yet at the same time, It's a miracle, it's an ecstasy. (*TL* 272)

Of all the manifestations of Christian culture that were available to Virginia Woolf, representations of the Virgin Mary were the most varied and had elicited the most complex reactions over time. Depictions and understandings of the Virgin Mary have had a rich and varied history throughout the Christian era and across traditions. The Orthodox Church sees her as the *Theotokos* or God-bearer, the human mother who carried and gave birth to God; in Orthodox iconography, which Woolf saw during her travels in Greece in 1906 and especially when she travelled there with Roger Fry in 1932, images of the Virgin are believed to provide direct contact with the divine itself. Mary is particularly venerated within the Catholic tradition through beliefs in the Virgin Birth, her power to make intercession for human beings and her working of miracles. She is commemorated in Catholic countries in a sequence of festivals marking her immaculate conception, her birth, the annunciation and her assumption into heaven: Woolf wrote powerfully about one such feast at Siena on 8 September 1908. Renaissance religious art represented the reverence in which she was held: Woolf knew this art from her visits to the National Gallery in London, and also from her travels in Italy, where she was particularly intrigued by the frescoes at the Collegio del Cambio in Perugia. And although Mary has a lesser place within the Protestant tradition, she is nonetheless significant for, as Miri Rubin points out, while she 'lost much of her devotional adornment and visual glamour', she 'gained an embedded quality as a symbol of good faith and Christian family values.'[1] The Virgin Mary therefore represents an ideal of purity which adds a strong, complex and longstanding religious and cultural impetus to the ideology of the Angel in the House, an ideology that persisted into Woolf's agnostic upbringing, as we have seen.

The cultural history of the Virgin Mary is therefore important to an understanding of religion and gender for, as Rubin notes, it leads us to 'reflect on the uses of the feminine in private yearnings and public supplications'.[2] And, as Marina Warner has argued in her groundbreaking study,

> Whether we regard the Virgin Mary as the most sublime and beautiful image in man's struggle towards the good and the pure, or the most pitiable production of ignorance and superstition, she represents a central theme in the history of western attitudes towards women.[3]

This has led to conflicting responses to Mary over the centuries. As Warner notes, she embodies a paradox that 'in the very celebration of perfect human woman, both humanity and women were subtly denigrated.'[4] Warner encourages a critical view of the Virgin Mary, but Julia Kristeva, responding to Warner in her essay 'Stabat Mater' shifts the emphasis to note that she also has an appeal for women, for she 'was able to attract women's wishes for identification as well as the very precise interposition of those who assumed to keep watch over the symbolic and social order'.[5] As this chapter will show, Woolf's responses to the Virgin Mary give evidence both of attraction and of a critique of patriarchal understandings of her.

Kristeva's essay is helpful for setting out three slightly different constructs of the Virgin Mary that help to explain cultural preoccupations with her, all of which are found in Woolf's writing. Kristeva notes first that as a virgin, Mary is associated with 'neither sex nor death', citing John Chrysostom's maxim that 'where there is death there is also sexual copulation, and where there is no death there is no sexual copulation either'.[6] Judged against her, no human being can match such standards, so all women are implicitly impure. Although Kristeva argues that this is a particular problem within Catholicism (she notes that the doctrine of the Immaculate Conception of Mary was ratified in 1854 as a challenge to the rise of feminism), she overstates the case when she claims that Protestantism is immune.

The second construct concerns power: Mary has been represented as Queen since the early sixth century, and as Lady (Madonna or Our Lady), reflecting feudal hierarchy, since the fourteenth century.[7] In this respect, doctrines of Mary incorporate Pagan conceptions of the mother goddess into Christianity; these beliefs sometimes arose in opposition to the doctrines of the official church.[8] Representations of Mary therefore have their place alongside other constructions of female deity, such as those uncovered by Jane Harrison; we can set the Virgin Mary in Woolf's work alongside her other representations of female power and divinity.

The third construct is of a Mary who represents human relationships: 'Mary as poor, modest and humble – Madonna of humility at the same time as a devoted, fond mother.' Referring to the *Nativity* by Piero della Francesca (1470–5), bought by the National Gallery in 1874, Kristeva argues that it is not as de Beauvoir argued, 'a feminine defeat because the mother kneeled before her barely born son', but an image that 'in fact consolidates the new cult of humanistic sensibility.'[9] Art therefore is a particular focus for Mary's humanity, both as the nursing Madonna and the grieving Stabat Mater or Mater Dolorosa. As Rubin has shown,

> the image of the mother – nurturing, suffering, and bereaved – became the emblem of European and then world Christian cultures: an image of solace and of exhortation, looking over to admonish, looking on to comfort. Artists of all traditions, Catholics, Protestants and others, continued to reproduce Mary and her son in their making of images of both a loving and a suffering humanity.[10]

There is a long tradition particularly of setting paintings of the Madonna and Child in contemporary or local contexts, such as the Renaissance artists' use of Italian landscapes as a backdrop for religious scenes. However, the modernist era saw particularly challenging recontextualisations, including Gauguin's Polynesian *La Orana Maria (Hail Mary)* (1891), Picasso's *Mother and Child* (1902) set in the squalor of the Saint-Lazare Prison, and Galo Ocampo's controversial non-Caucasian holy family in *Brown Madonna* (1938).

There were also particular examples from within Woolf's own family. Her aunt Julia Margaret Cameron pioneered photography as an art and some of her earliest pictures, taken in the 1860s, were pastiches of the Madonna and Child, for which she used her servant Mary Hillier as her model. This choice subverted class structures for, as Woolf noted in her introduction to Roger Fry's catalogue of Cameron's work: 'Boatmen were turned into King Arthur; village girls into Queen Guenevere . . . The parlourmaid sat for her portrait and the guest had to answer the bell' (*E4* 381). The performance of the photographs in Cameron's home was subversive, as were the finished objects: as Carol Mavor has shown, Cameron challenged Victorian ideals of feminine behaviour and also rejected the image of Mary as being associated with neither sex nor death, for her photographs are often sensual and her studies often show the infant Jesus in a pose more akin to the *pietà* than a babe-in-arms.[11]

During the last months of Woolf's life, Vanessa Bell became involved in the project of designing murals for Berwick Church with Duncan Grant, for which she painted the Nativity and the Annunciation, using her daughter Angelica as a model for the Virgin Mary in the latter. Bell's sketch for the Annunciation is the cover image for this book. Bell began painting these murals in the latter part of 1941 and they were installed in November 1942, and so they were painted in the aftermath of the deaths of her son Julian and her sister. Frances Spalding suggests that Vanessa accepted the commission, 'moved perhaps less by the Holy Spirit than by her admiration for Italian art,'[12] but adds that she 'put more of herself into the paintings than into any other of her mural decorations, for she used the religious subjects as an impersonal cloak for her own feelings and experience.' Noting that the paintings were made when Vanessa was also increasingly worried about Angelica's life-choices, Spalding argues that her painting of the Annunciation confirms the personal resonances, for 'the pose of the Virgin contains a deeply felt expression of resignation, of submission to the compound of joy and pain involved in maternal experience.'[13] With her simplicity of drawing, and her use of vibrant colours associated with Bloomsbury interiors, Bell brings the human element of religious painting to the fore. Bell's art therefore presents a particular way of using the Virgin Mary to reflect human experience.

'A very ideal type of mother'

An altogether more complicated representation of the Virgin Mary within Woolf's family was Burne-Jones's *Annunciation* (1879), for which Julia Stephen was the model. This representation of Julia came to be closely bound up with the ideologies of the family. Woolf held Julia responsible for her 'tea-table training' in flattering and sympathising with men, but it was Leslie who devised a systematic approach to preserving the mystique and veneration of womanhood in spite of his agnosticism. Key to this was the role played by Auguste Comte in his apostasy: Comte not only helped Stephen reject much of the Bible, but also influenced his thinking on the role of the family, particularly the mother, in social progress. Seeking to counter the destructive potential of individualism, Comte advocated a form of community modelled on that of primitive Catholicism. Comte's Positivism preserved traditional structures by translating Christianity into the 'Religion of Humanity': Comte replaced a transcendent God with 'le Grand Être' or the soul of humanity, which he saw as intrinsically female. Comte's ideas, which attracted followers in the Victorian era into the early twentieth century,[14] therefore reinforced Victorian ideals of womanhood and served to transmute Catholic veneration of the Virgin Mary into reverence for womankind in general.

Woolf therefore grew up in an environment in which the remnants of Christian ideas were used to enforce traditional ideas of womanhood. These were compounded after her mother's death, for they formed an important part of Leslie Stephen's memorialisation of Julia in his *Mausoleum Book,* where he drew on Comtean ideals of womanhood and the figure of the Madonna to remember Julia. Recalling their first meeting in 1866 he wrote: 'I do not remember that I spoke to her. I saw and remembered her, as I might have seen and remembered the Sistine Madonna or any other presentation of superlative beauty.'[15] Here Julia is silenced (if she had said anything, it is not recalled) but on the other hand she is a beautiful object inspiring reverence. This memory is of course overlaid with the cultural representation of Julia in Burne-Jones's painting, which was significantly made while she was pregnant with their first child.[16] As a model, Julia enacts a performance both of the Virgin Mary and of herself, presenting her maternity along with that of the Madonna. Stephen's recollection of Julia, influenced both by Comtean ideals and by religious art, was closely bound up with ideas of her perfection as a mother:

> The love of a mother for her children is the most beautiful thing in the world . . . [Julia] was a perfect mother, a very ideal type of mother; and in her the maternal instincts were, as it seemed, but the refined essence of the love which showed its strength in every other relation of life.[17]

Julia here becomes less a person in her own right than an epitome of maternal perfection. It renders her more mysterious, leaving the reader with a sense of what, rather than who, she was.

Stephen addressed *The Mausoleum Book* to Woolf and her siblings, and she re-read it while memorialising her parents in writing *To the Lighthouse*. As a result, the Madonna image was particularly influential on Woolf's memories of her mother and the idealisation of Julia hinders the act of remembering her as a human being. Woolf hints that this was still a problem late in her life, as she tries to recall her mother in 'A Sketch of the Past', struggling with the impression that her physical beauty and her motherhood were inseparable:

> I think I accepted her beauty as the natural quality that a mother – she seemed typical, universal, yet our own in particular – had by virtue of being our mother. It was part of her calling. I do not think that I separated her face from that general being; or from her whole body. (*MB* 82)

And Woolf also recalls her mother, Madonna-like, with Adrian, her youngest child and her favourite: 'Him she cherished separately; she called him "My Joy"', but this image is tinged with criticism for Woolf accuses Julia of favouritism, noting that no one else received such a concentration of love and attention. Woolf also testifies to the difficulties inherent in the act of remembering, of separating her mother from the narratives that developed around her: 'can I get any closer to her without drawing upon all those descriptions and anecdotes which after she was dead imposed themselves very quickly upon my view of her?' (*MB* 83).

Kristeva's insights on the Virgin Mary are helpful in examining Stephen's idealisation of Julia and Woolf's ambivalence towards her mother and motherhood. Kristeva notes that '[w]e live in a civilization where the *consecrated* (religious or secular) representation of femininity is absorbed by motherhood', and that 'Christianity is doubtless the most refined symbolic construct in which femininity . . . is focused on maternality.'[18] Kristeva shows that feminism, in rejecting these ideals, had tended to reject motherhood itself. Woolf's work is marked by ambivalence towards motherhood: she was deeply preoccupied with it, haunted by memories of her own mother and plagued with feelings of inadequacy against Vanessa's motherhood. Kristeva offers two strategies for dealing with these issues, both of which we will see in Woolf. The first is to recognise lived experience

(Kristeva's essay is noteworthy for interweaving lyrical reflections on her own experiences of motherhood with her theoretical discourse); the second is to emphasise the appeal that virginal motherhood held for both women and men.

Siena, 1908

While Woolf's upbringing with post-Christian agnostic ideas had stirred her ambivalence towards the Madonna, she encountered a strongly contrasting view of the Virgin Mary in Catholic Europe, when she visited Italy with Vanessa and Clive Bell in 1908. She recounts seeing a celebration of the Feast of the Virgin at Siena Cathedral, during a *flânerie* where she is a tourist and spectator rather than a worshipper (*PA* 385–6). She is struck by the otherness of Catholicism, but she finds it refreshing because the rite is not a 'military performance' like Anglican services, and the worshippers are not, she says, bound by 'clerical commands'. Woolf is fascinated by the beauty of the occasion: 'There were gorgeous priests, ministering here, with their backs to us, from which yellow satins gold embroidered, hung in stiff squares. One had a white hat, like the petal of a cyclamen, on his head.'

Woolf's notes that though the congregation were not part of this 'mystic rite' and though they did not understand it, they were nonetheless moved and faithful: 'their faith seemed warm & private, not to be regulated by any common need.' She speculates that the performance 'did represent to them the sacred body of their religion'; their faith is literally *embodied* and the rite has an iconographic function by which sights and sounds take them straight to the spiritual realm:

> I supposed that all the glories of the Heavens had this tangible form for them – the more impressive because of all these mysterious weavings & symbols.
>   They smell the flowers that grew in the holy fields; imagine the Cross risen, & the body upon it; it is all yellow stained, splendid, & remote. Are these priests – or are they not rather people who were present at the scene themselves?

Though Woolf does not admit to any religious experience of her own, she imputes such an experience to others, in their ability to know 'the glories of the Heavens' in 'tangible form'. The passage becomes even more vivid as Woolf goes on to use free indirect discourse to present the visions from their perspective. As they take up the position at the foot of the cross traditionally associated with Mary the Stabat Mater, witnessing 'the Cross . . . yellow stained, splendid, & remote', Woolf vicariously shares their experience. The strong visual appeal of the whole service, then, starts to have an iconographic effect for Woolf, as sights and sounds take her into the mystery. The scene emphasises female power, as the priests are feminised in their 'gorgeous' robes, their flower-like hats, and their spiritual self-surrender to Mary.

Art and iconography in *To the Lighthouse*[19]

These contrasting examples suggest that Woolf experienced the tension between two positions identified by Kristeva: an awareness that the Virgin Mary represents patriarchal ideals of womanhood and a sense of attraction to her. This tension comes into play particularly in Woolf's representation of the Madonna in *To the Lighthouse*, the novel in which she deals with the posthumous influences of her parents and explores ideologies of the family.

Woolf repeatedly interrogates comparisons between human mothers and the Virgin Mary as she frequently compares Mrs Ramsay and James with the Madonna and Child: the novel opens with mother and son together and James imagines a kind of halo around himself when he finds that his game becomes 'endowed . . . with heavenly bliss . . . fringed with joy' when his mother speaks. Mrs Ramsay similarly regards her son as the Christ-child, imagining him 'frowning slightly at the sight of human frailty' (*TL* 7–8). The pair are seen as objects of reverence by the family and their guests: particularly Mr Ramsay, who worships his wife and son, seeing them from a distance as 'lovely and unfamiliar', symbolic of the mother–child bond but with a religious impulse: 'who will blame him if he does homage to the beauty of the world?' (*TL* 51). Mr Bankes holds Mrs Ramsay in veneration, looking at her with what Lily Briscoe describes as 'love . . . distilled and filtered; love that never attempted to clutch its object; but, like the love which mathematicians bear their symbols, or poets their phrases, was meant to be spread over the world and become part of human gain.' The love is particularly religious and at this moment, Lily feels positively about the sacredness of womanhood: 'She took shelter from the reverence which covered all women; she felt herself praised' (*TL* 66).

However, the polyphonic nature of the novel enables Woolf to set this veneration in tension with voices questioning this process, and this is partly done by drawing attention to the potential for artifice within painting. Seeing Mrs Ramsay knitting and using James to measure her stocking for the lighthouse keeper's boy, the narrative voice draws attention to the 'painterly' quality of the two, and the constructed nature of the scene by commenting on her beauty and her silence. The scene ends with Mrs Ramsay kissing James on the forehead near a Renaissance painting, 'with her head outlined absurdly by the gilt frame, the green shawl which she had tossed over the edge of the frame, and the authenticated masterpiece by Michael Angelo' (*TL* 42). The presence of the painting suggests that the content of the picture is continuous with the scene (because it is present and visible) but also discontinuous (because it is marked off by its frame). The juxtaposition suggests that the picture is connected with Mrs Ramsay but also that it has nothing to do with her. Seen next to the Michaelangelo she seems to become a worthy subject for Renaissance religious art, but the frame which divides her from this painting suggests that she has nothing in common with it. In fact, the appearance of the frame around Mrs Ramsay is 'absurd', and her shawl is carelessly 'tossed' over it. This casual image accentuates the human side of mother and son, picking up on Mrs Ramsay's reflections about the inadequacy of her life, her 'shabby' home with its dirty floors, and James's misbehaviour: 'what demon possessed him, her youngest, her cherished?' (*TL* 37–8). Woolf challenges the religious ideology here, seeking instead to uncover the value and validity of lived experience.

The debates between Lily Briscoe and William Bankes in particular help to articulate the problems in seeing Mrs Ramsay as a Madonna figure. William Bankes speaks as an admirer of Renaissance religious art, who includes among his favourites Raphael, Titian, the Sistine Chapel and Michelangelo's work in Rome, and Giotto's paintings in Padua (*TL* 72, 79). Bankes believes in the holiness of the subject of these paintings, a parallel to his reverence for Mrs Ramsay, for he sees mother and child as 'objects of universal veneration' (*TL* 72). Lily, on the other hand, uses experimental artistic techniques to challenge these traditional approaches to art that ironically serve to belittle women. She strives to recover the 'real Mrs Ramsay' from the traditional iconography of womanhood, but also feels overpowered by traditional representations of women and by the fame of great painters. As a result, she cannot reject Bankes's view entirely: she tries to see Mrs Ramsay as 'unquestionably the loveliest of people . . . the best perhaps; but also, different too from the perfect shape which one saw there' (*TL* 67). Like Woolf trying to rescue her mother from the stories that had accrued to her and from the perfection attributed to her, Lily seeks the 'spirit' the 'essential thing' of Mrs Ramsay in a discarded and distorted object: 'had you found a glove in the corner of a sofa, you would have known it, from its twisted finger, hers indisputably' (*TL* 68).

However, Lily's painting ultimately works to preserve rather than subvert the 'perfect shape'. On one level, she rejects the values of Renaissance art by painting in the Post-Impressionist style: as several critics have pointed out, her work evades direct representation and concentrates instead on rendering what Roger Fry and Clive Bell termed 'significant form'.[20] Lily represents Mrs Ramsay, James, the hedge and a wall of the house in a mass of lines, shapes and colours. Her decision to paint Mrs Ramsay and James as a 'triangular purple shape' attempts to ignore Mrs Ramsay's physical beauty and the reverence that this attracts. But on another level, Lily does not subvert the reverential qualities behind Renaissance art, for the principle of significant form was not that art should destroy its object but preserve that object's essence. Roger Fry wrote that in the 'abstract world' of painting, specific characteristics of an object are 'reduced to pure elements of space and volume . . . these elements are perfectly co-ordinated and organized by the artist's sensual intelligence, [so that] they attain logical consistency.' When expressed in the texture of a painting, these elements 'retain their abstract intelligibility, their amenity to the human mind, and regain that reality of actual things which is absent from all abstractions'.[21] If Lily is painting in the Post-Impressionist mode, therefore, her purple triangle does not reduce Mrs Ramsay and James to abstractions, but it attempts to preserve the emotions, including the reverence they inspire in others. As Tickner and others have pointed out, the purple triangle is a version of the 'wedge-shaped core of darkness' which symbolises Mrs Ramsay's inner self.[22] Rather than subverting reverence for mother and child, then, Lily preserves it in a transformed state: as she tells William Bankes, she 'reverences' mother and child in her own way, and her painting is a 'tribute' to them. She convinces him that mother and child the 'objects of universal veneration' can be 'reduced . . . to a purple shadow

without irreverence' (*TL* 72, emphasis added). Lily's painting therefore has an iconographic effect.

More specifically, Lily's purple triangle does not obliterate the
figure of the Madonna but preserves it, for Renaissance paintings
of Madonna and Child were frequently composed in a triangular
shape, to reflect the iconography of three sides and three points as
a representation of the Trinity. This shape is seen in *Madonna and
Child* paintings by both of Mr Bankes's favourites: Raphael and
Titian.[23] Mr Bankes implies that modern artists will always work
in their shadow (as well as, perhaps inadvertently, that of one of
the most famous detractors of religion): 'We can't all be Titians
and we can't all be Darwins, he said; at the same time he doubted
whether you could have your Darwin and your Titian if it weren't
for humble people like ourselves' (*TL* 98). Lily specifically defends
herself against an unfavourable comparison with Raphael: 'She did
not intend to disparage a subject which, they agreed, Raphael had
treated divinely' (*TL* 238). While Lily does not claim to be treating the subject 'divinely' herself, she nonetheless agrees that the subject of mother and child needs to be treated with respect. While the
purple triangle remains enigmatic within the novel, one of its many
possibly functions is to evoke the iconography of mother and child
from Renaissance painting.

Woolf also uses these debates about art to investigate the ideologies
with which she had grown up, for Victorian photographers had drawn
on Renaissance conventions in their portraits of mothers and children
in an attempt to gain artistic credibility for their medium, and a triangular composition was often found in Victorian representations of
motherhood. There are examples of this in the photograph album that
Leslie Stephen compiled while writing *The Mausoleum Book*, such as
the one of Julia with Vanessa as a toddler, who is leaning against her
mother so that their heads form a point, with Julia's skirts shaping the
base of the triangle.[24] In describing Lily's abstract representation of
Mrs Ramsay and James as a dark triangle, then, Woolf alludes to the
composition of these photographs in a way that emphasises their links
with Renaissance paintings of Madonna and Child.

Such representations of motherhood in Victorian culture threatened to render the mother inaccessible and distant and a Protestant
symbol of unattainable perfection. Lily voices the difficulties this creates. She is urged by Mrs Ramsay to get married, presumably in
order to become a mother herself but this makes her feel inadequate,
'so little, so virginal, against the other' (*TL* 69).

Woolf addresses the problems generated by the reverence for motherhood by seeking to subvert or damage the Madonna's traditional perfect image. In the first part of the novel, Woolf inverts the idea of the virgin mother, as Cameron had done in her photographs, by ascribing powerful reproductive sexuality to Mrs Ramsay. Woolf's description of the relationship between Mr and Mrs Ramsay uses classic Freudian sexual imagery: she writes that Mrs Ramsay 'seemed to raise herself with an effort, and at once to pour erect into the air a rain of energy, a column of spray, looking at the same time animated and alive' (*TL* 52). As a result, Woolf supplants the doctrine of immaculate conception and perfect motherhood with images of fecund human, heterosexual reproduction.

Rather than embodying 'neither sex nor death', Mrs Ramsay is presented as the initiator of both. When Mrs Ramsay discovers that Minta Doyle and Paul Rayley have got engaged, as she had hoped, she reflects that 'the love of man for woman' bears 'in its bosom the seeds of death' (*TL* 135). Looking on, Lily feels as though Mrs Ramsay is making a human sacrifice, as though she 'led her victims . . . to the altar', playing on the ambiguity of the word 'altar' as a site of both marriage and sacrifice. (The story of Prue bears this out in 'Time Passes', when she dies in an illness connected with childbirth.) Lily's reaction draws attention to the greatest subversion of artistic convention in the novel. Traditionally, a male artist (presumably with sexual experience) would create an image of a pure and innocent mother; but here, a female artist, who admits herself to be 'little' and 'virginal' paints a woman who has eight children and threatens to initiate others into sexual experience and death.

The problem of death is a particular concern in the third part of the novel where the question of how to represent women in art (how to extract Mrs Ramsay or Julia Stephen from the iconography which surrounds them) becomes closely connected to the novel's elegiac concern of commemorating the dead. When Lily returns to her painting after Mrs Ramsay's death, she has to face the problem that her main subject is missing: the space where Mrs Ramsay had once sat with James is now empty. As Lily settles down to paint, she finds an antidote to the blank space when her mind throws up pictures which are quite different from the network of lines, shapes and colours which constitute her painting. One of these is an image of Mrs Ramsay as William Bankes might have seen her:

She looked now at the drawing-room step. She saw, through William's eyes, the shape of a woman, peaceful and silent, with downcast eyes. She sat musing, pondering (she was in grey that day, Lily thought). Her eyes were bent. She would never lift them. Yes, thought Lily, looking intently, I must have seen her look like that, but not in grey; nor so still, nor so young, nor so peaceful. (*TL* 239)

Although Lily is trying to remember Mrs Ramsay, the complex perspective taken in this passage suggests that she is comparing her memories with those of someone else: she sees Mrs Ramsay 'through William's eyes' or indeed in a photograph. Although Lily sees Mrs Ramsay in grey, she does not associate that colour with her, and this suggests the disparity between a black-and-white photograph and the colours of memory.

This image too, comes from Leslie Stephen's photograph album, for the picture of Mrs Ramsay 'with downcast eyes' resembles one in which Julia Stephen gazes downwards into a clump of flowers.[25] The eerie stillness of the vision is photographic, for a photograph freezes a person in one pose: as Lily says, Mrs Ramsay would never lift her eyes again. There is a close connection between photography and death. As Christian Metz has argued: 'Even when the person photographed is still living, the moment when she or he was has forever vanished. Strictly speaking, *the person who has been photographed* – not the total person, who is an effect of time – is dead.'[26] The particular Julia Stephen who was captured in this photograph will never raise her eyes because they have been frozen in the pose for as long as the photograph lasts. We know too (as Lily knew of Mrs Ramsay), that the person of Julia, who is now dead, will never raise her eyes either.

In her description of Lily's memories, Woolf suggests that though death is loss and a photograph is a signifier for something which is lost, the absence of a person can also be liberating: we can do what we like with a person's photograph, we can say what we like of the dead. Lily experiences a sense of this liberation from Mrs Ramsay: 'Oh the dead! she murmured, one pitied them, one brushed them aside . . . Mrs Ramsay has faded and gone, she thought. We can over-ride her wishes, improve away her limited, old-fashioned ideas' (*TL* 235–6). The greatest freedom Lily enjoys is the freedom not to marry, but to enjoy a long and platonic friendship with William Bankes.

Woolf articulates a number of reversals as Lily completes her painting. Lily is enabled to see Mrs Ramsay through Mr Bankes's eyes, as

Woolf views her mother in photographs in Leslie Stephen's album. Furthermore, Lily's black-and-white vision overturns the threatening, sexualised picture of motherhood presented earlier in the novel, by re-asserting the importance of chastity and purity associated with the Virgin Mary; and here, Woolf acknowledges what Kristeva later identified as the appeal that virginal motherhood held for both women and men. We can see this when we compare the photograph with *Convent Thoughts* by the Pre-Raphaelite painter Charles Collins. The women in both pictures gaze downwards as though contemplating the flowers. Julia's dress, though it has a slightly elaborate collar, is dark and has an apron, matching the nun's grey habit and scapular. Julia's hair is tied back in a severe French knot, while the novice's hair is covered by her veil; the close confinement of hair in these portraits suggests a particular curb on sensuality. In the photograph Julia is surrounded by white flowers (in 'Sketch', Woolf identified these as 'passion flowers', symbols closely associated with the Virgin Mary (*MB* 66)); Collins' novice contemplates a white passion flower surrounded by white lilies and waterlilies: flowers that represent purity, especially that of the Madonna. The lilies within the painting are matched by more flowers carved into the frame and the caption 'Siaam Liliam' ('as the lily'). As we saw in the previous chapter, Woolf found the idea of female monasticism to be liberating; in this scene in *To the Lighthouse*, she reconciles the image of the nun with that of a mother.

In Lily's photographic memory of Mrs Ramsay, the threatening images of motherhood and sexuality have been displaced. This is an important process for Lily, because the nun provides her with an image of a woman that does not define her by her sexual relations with men or by her ability to bear children. It provides Lily with an alternative to the negative images of herself as 'so virginal' and now, in her forties as 'a peevish, ill-tempered dried-up old maid.' Lily thus reclaims the figure of the Madonna as a virgin mother to make her an icon for women who renounce marriage and motherhood.

Lily's thought processes on completing her painting vacillate between contradictory forces. The first vacillation is between ordinary experience and iconographic experience of the divine, those two contrasting aspects of cultural representations of the Virgin Mary: 'One wanted, she thought, dipping her brush deliberately, to be on a level with ordinary experience, to feel simply that's a chair, that's a table, and yet at the same time, It's a miracle, it's an ecstasy' (*TL* 272).

Lily also goes through a complex vacillation between attempting to recover Mrs Ramsay from the traditional iconography of womanhood and motherhood which had enclosed her, and committing her to the past by endorsing those images. Lily also veers between attempting to overcome death through reviving her memories of Mrs Ramsay and enjoying the freedom which Mrs Ramsay's death has produced. These conflicting emotions are evident in Lily's final vision before completing her painting. As she sits looking at the empty steps of the cottage, someone comes into the room inside. Her or his presence changes her view of the scene, for it casts an 'odd-shaped triangular shadow' on the step, piquing Lily's interest. The shadow re-creates the purple triangle which Lily had painted ten years earlier to represent Mrs Ramsay and James. Lily is seized by the 'old horror' of desperation to know Mrs Ramsay, but this gives way to an imaginary vision of her, as she 'sat there quite simply, in the chair, flicked her needles to and fro, knitted her reddish-brown stocking, cast her shadow on the step' (*TL* 272). The vision (which evokes another of the photographs from Leslie Stephen's album)[27] encapsulates many of the contradictions which Lily entertains in her final vision, for she comes close to discovering the ordinary woman behind the ideal image, but she does not lose the aura of adoration which surrounds her. Mrs Ramsay's reappearance is 'part of her perfect goodness to Lily', while the shadow on the step is a version of the holy triangle, the perfect shape of Madonna and Child.

In her visual and verbal allusions to the figure of the Madonna, therefore, Virginia Woolf may be seen to rationalise the ideals of womanhood that the figure had traditionally embodied, including those propounded by the Victorians and by Leslie Stephen in particular. The imperatives associated with that idealised image are clearly aligned with an age that has passed: Mrs Ramsay, like Julia Stephen, is dead and gone, and her views and example can be disregarded by members of the next generation, such as Lily (and by implication, by Woolf herself). The Madonna's virginal status gives Lily permission to live happily as an unmarried woman; this icon of the ideal family becomes reappropriated as a sympathetic symbol for her as a spinster. And yet, now that these problematic associations have been set at a distance, Woolf can allow space for the beauty and holiness of the Madonna figure to be a positive representation of womanhood: as a representative of humanity, the Madonna shows the sanctity of the human condition, showing that womanhood can indeed be sacred.

Art and abstraction in *The Waves*

Woolf returns to the figure of the Virgin Mary in a short but significant passage in *The Waves*, when Bernard visits the Italian Room at the National Gallery as he struggles to take in the news of Percival's death (W 120–5) and the Madonna is brought to bear very starkly on the anguish of death and bereavement. Bernard's situation encompasses both sex and death, for he has recently become a father and his feelings about the two events are indistinguishable: 'which is sorrow, which is joy?', and he needs time to reflect on the centrality of death to the human condition by considering 'what death has done to my world.' Woolf questions the validity of Christian consolation by having Bernard stray into a gallery of religious paintings at a time when he feels anger and defiance towards a figure in the sky, a stereotypical image of the Christian God. This figure is 'abstract, facing me eyeless at the end of the avenue, in the sky . . . that blank and brutal face', echoing Woolf's representation of God as a vindictive, 'spiteful' being who 'likes . . . to take away, to destroy' (D1 166; L4 372). Bernard blames the figure for 'inflict[ing] meaningless death' at 25 on someone who should have lived to be 80, and turns away defiantly saying, 'you have done your utmost.' Bernard struggles to find elegiac consolation: he first insists (like Clarissa Dalloway) that 'you exist somewhere. Something of you remains', and imagines himself having a private dialogue with Percival, but he immediately qualifies this by asking 'for how long?', voicing an awareness that the world will quickly move on without Percival in it.

Bernard does not go to the gallery to seek out particular paintings, but simply to step out of a hectic world and the rapid passage of time in order to enter a timeless space where artists of all eras are exhibited together. In keeping with his emotional state, Bernard only sees snatches of the paintings: Woolf does not identify any particular pictures but simply notes fragmentary details of the religious art of the Italian Renaissance.[28] There are 'saints and blue madonnas', reflecting the traditional depiction of Mary wearing blue as a colour of purity. There are pillars, features of classical architecture, often depicted in ruins to symbolise the fall of Paganism. There are the 'pricked ears' of the olive branches, a feature of the Italian landscape used to represent peace (as, for example, in Andrea Previtali's *The Virgin and Child with a Shoot of Olive*). The 'ruffled crimson against the green lining' picks up on the attention that Renaissance artists often paid to texture (as in Dosso Dossi's *The Adoration of the Kings*, in which the Virgin is in a ruffled red dress, with green lining to her blue cloak). The 'orange light behind the black' reflects a tendency towards dramatic backdrops (as in Titian's *The Holy Family with a Shepherd*, with its orange sky behind black cliffs). However, the most important thing about these details is their emotional impact for Bernard: 'ruffled' is disturbing, 'pricked' is harsh, and the strong colours of orange and black suggest violence. 'Blue madonna' does not only describe Mary's clothing: it gives her a deathly hue to match Bernard's frame of mind.

Significantly, Woolf brings together fragments from both the Nativity and the Crucifixion: this is fitting, because Mary as both the nursing mother of the Nativity and the grieving mother of the crucifixion encapsulates the conflict of emotions that Bernard is experiencing. This juxtaposition becomes even clearer in Bernard's reprise of this scene in his summing up: 'Madonnas and pillars, arches and orange trees, still as on the first day of creation, but acquainted with grief, there they hung, and I gazed at them' (W 211–12). Timescales are blurred into one: the Nativity, with its arches, orange trees and Madonna, is elided with Eden and the first day of creation; both creation and Nativity are imbued with sorrow, from the allusion to Isaiah's prophetic foreshadowing of Christ as 'a man of sorrows, and acquainted with grief' (53:3); the hanging of the pictures is elided with Christ's hanging on the cross; and the watchful 'gaze' of Mary as Stabat Mater is folded in with Bernard's contemplation of the images.

The emphasis Woolf places on art conveying emotion, particularly through the use of shape and colour, suggests that she is rendering Renaissance art in Post-Impressionist terms, as she did with Lily Briscoe's purple triangle: the paintings are reduced to abstract 'lines and colours' and 'fragments'. Indeed, Bernard's description of the 'blue madonna' recalls Picasso's Blue Period *Mother and Child*. However, just as Lily's purple triangle served to accentuate rather than destroy the reverence accorded to mother and child, so Woolf's creative vandalism of Renaissance art points to the power of art to speak to the emotions. Bernard turns to other people's pictures in order to allay the traumatic visions of Percival's accident from his own imagination ('the incessant activity of the mind's eye, the bandaged head, the men with ropes'). But more than this, he wants to go beyond words, using visual stimuli as an antidote to his ability to 'make phrases so easily'. He seeks what Woolf had noted in her essay 'Pictures', which was the power of visual art to expose the inadequacy of language: 'As we gaze, words begin to raise their feeble limbs in the pale border-land of no man's language, to sink down again in despair' (*E4* 245).

Paradoxically, however, Bernard wants to 'find something unvisual beneath.' This partly refers to his desire to go beyond representation and visual cues to the visceral, physical process of painting, for Bernard thinks that '[p]ainters live lives of methodical abstraction, adding stroke to stroke'. As Maggie Humm has noted, Woolf had 'deep knowledge of the painting processes, particularly the use of color.'[29] However, the scene also affirms the iconographic power of art to access the sacred. This is seen in Bernard's final thoughts before rousing himself to leave the gallery, where he glimpses something fleeting that he cannot fully grasp: 'Something lies deeply buried. For one moment I thought to grasp it. . . . After a long lifetime, loosely, in a moment of revelation, I may lay hands on it, but now the idea breaks in my hand.'

It is enlightening to compare these reflections with Woolf's ideas about religious art that she had sketched many years earlier, on seeing the Perugino's frescoes in Perugia in 1908 (*PA* 392–3). Those frescoes depict group tableaux from the life of Christ, one of which is a Nativity, and Woolf was struck by the Perugino's composition of the scenes:

> I conceive that he saw things grouped, contained in certain & invisible forms . . . all beauty was contained in the momentary appearance of human beings. He saw it sealed as it were; all its worth in it, not a hint at past or future.

The paintings reach beyond the human to the spiritual or 'invisible', from physical beauty to a representation of beauty as an abstract quality; and from time to timelessness. Woolf therefore shows Bernard, in the timeless space of the gallery, experiencing painting as an 'infinitely silent' art that reaches beyond speech. Bernard adds that the only things that survive are 'Line and colours'; this echoes Woolf's observation on the power of the relationship between 'lines & colours' to bring the group together in the Perugino's frescoes.

Woolf recognised in 1908 that this had parallels with her own art: '[I] achieve a symmetry by means of infinite discords . . . some kind of whole made of shivering fragments.' In this scene in the gallery,

Woolf similarly holds the broken and fragmentary in tension with a desire for wholeness: it therefore forms a stepping-stone towards her theory of her own writing in 'A Sketch of the Past', where a 'moment of being' goes beyond the visible to 'a revelation of some order; it is a token of some real thing behind appearances'. Writing becomes a way of overcoming painful experiences, giving her instead 'a great delight to put the severed parts together' (*MB* 72). With the 'moments of being', she makes explicit what is also evident in the gallery scene: that elegiac consolation can only be achieved through acknowledging the pain of severance.

These three interrelated passages are also concerned with the relationship between God and humanity. Woolf remarks on how the human figures in the frescoes are related to one another rather than to God: the structure of many of the paintings shows this clearly, as the human figures are at the foot of the fresco, clearly divided from divine figures in the top part. The beauty is in human beings, not in a distant god-figure. Bernard defies the stereotypical figure of a God in the sky. By contrast, in the 'moments of being', Woolf locates the 'thing itself' in humankind for 'there is no God'. Woolf moves towards this perception of the divine in humankind in the gallery scene, for she uses the Madonna to affirm the importance of humanity and the presence of the divine within it. Amid Bernard's painful and confused glimpses of the paintings, he suddenly sees the Madonna as a suffering human being: 'Behold, then, the blue Madonna streaked with tears.' It is the counterpart to Lily's vision of Mrs Ramsay 'quite simply' sitting and knitting on the step. The human sympathies of the Mater Dolorosa give expression to Bernard's emotion. Bernard adds that '[t]his is my funeral service': the Madonna's appearance acts as an alternative to the word-laden rites of the church by providing an expression for Bernard's emotion. The Madonna does not explain away death and suffering; she simply shares human grief. As Kristeva notes, Mary has the power to reach beyond language, for milk and tears, the signs of the Mater Dolorosa, are 'metaphors of non-speech, of a semiotics that linguistic communication does not account for. . . . The Mother and her attributes, evoking sorrowful humanity, thus become representatives of a "return of the repressed" in Monotheism. They re-establish what is non-verbal.'[30] In this image, Woolf presents a purer image of the Madonna, detached from patriarchal explanations, emphasising her visceral association with raw emotions along with her humanity as she weeps for Bernard.

Conclusion

Woolf's engagement with the figure of the Madonna is as complex and varied as the Christian tradition had made her. Woolf was fully aware of ways in which the Madonna had been appropriated by patriarchy didactically as an image of an impossible perfection (enforcing ideologies of purity in particular), but equally she was aware of how Mary could be used to affirm a celibacy that involved freedom from men and patriarchal appropriations of the female body and female sexuality. Woolf was also aware of the iconographic potential of an image of woman who had such ready access to the sacred and equally she was drawn to a figure of a woman who gave such solemnity to an array of complex human emotions. Woolf's meditations on religious art, in which the Virgin Mary has an important place, were also closely implicated in her reflections on her own method as a writer and her desire to convey reality, both sacred and ordinary.

Notes

1. Rubin, *Mother of God,* p. 400.
2. Ibid., p. 413.
3. Warner, *Alone of All Her Sex,* p. xxiii.
4. Ibid.
5. Kristeva, 'Stabat Mater', p. 180.
6. Quoted Ibid., p. 165.
7. Ibid., p. 170.
8. Ibid., p. 164.
9. Ibid., p. 171.
10. Rubin, *Mother of God,* p. 413.
11. Mavor, *Pleasures Taken,* pp. 48, 47.
12. Spalding, *Vanessa Bell,* p. 318.
13. Ibid., pp. 320, 321.
14. Pickering, *Auguste Comte,* pp. 571–2.
15. Stephen, *Mausoleum Book,* p. 31.
16. Julia Stephen, *Julia Duckworth Stephen,* p. xv.
17. Stephen, *Mausoleum Book,* p. 83.
18. Kristeva, 'Stabat Mater,' p. 161.
19. The following section is partly based on my article, de Gay, 'Behind the Purple Triangle'.
20. See for example, Flint, 'Drawing the Line'; Tickner, 'Vanessa Bell', p. 79.
21. Fry, *Cézanne,* pp. 58–9.

22. Tickner, 'Vanessa Bell', p. 79.
23. See, for example, Raphael's *Mackintosh Madonna* in the National Gallery.
24. Smith College, image 36j, online.
25. Ibid., image 38b.
26. Metz, 'Photography and Fetish', p. 84, emphasis in original.
27. Smith College, image 37d.
28. Knight suggests that Bernard is contemplating one (unidentified) Titian painting of the Stabat Mater, but the scene conjures up a disjointed range of pictures. Knight also suggests that 'the passage seems to find inspiration in Eliot' (*Omissions*, p. 95) but, as we have seen, Woolf's interest in the Virgin Mary was longstanding and personal.
29. Humm, 'Woolf and the Visual', p. 298.
30. Kristeva, 'Stabat Mater', pp. 173–4.

Chapter 7

How Should One Read the Bible?

The Library of Leonard and Virginia Woolf at Washington State University, Pullman, contains seventeen volumes which are either bibles or books of the Bible, making it the book with the most duplicate copies in the entire collection. This statistic, in itself, would suggest that the Woolfs had a significant knowledge of and interest in this Christian text, but we need to temper this observation with Virginia Woolf's advice in both *Jacob's Room* and *Between the Acts* that we must be cautious about judging a person by their library: books can be owned 'in deference . . . to someone else's standard', they may have been prizes (*JR* 49), and they may be impulse purchases, so that if they are 'mirrors of the soul', they are as likely to reflect 'the soul bored' as 'the soul sublime' (*BA* 12).

One's library therefore tells a variegated story that is both communal and personal and, as Diane Gillespie shows in her introduction to the Pullman collection, the Woolfs' books came from a variety of sources. Besides books that the Woolfs bought for themselves, there are: books Virginia inherited from Leslie and Julia Stephen and her wider family; Leonard's books accumulated at St Paul's School, at Cambridge and in Ceylon; and gifts and presentation copies, including review copies or books donated by authors in the hope of attracting the interest of the Woolfs as influential literary figures. The Bible features among nearly all of these categories, and so its significance for them, both personal and cultural, was multifaceted.

In recognising that the Woolfs' library was part of a communal narrative, we need to acknowledge that the composition of the collection also reflects competing perceptions of the Bible. The nineteenth and early twentieth centuries saw a shift away from perceiving the Bible as divinely inspired scripture towards seeing it as a text that was susceptible to textual scholarship and literary criticism.[1]

As Benjamin Jowett argued in 1860, 'the Bible ought to be read like any other book – in other words, our aim ought to be to recover the authors' original meaning within their own context.'[2] Jowett's point is that the Bible was a set of works by men and not the Word of God. Leslie Stephen had rejected the notion of scriptural authority and Virginia Woolf had inherited his own agnostic writings as well as sceptical works that had influenced him.

The concept of the Bible as a source of historical truth had been steadily eroded within academic circles, starting with the Higher Critics of the Tübingen School, who tested biblical accounts against archaeological evidence. David Strauss's *Life of Jesus Critically Examined*, introduced to English readers by George Eliot's translation of 1864, presented the Bible as polemic rather than documentary, arguing particularly that the concept of Christ was constructed from over-interpretations of the life of the historical Jesus. Feuerbach contributed to the idea of the Bible as a human construct with God being an expression of the divine within humankind. Feminist scholarship built on this observation at the end of the century with Elizabeth Cady Stanton's *The Women's Bible,* which argued that men had engineered scripture to ensure the subjection of women.

Another view, which follows on from seeing the Bible as any other text, is to see it as literature, a work in the Western canon, with all the ideological implications that carried, but also as a work of literary beauty, meaning and insight. Efforts were made in the early twentieth century to improve religious literacy in education, and these were supported by anthologies such as W. L. Courtney's *Literary Man's Bible* and R. G. Moulton's *Modern Reader's Bible* (both 1907), and E. S. Bates's *The Bible: Designed to be Read as Literature* (1937).

However, as we have seen, the story of changing religious beliefs in this period did not follow the simple trajectory of scepticism replacing faith, and there were still powerful voices arguing for the sanctity of scripture. These sometimes became more vocal in the face of challenges: for example the Cambridge Intercollegiate Christian Union was formed in 1910 as a breakaway group from the Christian Union in protest against the latter's endorsement of new approaches to the Bible. Virginia Woolf was aware of historical expressions of literalist ideology from her tomes such as Henry Venn's *The Complete Duty of Man* and Sir James Stephen's *Essays in Ecclesiastical Biography*, but these views were perpetuated in her own generation by her cousins. She also had the gentler examples of Caroline Emelia Stephen and Violet Dickinson, as well as the influence of Ethel Smyth later in life. Woolf therefore lived in a context in which scepticism performed a fugue with liberal humanism, devotion and literalism. In various ways, all these movements had an impact on the composition of the library and on Virginia Woolf's reading of the Bible.

A tour of the library

Two volumes owned by Virginia (both in the Authorized Version) bear the date of her birthday. The first volume, an edition from 1683, is labelled with her distinctive AVS bookplate along with the date of her nineteenth birthday, '25th Jan 1901'.[3] There is no dedication in this volume and, due to the uncharacteristically long gap in Woolf's letters and her diaries for this time, we do not know for certain whether it was a gift. However, the date suggests that the book may have been a gift or purchased with birthday money, and may have been treasured for that reason. The year 1901 also places her acquisition of the volume within the period when she was in close contact with both Caroline Emelia Stephen and Violet Dickinson, making it less surprising that an agnostic's daughter would acquire a copy of the Bible. Additionally, Woolf would have appreciated the book for aesthetic and antiquarian reasons: it had passed through many hands, as the signatures on the flyleaf show, and by adding her bookplate Woolf was placing herself within the book's history.

The second bible was definitely a present, signed by Violet Dickinson on Woolf's twenty-fifth birthday,[4] one of many religious books that Violet gave her during their period of close friendship. The Bible formed part of Woolf's religious dialogue with Violet at this time: for example, when she alludes to the Book of Ruth, a story of female friendship, in a letter to Violet, adding 'I wish I knew my Holy Bible better' (*L1 96*). The volume was also a token of friendship and Woolf would have kept it as a reminder of Violet's affection. This gift, entwining friendship and religious influence, can be read in the light of Patrick Buckridge's analysis of the exchange of books:

> [M]odern gift-exchange within families is capable of nourishing affective bonds between individuals, premised on the mutual affirmation of valued roles, relationships and aspirations, and of entering into the same cycle of giving, receiving and reciprocation as that described by cultural anthropologists.[5]

The gifts from Violet certainly nourished the bonds between the two women, but they also carried Violet's hope that Woolf would share her feelings.

Leonard Woolf also brought a presentation copy to the collection: a copy of the Authorized Version inscribed by his mother Marie Woolf in 1901. Unlike the present from Violet to Virginia, this gift was not loaded with religious significance but it does suggest that they saw the Bible as an important cultural text, regardless of their Jewish background.[6] Indeed, given that Leonard had been educated at a church school and was starting at Cambridge University, the gift speaks of the normative value of the Christian culture in which Leonard was being educated. The final presentation copy (the Authorized Version from 1909), is from Leonard and inscribed 'To my dear wife Virginia Woolf'.[7] This could be read in similar terms to Marie Woolf's gift, a recognition that the Bible was common cultural currency for both Leonard and Virginia, despite their religious positions; but it also indicates that the Bible was a book that interested them both.

The collection also includes two presentation copies of books of the Bible that can be related to the gift economy of Bloomsbury. The first is an inscribed copy of the Book of Job given by Lytton Strachey to Leonard in 1901. As Stephen J. Vicchio has argued, this book came to have wide appeal in the twentieth century, because the figure of a man fighting against his lot struck a chord in the modern world. He notes that in the twentieth century the 'iconoclastic side of Job is frequently highlighted at the expense of the patient Job. Job is frequently seen as an existential hero, in the tradition of Prometheus, who defiantly holds fast to his own integrity.'[8] Strachey's dedication therefore fittingly contains a lengthy quotation from Shelley's *Prometheus Unbound*, and the gift speaks of shared values, not of faith but of worldview. Woolf read Job as a young woman (*CE2* 35) at an age when she was struggling to come to terms with multiple bereavements, and it remained an important touchstone for her resentment of a God she saw as cruel. As she wrote to Nelly Cecil in 1922: 'I read the book of Job last night – I dont think God comes well out of it' (*L2* 585).

The final example in this group reflects the aspirations of the donor: Stella Benson sent Virginia a signed copy of her 1931 novel, *Tobit Transplanted*, a retelling of the Book of Tobit set in Russia, which included the text of the Apocryphal book.[9] The book had also been recommended by both Ethel Smyth and Nelly Cecil, and

Woolf initially resisted reading it. This was partly because she suspected that Benson's motive was conversion and partly because she had disliked Benson's earlier collection of short stories: she told Ethel that 'I will try to read Tobit one of these days, but the repulsion of the earlier book, whatever it was, still poisons my mind' (*L4* 333).

The next volume had complex associations: Constantine Tischendorf's edition of the New Testament, which had belonged to Julia Stephen's first husband Herbert Duckworth.[10] This is the only inherited text that has made its way into the Pullman collection, which is surprising given the family's long religious history. 'A Sketch of the Past' provides a clue as to why Virginia Woolf may have hung on to this volume specifically. Recalling her mother, Woolf writes:

> Once when she had set us to writing exercises I looked up from mine and watched her reading – the Bible perhaps; and, struck by the gravity of her face, told myself that her first husband had been a clergyman and that she was thinking, as she read what he had read, of him. (*MB* 82)

If this is the volume associated with this memory, then it has complex associations: it enabled Woolf to read and touch a book that her mother had read, reconnecting with her mother, as, in turn, she had imagined her mother connecting with her late husband by reading and touching a volume that he had read. Here, the Bible is of significance not only as a book but as a 'thing'. Since, as Bruno Latour has argued, 'things do not exist without being full of people',[11] this volume is full of Herbert Duckworth and Julia Stephen.

This edition may also have appealed to both Leonard and Virginia for its textual scholarship, for it contains details of variant readings from three ancient sources: the Vatican Codex, Alexandrine Codex and Sinaitic Codex. Two other volumes in the library in particular give evidence of this interest: an edition of the Apocrypha from 1833, inscribed by Leonard in 1900, which starts with a list of variant readings between 1611 and 1613,[12] and an edition of the Apocrypha, published by OUP in 1927, with extensive editorial notes. The Woolfs had a copy of the World's Classics edition of the same text, published the previous year without notes, suggesting that the volume was bought for its annotations.[13]

It is true that Leonard was more interested in biblical scholarship than Virginia, and three of the volumes in the collection were his own rather than shared. The first was a Tamil translation which dated from his time in Ceylon: an indication of his colonial role there and of the significance of the Bible as a cultural text. The second was a Hebrew edition of the Old Testament from 1940. The third was the New English Bible New Testament of 1961, the only volume in the collection of biblical texts that was published after Virginia's death, an example of cutting-edge scholarship at the time that drew on recent discoveries of the Dead Sea Scrolls and translated the Bible into modern English.[14] That is not to say that Virginia Woolf was not interested in biblical scholarship or in competing interpretations of the Bible, for she used Renan's *Life of St Paul* in *Three Guineas* to show the human side of a religious figure and reduced his prescriptions to his personal psychology (*3G* 236).

Three further volumes in the collection give evidence that the Bible appealed to both Woolfs for their shared interest in languages and translation. Virginia owned an 1888 edition of the Greek New Testament, in which a short passage (Acts, Chapters 3–9) is heavily annotated with translation notes. While it is unclear whether these notes were hers, the fact that she owned the volume suggests that her interests in Greek were not limited to the classical works she studied with Janet Case and at London University.[15] It is certain that both Virginia and Leonard annotated their 1861 Scholz edition of The Greek New Testament, showing their shared interest in translation scholarship, and Virginia's notes show that she was at this stage an accomplished reader of the Greek.[16] The Woolfs also owned a Latin edition of the Bible, though there is no indication that either of them studied this.[17]

Virginia Woolf also used bibles for bookbinding practice: she bought a five-volume set of biblical books from World's Classics for this purpose, one volume containing the Four Gospels and Acts (1929) and a four-volume set comprising the Old Testament (1931).[18] Woolf's skills here are rather rudimentary, and perhaps her intentions were slightly iconoclastic, not unlike her purchase of a book of prayers by Isaac Watts to make a notebook by cutting out the pages and using the cover as a binding for her own journal (*PA* 160).

This survey shows the range of reasons why the Woolfs owned bibles: while they did not see its devotional significance for themselves, they owned bibles given to them by people who did; they owned bibles for reasons of language and scholarship, often to pursue sceptical arguments; and they owned bibles as artefacts and as emotionally loaded 'things'. But they also owned copies of the Bible because it was a book: one of many in the Western Canon and one among many items in their collection, and so a further reason for their interest was its literary value. Indeed, Woolf described the *King James Bible* as 'a translation of singular beauty' (*3G* 196). The Bible was a text with great cultural and literary resonance: no one who read Milton or Dante, for example, with the attention that she gave them, could do so without knowing their biblical sources.

The rest of this chapter will explore how these varied and complex reasons for owning bibles had an impact on Virginia Woolf's equally varied and complex use of biblical themes and ideas within her work. The chapter will focus on four approaches found in her work: her sceptical, selective use of biblical texts for purposes of political argument; her rhetorical use of biblical ideas and Evangelical ideas about the Bible to explore and defend the value of literature; her use of biblical ideas to define her conception of life; and finally, her use of extended allusions to the Passion narrative to test the doctrine of salvation.

A discerning reader

The Bible is a compendium of different texts and Woolf's reactions to them varied. This can be seen in her description of the chapel service in *The Voyage Out*, where she presents Psalms 56 and 58 as harsh and violent (*VO* 263). She quotes verses where the psalmist speaks of being oppressed by his enemies ('man goeth about to devour me'; 'all that they imagine is to do me evil' (Ps. 56:1, 5)) and where he calls for vengeance ('break their teeth, O God, in their mouths' (Ps. 58:6)), but misses out the more positive lines such as the conclusion to Psalm 56: 'For thou hast delivered my soul from death, wilt not thou deliver my feet from falling, that I may walk before God in the light of the living.' Woolf criticises this Old Testament scripture and dismisses it as an irrelevant product of a bygone age when she notes that the congregation are shocked by 'the sudden intrusion of this old savage . . . the ravings of the old black man with a cloth around his loins cursing with vehement gesture by a camp-fire in the desert.'

By contrast, she presents the gospel reading in this scene positively, for it makes the congregation think of the 'sad and beautiful figure of Christ' (ibid.). Woolf's language conveys a sense of living presence and continuing relevance: 'While Christ spoke they made another effort to fit his interpretation of life upon the lives they lived.' Woolf's phrasing here implies that Christ is speaking to the congregation in the present moment. Here Woolf reads the Bible in the lively and imaginative way she approached many literary texts: the congregation hear the words of Christ just as she enjoyed 'listening' to the voices of authors, such as Coleridge or Sir Thomas Browne. However, it is notable that Woolf always used the reverential word Christ ('the anointed one') rather than Jesus, the name of the historical figure, and that she sees his words as a guide for living, suggesting that she was not entirely persuaded by the arguments of the Higher Critics on this point.

Woolf does not disparage the teachings of Christ and indeed in *Three Guineas* she criticises the church for undermining them: as Froula notes, Woolf does not throw out the baby of the gospels with the bathwater of the church.[19] In this, Woolf also echoes Caroline Emelia Stephen's call to '*listen* to the Christianity of Christ himself', having 'disentangled' it from the Christianity of the churches.[20] Woolf goes even further to claim Christ for pacifism and feminism. The argument starts obliquely when she quotes Wilfred Owen's statement that 'one of Christ's essential commands was: Passivity at any price . . . pure Christianity will not fit in with pure patriotism' (*3G* 93), and later when she quotes an American feminist-pacifist organisation who argued that Christ 'taught that war is unchristian' (*3G* 126).[21] The theme comes to the fore when Woolf claims Christ for feminism, arguing that men's stranglehold upon the professions is anti-Christian for being rooted in economic jealousy: 'A great authority upon human life, you will remember, held over two thousand years ago that great possessions were undesirable' (*3G* 151). She goes on to stage a debate in which she positions her opponents, and not herself, as opponents of Christianity: it is they who want to read Christ's teachings as relevant only to the past, for she imagines them replying 'with some heat' that 'Christ's words about the rich and the Kingdom of Heaven are no longer helpful to those who have to face different facts in a different world' (*3G* 151). Woolf's allusion to Matthew 19:24 here ('It is easier for a camel to go through the eye of a needle, than for a rich man to enter into the kingdom of God'), makes it clear that she knows this text and expects her opponents to know it too. She chides them for downgrading it to a text of historical interest only, for she invokes it as a precept that has continuing relevance, citing Pierpont Morgan as a contemporary example of someone whose excessive wealth makes him tyrannical. And as we saw in Chapter 3, Woolf plays the words of Christ against those of St Paul, using Higher Criticism to reduce Paul's prescriptions for female behaviour and his teachings on head coverings to expressions of his own psychology and preferences.

Reading literature, reading the Bible

The second approach to the Bible that can be seen in Woolf's work is to draw on ideas about the Bible to raise the status of literature. On the one hand, Woolf did not see the Bible as superior to other works and certainly not as an authoritative source, but on the other, she valued some literary texts highly, seeing them as sources of a particular kind of truth. Woolf is not being frivolous when she describes Wordsworth, Coleridge and Shelley in 'The Pastons and Chaucer' as 'priests', who 'lead you straight up to the mystery', giving us 'text after text to be hung upon the wall, saying after saying to be laid upon the heart like an amulet against disaster' (*CE3* 13). Woolf turned to literature for solace, for encouragement, and for inspiration: for example, she described books as 'the greatest help and comfort' during Stella's illness (*PA* 79).

In 'How Should One Read a Book?' (1926), Woolf uses Evangelical concepts of the Bible to defend the value of reading literature, for this essay has significant congruencies with Henry Venn's instructions on reading scripture in *The Complete Duty of Man*. Although Woolf's friendly opening gambit that she is only going to offer suggestions seems to be diametrically opposed to Venn's didactic approach, parallels quickly emerge: Woolf points the reader in search of truth, offering a method for taking from 'each [book] what it is right that each should give us.' Both Venn and Woolf say that the reading process should start with a humble disposition: Venn urges the reader to 'lift up our hearts to him to teach us the true meaning of sense of what we are going to read'; while Woolf says that we should 'banish . . . preconceptions when we read. . . . Do not dictate to your author . . . try to become him . . . open your mind as widely as possible'. Like Venn, Woolf saw this process as leading to revelatory experience, for it will 'bring you into the presence of a human being unlike any other', and lead to a deeper appreciation of the art of the author(-god) as 'maker' of a fictional world (*CE2* 2–3). Like Venn, Woolf emphasises the need for a sincere, personal response to the text: Venn urges the reader to experience 'correspondent affections' to the text and to recall it in reflection and meditation in order to find its meaning 'beautifully unfolded'; Woolf notes that after the 'dust' of our first impressions has settled, we find the book will 'float to the top of the mind as a whole'.

The parallels between Venn and Woolf are not coincidental. They may be explained in part as an attitude inherited over the generations. Leslie Stephen's insistence upon careful reading and re-reading, encapsulated in his dictum that 'if a book's worth reading, it's worth reading twice' has echoes of the Clapham approach to devotional reading; he recommends a state of self-abnegation when he urges us to 'read a book in the true sense – to read it, that is, not as the critic but in the spirit of enjoyment – is to lay aside for the moment one's own personality, and to become part of the author'.[22]

However, Woolf also reacts against Clapham, for she moves beyond the devotional approach to strike a more assertive note: the final phase of reading, she says, is to stand back and pass judgement on a text. In a riposte to Venn's dictum against novels, Woolf recommends fiction as a source of truth, and the closing lines of the essay parody the Evangelical belief that the Bible provides all that is necessary for salvation:

> Yet who reads to bring about an end, however desirable? Are there not some pursuits that we practise because they are good in themselves, and some pleasures that are final? And is not this among them? I have sometimes dreamt, at least, that when the Day of Judgment dawns and the great conquerors and lawyers and statesmen come to receive their rewards – their crowns, their laurels, their names carved indelibly upon imperishable marble – the Almighty will turn to Peter and will say, not without a certain envy when he sees us coming with our books under our arms, 'Look, these need no reward. We have nothing to give them here. They have loved reading.' (CE2 11)

Behind the humour of this anecdote, we see Woolf's belief that literature offered its own form of salvation *and* that such benefits were to be found in time and not in the hereafter.

In 'On Being Ill', written in the same month, Woolf shows how it is literature rather than preaching that gives solace to the critically ill patient whose mind has turned to the 'universal hope – Heaven, Immortality'. She castigates a newspaper article on the subject by the

Bishop of Lichfield as 'vague', 'weak, watery, inconclusive', assert-ing that it requires 'time and concentration' to imagine Heaven.[23] It falls to poets to do this, for heaven 'needs the imagination of a poet . . . The duty of Heaven-making should be attached to the office of Poet Laureate.' Heaven is real because it is the product of the cre-ative imagination: 'since men have been wishing all these ages, they will have wished something into existence; there will be some green isle for the mind to rest on even if the foot cannot plant itself there' (*E4* 322–3).

Here we see how literature relates to Woolf's elegiac project in her writing: Woolf repeatedly wrote about her lost loved ones in her fiction and literature offers the possibility of immortalising people in text (much as Shakespeare had hoped to do in his sonnets). Leonard Woolf suggested, too, that she believed that she would attain immor-tality through her books.[24]

'Life or spirit, truth or reality, this, the essential thing'

Woolf draws closely on biblical images to explore her ideas about how literature might offer its own form of salvation. She presents her most fully developed account of these in 'Modern Fiction' where she argues that the writer should seek to convey 'life', which she describes as 'a luminous halo, a semi-transparent envelope surround-ing us from the beginning of consciousness to the end' (*CE* 106). Life is a spiritual entity rather than a material one, and she castigates H. G. Wells, John Galsworthy and Arnold Bennett for being 'materi-alists' and champions James Joyce and, even more so, the 'saintly' Russians for being 'spiritual' writers. Woolf's distinction between the spiritual and material has been considered in relation to many differ-ent discourses, such as Cartesian dualism or Platonic idealism, but the conjunction of terms here – halo, saintliness, spirit – also encour-ages us to read it in religious terms, for the division between body and spirit is part of Christian discourse, developed particularly in St Paul's argument for the supremacy of the life-giving Holy Spirit over deathly sin (Romans 8), and in his distinction between the virtuous and life-giving fruits of the spirit and the sinful and deathly works of the flesh (Galatians 5).

Woolf begins 'Modern Fiction' by suggesting that writing is a spir-itual quest in which writers stumble along in the 'plain', lacking the 'lofty pinnacle' from which to see where they are going and therefore not knowing whether they are heading for success and life in 'fertile land' or failure and death in 'dust and the desert'. This opening paragraph invokes the Exodus, in which the people of Israel travelled through the desert in search of the promised land, and where God was a distant figure on the mountain-tops. Woolf therefore implies that writing is a vocation and a pilgrimage, the alternatives of 'fertile land' and 'dust and desert' offering a choice between works that will survive and works that will not: a literary version of salvation and damnation.

Woolf warns that the popular writers of the day, Wells, Galsworthy and Bennett, exemplify the perils of materialism that can lead to producing writing that does not survive. She notes that their work has not yet stood the test of time because they are still living or as she puts it, existing 'in the flesh', a pejorative term that emphasises individual mortality. She castigates them for cheapening their work by paying attention to material things, leaving the reader 'disappointed' because 'they are concerned not with the spirit but with the body'. They mislead the reader by valuing things that will not last, spending 'immense skill and immense industry making the trivial and transitory appear the true and the enduring' (CE2 104–5). The distinction that Woolf evokes here parallels the idea from Romans: 'to be carnally minded is death; but to be spiritually minded is life and peace' (8:6); and 'if Christ be in you the body is dead because of sin; but the Spirit is life because of righteousness' (8:10).

Woolf invokes a specifically religious register to suggest that if these writers have any notions of eternity or of what is good and lasting, then they are cheap ones. She argues that Bennett's characters concern themselves with the material luxuries of middle-class vulgarity to an extent that occludes any higher purpose, so that 'the destiny to which they travel so luxuriously becomes more and more unquestionably an eternity of bliss spent in the very best hotel in Brighton.' The bathos of juxtaposing 'an eternity of bliss' with a mere hotel underlines how Bennett has sold his characters short. She sees Wells's characters as lacking spiritual substance, too:

> what more damaging criticism can there be both of his earth and of his Heaven than that they are to be inhabited here and hereafter by his Joans and his Peters? Does not the inferiority of their natures tarnish whatever institutions and ideals may be provided for them by the generosity of their creator? (CE2 105)

She casts Wells as the creator-god of his fictional worlds, but argues that he is too concerned with physical welfare to develop meaningful characters: as she adds in 'Mr Bennett and Mrs Brown', he is too interested in creating utopias to be interested in character (*CE1* 327). Woolf later warns that writers who follow this method will not only miss out on what is good and enduring, but will actually produce a dead body of work: in trying to please audiences by providing plot, comedy, tragedy and love interest, they create an 'air of probability *embalming* the whole' (*CE2* 106, emphasis added).

By contrast, and with a tone of Evangelical seriousness, Woolf argues that literature should be about something more 'worth while', and it needs to invoke life in order to do this, for 'perhaps without life nothing else is worth while.' Woolf's advice for finding 'life' is to examine 'an ordinary mind on an ordinary day'. This famous passage is rightly regarded as reflecting an interest in psychology that Woolf shared with her fellow modernists, an 'inward turn' that was strongly inspired by the work of Freud and Jung. However, once we are attuned to the religious significance of the essay, we can also see that Woolf is advocating a method akin to the Evangelical spiritual journal, a process of finding life by 'look[ing] within', and reflecting on 'an ordinary mind on an ordinary day' to see its spiritual significance:

> life is a luminous halo, a semi-transparent envelope surrounding us from the beginning of consciousness to the end. Is it not the task of the novelist to convey this varying, this unknown and uncircumscribed spirit, whatever aberration or complexity it may display, with as little mixture of the alien and external as possible? (*CE2* 106)

Woolf's emphasis here is moralistic: root out the trivial, focus on the spiritual. She urges writers to practise the virtues of 'courage and sincerity', and suggests at this point that there may be a correct approach to writing, for the spiritual is the 'proper stuff of fiction'.

Woolf continues to draw on moral distinctions between life and death when she turns to the writers she considers to be more satisfactory. Woolf suggests that young writers of her day 'attempt to come closer to life', and on the basis of reading *A Portrait of the Artist as a Young Man* and the early instalments of *Ulysses*, cites James Joyce as an example of a 'spiritual' writer whose techniques capture the activities of the mind and consciousness. Significantly, she chooses the cemetery scene in *Ulysses* as a passage that captures life, even as it contemplates death and burial. However, she finds Joyce limited because of his egotism and his crudity: when Harriet Weaver brought the Woolfs some manuscript material of *Ulysses* (appropriately hidden in a brown paper bag), in the hope that they would publish it, Woolf wrote in her diary about the disparity between Weaver's smart and demure appearance and the contents of Joyce's novel: 'How did she ever come in contact with Joyce & the rest?' Woolf asks, 'Why does their filth seek exit from her mouth? Heaven knows' (*D1* 140). Clearly, Joyce is too concerned with the works of the flesh, with too much fornication and uncleanness (Galatians 5:19) for Woolf's liking. By contrast, the authors Woolf finds the most appealing are the Russians (Chekhov in particular), who exhibit 'saintliness' in their 'sympathy for the sufferings of others, love towards them, endeavour to reach some goal worthy of the most exacting demands of the spirit' (*CE2* 109). The Russians, then, exemplify the fruits of the spirit, including love, gentleness and goodness (Galatians 5:22).

However, just as Woolf's argument appears to reach its logical conclusion, she pulls back by suggesting that such elevated writing is not in the English character: the Russian worldview is ultimately too gloomy, too concerned with suffering and submission; the English mindset requires comedy and resistance. Just as Woolf was often struck by the 'otherness' of people's religiosity, she concludes that such elevated writing is not in the English character. Significantly, she distances herself from the Evangelical perspective she had adopted by reasserting the importance of the body: 'English fiction from Sterne to Meredith bears witness to our natural delight in humour and comedy, in the beauty of the earth, in the activities of the intellect, and in the splendour of the body' (*CE2* 109–10). Ultimately, Woolf suggests that a balance is needed between the body and the spirit in a literary work if it is to be effective.

'Life came breaking in as usual'

Woolf continues to engage with these biblical concepts about salvation and what it means to be truly alive in *Mrs Dalloway*: the novel in which she put her ideas from 'Modern Fiction' most fully into practice in her own work by making her first sustained attempt to present 'life' through examining an 'ordinary mind on an ordinary day'. The binary opposition of life and death was central to her conception of this novel, as she wrote in her diary: 'I meant to write about death, only life came breaking in as usual' (*D2* 167). The question of mortality had become more urgent for Woolf after a heart scare,[25] but a more immediate impetus that day had been a visit from Violet Dickinson during which they had discussed death and immortality (*D2* 166). It is not surprising, then, that the question of life and death carries a Christian resonance. Peter Walsh hears the bell of St Margaret's Westminster, and reflects that it 'tolled for death that surprised in the midst of life' (*MD* 45), a sentiment echoed by Clarissa when she hears the news of Septimus's suicide and thinks, 'in the middle of my party, here's death' (*MD* 164). These quotations have a liturgical allusion, echoing the phrase 'In the midst of life we are in death' from The Burial of the Dead in *The Book of Common Prayer* (which is in turn derived from the key passages on life and death in Romans 8 and Galatians 5).

As in 'Modern Fiction', Woolf locates her exploration of questions about life and death within a wider concern to find the permanent amid the ephemeral. Clarissa loves 'life; London; this moment', but is aware that these are transient. She is reminded of death in the pleasures of the city and its consumerist buzz, and again she is reminded of death in the party, despite the thrills of the food, the clothing, the conversation. Woolf admitted when writing the novel that she initially found Clarissa too 'tinselly' until she probed deeper to investigate her memories, but Woolf's study of Clarissa goes further than her psychology to explore something that she refers to using the religious term of the 'soul'.

The novel makes an appraisal of Clarissa's spiritual condition comparable with Evangelical soul-searching. Clarissa has shown resilience at her sister's death, determining to 'behave like a lady' and then developing an 'atheist's religion' of 'doing good for the sake of goodness' (*MD* 70). On the other hand, her hatred of Miss Kilman is corrosive and explicitly harmful to her soul, a 'brutal monster' stirring in 'the depths of that leaf-encumbered forest, the soul.' Such is the extent of its influence that it threatens her contentment in material comfort, making her feel 'as if the whole panoply of content were nothing but self love! this hatred!' (*MD* 11). The feeling of hatred rises and subsides in Clarissa several times during the novel, even at the party, when it leads her to feel the 'hollowness' of her successes.

Peter Walsh is especially critical of Clarissa's spiritual state, and we are told that he has enjoyed talking about the 'defects of her own soul' (*MD* 7). In his view, one of her worst faults is to be judgemental. Ironically, he sees her disgust at an unmarried mother as being 'the death of the soul' (*MD* 53–4). This moral judgement (which Evangelicals would find perfectly justified) is for Peter a deathly lack of empathy. There are clear resonances here of the twentieth-century tendency to see salvation and damnation not as states to be determined in the hereafter, but to be experienced in the present.

As in her conclusion to 'Modern Fiction', Woolf recognises that, while spiritual health is one measure of what it is to be truly alive, the body and sexuality are also important. Clarissa's love for Sally Seton is redemptive, but by contrast, the mortification of the flesh practised by Miss Kilman, the only major character to be a committed Christian, is not life-giving. It is easy to castigate Miss Kilman as a satirical attack on Christianity *per se,* but if we discount the most vehement attacks on this 'monstrous' woman as expressions of Clarissa's hatred, as Lewis suggests, then we can see her as a pathetic and damaged figure, a study of why someone might turn to faith for consolation for deep personal bitterness.[26] Miss Kilman's struggles to subdue the flesh are not motivated by a desire to strengthen the spirit so much as an outlet for deep-seated 'turbulent and painful' self-hatred sparked by an awareness that '[s]he could not help being ugly; she could not afford to buy pretty clothes' (*MD* 115). Clarissa is therefore close to the mark when she observes of Miss Kilman that 'all her soul rusted with that grievance sticking in it' (*MD* 11).

Mrs Dalloway therefore sets out a series of questions about what it means to be alive. Both Clarissa and Peter, though atheists, are aware that 'in the midst of life we are in death', while Miss Kilman's faith is stultifying rather than life-giving. Septimus contributes to this chorus, for one of his many observations reverses the theme of death-in-life: 'I have been dead, yet am now alive' (*MD* 62). Although the image of rebirth could be examined in relation to a wide range of religious traditions, there is much in Septimus's heightened, religious language that alludes to the Christian idea of resurrection. After all, it is Septimus rather than Miss Kilman who declares, 'There is a God' (*MD* 22). Septimus's reference to resurrection relates to the fact that he has survived the war when so many others have not. It is also a metaphor of religious conversion, of dying to sin and rising to new life (Romans 6: 1–14), and the syntax of his statement echoes that of John Newton's hymn, 'Amazing Grace': 'I once was lost, but now am found / Was blind but now I see'. Septimus's description of himself as a 'wretch' (*MD* 82) is a further allusion to Newton's testimony that grace 'saved a wretch like me'.

Woolf's Passion Trilogy

Woolf's explorations of life and death, the soul and salvation in *Mrs Dalloway* are situated within a wider framework of biblical motifs, and this leads us to a further way in which Woolf uses the Bible in her work: as the source for an extended set of literary allusions. *Mrs Dalloway* represents the start of Woolf's interrogation of the story of the Passion that she develops in *To the Lighthouse* and *The Waves*: a cycle that I will call Woolf's 'Passion Trilogy'. In each of these novels, Woolf identifies one or more characters with the figure of Christ, and her frame of reference becomes wider over the course of the trilogy, from allusions to the crucifixion and resurrection in *Mrs Dalloway*, to a narrative arc from the Fall to the resurrection in *To the Lighthouse*, and an arc from the Fall through to the Last Judgment in *The Waves*. In each case, Woolf applies the Passion narrative to human characters and the present day, but in each case she uses these story lines to test the Christian doctrine of salvation.

Woolf's use of biblical allusions can be situated within a context of modernist intertextuality. Her use of a biblical framework as a structuring device owes something to Joyce's use of *The Odyssey* as a structure for *Ulysses*; Eliot's use of Fraser's *The Golden Bough* and Weston's *From Ritual to Romance* in *The Waste Land*; and Lawrence's use of biblical motifs in *The Rainbow*. However, Woolf uses literary quotations very differently from Joyce and Eliot, for instead of referring back to a source as a site of authority, she engages in a process of reinterpretation and recontextualisation: as Anne Fernald notes, Woolf plays 'at once with the syntactic greatness of an early work and her distance from it as a modern feminist reader.'[27] The fact that Woolf saw the Bible as literature, not scripture, enables her to do this. Woolf's use of biblical narratives is parodic in the sense that Linda Hutcheon has described it: not satire, but 'extended repetition with critical difference'.[28]

The Christ-figure in *Mrs Dalloway* is Septimus, who describes himself as 'the greatest of mankind . . . lately taken from life to death, the Lord who had come to renew society' (*MD* 23, echoed 87). While it could be argued that Septimus's thoughts are hallucinations, an indictment of Christianity as irrational and delusional, such a reading would undermine the level of empathy with which Woolf treats Septimus's experience of mental illness and the level of antagonism she expresses towards the psychiatric profession. The only person who labels Septimus as having a Messiah Complex is the unreliable Sir William Bradshaw, who insists that 'these prophetic Christs and Christesses, who prophesied the end of the world, or the advent of God, should drink milk in bed' (*MD* 89). The bathos of this sentence shows the inadequacy of Bradshaw's treatment regimes, his inability to grasp important truths, and his failure to acknowledge the significance of his patients' feelings. Furthermore, Septimus does not seek self-aggrandisement: he is aware that being 'the Lord' means 'suffering for ever, the scapegoat, the eternal sufferer, but he did not want it' and, in a gesture that recalls Christ's prayer at Gethsemane, 'Let this cup pass from me' (Matthew 26:39), he puts 'from him with a wave of his hand the eternal suffering, that great loneliness' (*MD* 23).

This identification between Septimus and Christ is reinforced by his compulsion to take the sins of society upon himself. Woolf makes it clear that Septimus is suffering as a result of being forced to lose his humanity, a loss that society and the medical profession are unwilling to acknowledge. As a soldier, Septimus had had to embrace death by killing others and accepting the losses of his comrades with *sang froid,* and he had been rewarded for doing so. However, by the present day of the novel, he has come to see this behaviour as a crime against humanity: 'the sin for which human nature had condemned him to death; that he did not feel' (*MD* 81–2). Although a medical reading of this statement would simply see it as an expression of suicidal tendencies, the language of 'sin' and 'condemnation' alludes to the religious maxim that 'the wages of sin is death.' Like Christ (Romans 4:25), Septimus takes the sins of others upon himself and is punished in their place.

The novel persistently represents Septimus's death as sacrificial. It is significant that he commits suicide when he is at his happiest, in a moment of contentment and laughter with Rezia: 'He did not want to die. Life was good.' He only throws himself from the window when they are about to be interrupted by Dr Holmes. It is both a spur-of-the-moment act (he chooses the method hastily), and a gesture of defiance towards Holmes and Bradshaw, and its sacrificial nature is shown in his final words: 'I'll give it you' (*MD* 133–4).

The sacrificial element becomes clearer in Clarissa's reaction to the news, for she articulates clearly that Septimus had died in her place and for her faults: 'it was her disaster – her disgrace. It was her punishment . . . She had schemed; she had pilfered. She was never wholly admirable' (*MD* 166). Clarissa therefore sees Septimus as a saviour figure, and her reaction to Septimus's suicide leads to her overcoming her fear of death: 'Death was defiance. Death was an attempt to communicate, people feeling the impossibility of reaching the centre which, mystically, evaded them; closeness drew apart; rapture faded; one was alone. There was an embrace in death' (*MD* 165). Clarissa's reaction to Septimus's death creates a connection between them, despite the fact that they had not known one another in life: it is an outworking of her theory from much earlier in the novel that we live through one another (*MD* 8). Ironically, too, what Clarissa recognises in Septimus's suicide is the Evangelical concept of the 'good death': the exemplary conduct of a dying person teaching others how to live and die.

Although Septimus talks about resurrection in the early part of the novel, it is Clarissa who ultimately experiences resurrection. It is she who gets a new lease of life, as her thoughts move on from death to a renewed joy in life. Her observation 'she had never been so happy', though following on from a memory of her youth, actually applies to the present: 'No pleasure could be equal . . . this having done with the triumphs of youth, lost herself in the process of living, to find it, with a shock of delight, as the sun rose, as the day sank' (*MD* 166). Significantly, the resurrection is to life in this world, and not the hereafter. It is a motif throughout, starting with Clarissa's recovery from a potentially life-threatening illness and the restoration of society after the War ('it was over; thank Heaven – over' (*MD* 4)), and which recurs at the party when Peter is pleased to see Clarissa's Aunt Helena, having thought that she was dead.

The presence of allusions to the Passion in *Mrs Dalloway* can be read as an indication that Woolf was drawn to the story of Christ as the 'sad and beautiful' figure who was also a moral arbiter. As Emily Griesinger suggests, the novel shows, 'at least hesitating admiration of Christ and the Christ-story.'[29] Woolf may have had additional impetus for this when she visited Madrid at Easter 1923 in the early stages of writing the novel, for she wrote to Jacques Raverat: 'Here we have been following the Crucifixion and Last Supper through the streets, and again I felt entirely sympathetic, which one couldn't imagine doing in Piccadilly' (*L3* 24). In using the story of the Passion to inform her representation of Septimus, however, Woolf focuses her biblical allusions on a human character rather than a divine or supernatural being so that, rather than endorsing faith in Christ, Woolf emphasises the value of a human life and how it can have meaning for others. Septimus has performed a spiritual function for Clarissa in helping her see life and death differently, and so the Passion references contribute to Woolf's development of a theme of life coming from death and the redemptive possibility of change and renewal in this life.

To the Lighthouse

Allusions to the Passion are more persistent in *To the Lighthouse* and Woolf resumes the theme of 'in the midst of life we are in death' with greater rigour and intensity and with a heightened consciousness of mortality. Rather than showing death intruding on life as in *Mrs Dalloway,* this novel is imbued with the sense that we are born to suffer and die. So, although Mrs Ramsay's party is interrupted by news not of a death but of an engagement, Mrs Ramsay reflects that this 'love of man for woman . . . bear[s] in its bosom the seeds of death' (*TL* 135). This continues Mrs Ramsay's earlier thoughts that her children will 'grow up and lose all that,' for life itself is 'terrible, hostile, and quick to pounce on you' (*TL* 80–2). Where *Mrs Dalloway* identified 'works of the flesh' that crush the spirit and suppress positive ways of living, *To the Lighthouse* emphasises that mortality is endemic to the human condition.

This insight is enhanced by Woolf's taking the biblical narrative back to the Fall and original sin. James remembers his childhood in Edenic terms: he recalls a traumatic sense of the loss of innocence akin to seeing 'a waggon crush ignorantly and innocently, someone's foot' and wonders 'in what garden did all this happen?' (*TL* 249–50). As a result, the human condition is one of unavoidable suffering, as Mrs Ramsay acknowledges: 'There were the eternal problems; suffering; death; the poor. There was always a woman dying of cancer even here' (*TL* 82). Mrs Ramsay's pessimism makes her good works more urgent and sincere than the generalised kindness of Clarissa Dalloway or the grim self-sacrifice of Doris Kilman. Mrs Ramsay has the gift of being fully present to people in their suffering, as Lily thinks: 'eyes that are closing in pain have looked on you. You have been with them there' (*TL* 264). Mrs Ramsay is self-critical about her motives for offering help, aware that 'all this desire of hers to give, to help, was vanity . . . for her own self-satisfaction' (*TL* 58), but she also hopes that by making case-notes 'she would cease to be a private woman whose charity was half a sop to her own indignation' and become 'an investigator elucidating the social problem' (*TL* 15). Mrs Ramsay's motivations follow on from her perception that it is a 'lie' to think that 'we are in the hands of the Lord'; if God cannot help us, then good works are necessary to alleviate human suffering and not to secure personal salvation.

Allusions to Christ in *To the Lighthouse* are fragmented across different characters. This novel is peppered with allusions to the story of Christianity, even in passing details such as the rooks that Mrs Ramsay names Mary and Joseph and Jasper tries to shoot. Mrs Ramsay and James are compared to the Madonna and Child, but Cam also sees James, somewhat resentfully, as the God of the Old Testament, 'the law-giver, with the tablets of eternal wisdom laid open on his knee . . . most god-like' (*TL* 227). Mrs Ramsay sees her husband as Christ-like, 'She was not good enough to tie his shoe strings, she felt' (*TL* 46; cf. Mark 1:9). The allusions convey a sense of the sanctity of home and family, but this is counterpoised by an emphasis on the everyday, as Lily Briscoe reminds us, '[i]f you are exalted you must somehow come a cropper' (*TL* 63).

Beyond these local allusions, however, the novel traces the pattern of the Passion narrative, starting with the dinner party, which is Mrs Ramsay's Last Supper. As Christ 'knew that his hour was come that he should depart out of this world' (John 13:1), so Mrs Ramsay comes to the meal with a sense of finality, 'a sense of being past everything, through everything, out of everything' (*TL* 112). As Christ commanded his disciples to remember him at Communion ('do this in remembrance of me' (1. Corinthians 11:24)), so Mrs Ramsay is aware that people will remember her by the dinner and that the communion, or 'community of feeling' that she has generated will be passed on: 'Paul and Minta would carry it on when she was dead'.

'Time Passes', Woolf's bleakest piece of writing, is an extended allusion to the crucifixion. Again the story is refracted onto several characters, for the section sets Christ's death alongside many others: the war dead, Prue and Andrew Ramsay, and especially Mrs Ramsay. The section is set in a profusion of 'immense darkness' that lasts not only a single night (joining the two single days of 'The Window' and 'The Lighthouse'), but a period of ten years during which 'night succeeds to night', echoing the unnatural darkness over the land from the sixth hour to the ninth hour at the crucifixion (e.g. Matthew 27:45). Like the crucifixion, it is a confrontation between good and evil: well-intentioned people, 'divine goodness', and spiritual searchers on the beach are pitted against the war and multiple deaths. Woolf also describes it as the action of divinity on the sinfulness of human nature:

> It seemed now as if, touched by human penitence and all its toil, divine goodness had parted the curtain and displayed behind it, single, distinct, the hare erect; the wave falling; the boat rocking, which, did we deserve them, should be ours always. (*TL* 174)

The parting of the curtain recalls the moment in the crucifixion narrative when 'the veil of the temple was rent in twain' (e.g. Mark 15:38). The soft consonants and lulling cadences of Woolf's rendition make it seem less traumatic than the biblical verse, but in theological terms it is much harsher. The tearing of the veil of the temple is often interpreted as a revelatory moment in which humankind is brought closer to God,[30] but in Woolf's version, sin remains because good works or 'toil' do not deserve a reward and because penitence is not enough: 'alas, divine goodness, twitching the cord, draws the curtain; it does not please him . . . For our penitence deserves a glimpse only; our toil respite only' (*TL* 174).

This confrontation is not treated as an intellectual matter for theological debate, however, for 'Time Passes' raises immensely painful questions. Immediately after 'divine goodness' has withheld forgiveness, the narrator notes that no one would find answers on the beach: 'no semblance of serving and divine promptitude come readily to hand'. This failure to find an answer is immediately juxtaposed with the news of the death of Mrs Ramsay: '[Mr Ramsay stumbling along a passage stretched his arms out one dark morning, but, Mrs Ramsay having died rather suddenly the night before, he stretched his arms out. They remained empty]' (*TL* 175). The proximity of these passages shows the hopelessness of the quest: the searchers lack an answer and Mr Ramsay's arms remain empty. A similarly harsh juxtaposition occurs with the next appearance of searchers: although they come in the Romantic belief that the natural world can assure them that 'good triumphs, happiness prevails, order rules' (*TL* 180), the air of hope is crushed by the interpolation of Prue Ramsay's death in childbirth: the most extreme demonstration of human mortality and the cruelty of nature.

Woolf's allusions to the crucifixion continue as the war starts to intrude on the silence of the empty house: 'the rock was rent asunder', and 'some glass tinkled in the cupboard as if a giant voice had shrieked so loud in its agony that tumblers stood inside a cupboard vibrated too' (*TL* 181). The word 'asunder' is a common biblical term: the rending of the rock alludes to the earthquakes that accompany the crucifixion, while the shrieking of the giant voice echoes the cry of Jesus: 'And about the ninth hour Jesus cried with a loud voice, saying *"Eli, Eli lama sabachthani?"*, that is to say, "My God, my God, why hast thou forsaken me?"' (Matthew 27:46). This biblical verse brings the crucifixion narrative to the point of god-forsakenness, Luther's *Deus absconditus*,[31] and this is the point when Woolf's searchers despair of any answer. As the death of Andrew Ramsay in France is reported and a warship is seen making a 'purplish stain' on the bay, the searchers give up: 'to pace the beach was impossible; contemplation was unendurable' (*TL* 182–3).

'Time Passes' presents widespread loss: the deaths of individuals; the end of the whole pre-war way of life, a world organised around family, marriage and the separate spheres; and the decay of the house. There are even hints at the wholesale destruction of humanity: 'there was scarcely anything left of body or mind by which one could say "This is he" or "This is she"' (*TL* 172). By setting this narrative of destruction alongside allusions to the crucifixion, however, 'Time Passes' demonstrates the biblical precept that all are 'crucified with Christ': the old way of life put to death to make way for the new. This life emerges in 'Time Passes', as it does at the resurrection, as dawn begins: 'that moment, that hesitation, when dawn trembles and night pauses' (*TL* 188; cf. Matthew 28:1). The agent of resurrection is the comical Mrs McNab and, ironically, she now emerges as a Christ-like figure. As if engaged in the harrowing of hell, she rescues the Waverley novels from oblivion and resurrects Mr Ramsay like a projection of moving film: 'in a ring of light she saw the old gentleman lean as a rake, wagging his head . . . talking to himself' (*TL* 190). Mrs McNab, Mrs Bast and George restore the house and garden, and, as if to confirm the redemptive significance of their work, Woolf describes the culmination of their efforts in an allusion to the last words of Christ: 'it was finished' (*TL* 192; cf. John 19:30). The final section of 'Time Passes' sees a new day break with order restored: 'peace had come. Messages of peace breathed from shore to shore' (*TL* 193). The searchers now have their answer: 'whatever the dreamers dreamt holily, dreamt wisely' is confirmed, and the 'beauty of the world' (which Mr Ramsay had worshipped in his wife and son) can be heard again.

But clearly this is not enough. Although 'Time Passes' ends on a hopeful note, 'The Lighthouse' goes on to ask what this really means for those who, like Mr Ramsay, are grieving and for those who, like Lily Briscoe, still have unanswered questions. In other words, the resurrection rings hollow for those who continue to suffer. Indeed, Woolf disputes the idea that the crucifixion happened 'once for all' (Hebrews 10:10). The redemptive act is not singular but repetitive because the novel ends with two further allusions to Christ's last words, on Mr Ramsay's arrival at the lighthouse ('"He has landed," [Lily] said aloud. "It is finished." (*TL* 280)) and on Lily's completion of her painting: ('She drew a line there, in the centre. It was done; it was finished' (*TL* 281)).

The question that Lily Briscoe poses at the start of the section, 'what can it all mean?' (*TL* 197), resonates throughout 'The Lighthouse', and she turns to her painting as an antidote to the emptiness and unreality that she experiences on returning to the island. In a clear echo of 'Modern Fiction', Lily's attempt to paint Mrs Ramsay is also an attempt to capture life, to confront 'this other thing, this truth, this reality' (*TL* 214). Furthermore, Lily comes to realise that it is Mrs Ramsay who holds the key to this problem, as it is she who has the ability to offer 'little daily miracles', some 'revelation', through her ability to transcend time: 'Mrs Ramsay saying "Life stand still here"; Mrs Ramsay making of the moment something permanent' (*TL* 218). Lily makes progress through reviving Mrs Ramsay in her memory. She remembers Mrs Ramsay's authoritative nature: 'Do this, she said, and one did it', a phrasing that gives her words a sense of divine command through an echo of the story of healing of the centurion's servant (Matthew 8:9). Lily starts to call her name, as if in prayer ('if they shouted loud enough Mrs Ramsay would return' (*TL* 243)). While there are possible parallels here with Forster's *A Passage to India*, where the Indians pray for Mrs Moore's help, unlike Forster, Woolf does not see this as delusory: when Mrs Ramsay eventually reappears, it is a resurrection moment that is 'part of her perfect goodness to Lily' (*TL* 272), and it enables Lily to complete her painting.

Woolf also ponders questions of salvation in Mr Ramsay's journey, which is physically and spiritually tougher than Lily's. He sails to the lighthouse as a 'ritual' to do honour to Mrs Ramsay's memory, setting out religiously in a 'little procession' with his two teenaged children. His struggle is threefold. First, he is overwhelmed by grief for his wife. Second, he is facing his own mortality: Lily notes his 'extreme decrepitude' and she thinks fatalistically that 'there was no helping Mr Ramsay on the journey he was going' (*TL* 209). But third, more so than Lily, Mr Ramsay is beset with doubts. These can be seen in his repetitive recitation of lines from William Cowper's 'The Castaway'. The poem recalls a shipwreck and so it fits in with Mr Ramsay's questioning Macalister about the storms of the previous winter. The quotation and Mr Ramsay's preoccupation with the shipwreck seem melodramatic, given that the day is calm and sunny, but these lines from Cowper's poem point to a deeper crisis. Cowper, an Evangelical hymn writer and religious poet, suffered from depression for the whole of his life, and wrote 'The Castaway' during a severe episode when believed himself to be damned. The core of the poem tells a story of a man who falls overboard in a storm and cannot be rescued despite the efforts of his friends, who eventually have to abandon him to save their own lives. In the framing verses, the narrator aligns himself with the castaway, but he is in a worse state because he is 'a destin'd wretch', condemned not by events but by predestination. The full final verse speaks of the absence of divine help, either physical or spiritual:

> No voice divine the storm allay'd,
>   No light propitious shone:
> When, snatch'd from all effectual aid,
>   We perish'd, each alone:
> But I beneath a rougher sea,
> And whelm'd in deeper gulfs than he.

Cowper had been a favourite poet of Leslie Stephen's, which is another reason why Mr Ramsay should quote him. Woolf had read Cowper at her father's recommendation, and chose to re-read him for herself in 1908–9. Cowper therefore expresses the religious doubts of Stephen and of Woolf. But by landing Mr Ramsay safely on the lighthouse, Woolf envisages spiritual safety for the character and her father. Mr Ramsay's actions of leaving the boat as if 'leaping into space' and springing 'like a young man' suggest that the arrival at the lighthouse is a metaphor for his death (his children stand up in the boat, but they don't make the leap themselves). Lily's words 'it is finished' echo this sense of finality. They suggest a kind of salvation, but not a Christian one, for Mr Ramsay leaps as if saying 'there is no God.' Mr Ramsay has redeemed himself through love, an act of reverence from husband to wife; restitution for his scepticism, ten years earlier, that the trip would not happen.

In this second novel of the Trilogy, Woolf again shows aspects of biblical narratives being enacted in the lives of ordinary people. As with *Mrs Dalloway,* biblical allusions serve to emphasise the importance and sanctity of human relationships, showing that an individual has value for others after their death and that an individual continues to exist in the memories and imagination of others. Yet, Woolf does this alongside discourses of profound scepticism: it is a lie to say that 'we are in the hands of the Lord', and there is no possibility of a redemptive act that will save the human condition 'once for all'. Instead, the novel suggests momentary solace and insight can be found in the 'little daily miracles' of ordinary life (*TL* 218).

The Waves

Woolf's vision is altogether bleaker in *The Waves,* for instead of celebrating the value of human lives, her keynote is the insignificance of the individual. Once more, she tests Christian consolations against painful realities as she continues her meditation on the theme of 'in the midst of life we are in death', for the tragic death of Percival is central to the novel and the incident is replayed traumatically by its characters. Human mortality and the corruptibility of the flesh are emphasised throughout: even before Percival's death Bernard, still a young man and in the midst of a busy London street, reflects that although 'we insist, it seems, on living', the wider world is indifferent to our existence and in the scheme of things we are nothing: 'we are only lightly covered with buttoned cloth; and beneath these pavements are shells, bones and silence' (*W* 89). The references to mortality, ageing and decay become more intensive from middle age onwards, when Bernard realises that 'I have lost my youth' (*W* 147), and by the final episode, as an old man near death, he sees humanity as mere stinking meat: 'Disorder, sordidity and corruption surround us. We have been taking into our mouths the bodies of dead birds' (*W* 234). This takes to an extreme the concept that 'in the midst of life we are in death', for the very means of preserving physical life is eating the flesh of dead animals.

As with the other novels in the Passion Trilogy, these reflections are offered against the framework of a biblical narrative: this time, an even broader arc from creation, Eden and the fall, to the crucifix-ion and on to the apocalypse, final judgement and the new heaven and new earth of Revelation. Woolf's creation narrative includes a godlike female presence for the sky lights up at sunrise 'as if the arm of a woman couched beneath the horizon had raised a lamp' (W 3). The Judaeo-Christian narrative of creation is imbued with female presence and agency and the image of 'light arising' echoes the title of Caroline Emelia Stephen's work of Quaker spirituality. The characters spend their childhood in an Edenic garden, an asso-ciation strengthened by Bernard's description of it in his summing-up: 'In the beginning there was the nursery, with windows opening on to a garden' (W 192), which alludes to both the opening line of Genesis and its echo in the opening of St John's Gospel. Behind this scene there are images of a solitary woman: Bernard and Susan make a secret visit to Elvedon, with the 'close-clipped hedge of the ladies' garden', in which they see a lady writing. This lady is the first of many unnamed figures encountered by the characters, but here it could be read metafictionally as the author-god(ess) of the text. This garden, like Eden, is the site of a fall: not the cosmic fall of Genesis or *Paradise Lost,* but the human child's discovery of sexuality and death, for innocence is 'shattered' with Jinny kissing Louis, bringing about an awareness of sexual attraction and awak-ening jealousy in Susan. This is followed by knowledge of death when Neville overhears news of a suicide and observes, 'I will call this stricture, this rigidity "death among the appletrees" for ever' (W 8, 17).

Like other novels in the Trilogy, *The Waves* represents the story of Christ in a human figure – in this case, Percival, based on Thoby. Neville and Bernard attribute divine powers to Percival. Bernard imagines him as 'a God' in his authoritative dealings in the colo-nies (W 107); Neville sees his arrival among his friends as restoring order from the 'reign of chaos' (W 96), a phrase that recalls the rebel angels in Milton's *Paradise Lost* (1, 543) and thus attributes cosmic significance to Percival's actions. However, in line with the novel's tone of hopelessness, the suggestions of Percival's power are under-cut. So, although the gathering of friends for a farewell meal before his departure to India is his Last Supper, there is no hope that any-thing permanent has been achieved. Bernard says that they have been drawn into 'communion' (W 99), but qualifies this by adding that 'we have come together . . . to make one thing, not enduring – for what endures?' and Jinny observes that 'we shall perhaps never make this moment out of one man again' (W 99, 114). Moments of insight are fleeting and nothing endures. The party is followed by a moment of 'agony' akin to Gethsemane, albeit for Neville rather than Percival (W 115; Luke 22:44).

Percival's death, which is placed in abrupt juxtaposition to the party scene with Neville's stark announcement that 'He is dead', is an allusion to the crucifixion but without its redemptive capacity. The crucifixion appears in the religious art that Bernard views in the National Gallery and in Neville's image that 'the lights of the world' have gone out, evoking the hours of unnatural darkness and also offering a negation of Holman Hunt's famous painting of Christ at St Paul's Cathedral. Neville knows that light would only return if Percival's accident could somehow be undone and he knows that though there is a fall there is no redemption: recalling his child-hood experience, he notes that 'there stands the tree which I cannot pass.' This tree merges the tree of knowledge from Eden with the tree of the cross, but the latter does not cancel out the former as in Christian theology because, instead, 'we are doomed' (W 119–20). Bernard rails against a 'blank and brutal' face in the sky. It is signifi-cant that Louis, the only speaker to profess a religious faith, does not have a monologue in this episode. Instead his views are repre-sented in Rhoda's bitter observation that Louis's comments would be trite: 'He says ... he will shepherd us if we will follow. If we submit he will reduce us to order. Thus he will smooth out the death of Percival to his satisfaction' (W 127). Contained within Rhoda's summary, the figure of the good shepherd and advice to submit to Christ become shallow explanations that ignore the realities of suf-fering and loss.

Bernard thinks of Percival as a 'judge', which not only indicates the intended career of Percival and Thoby, but also alludes to Christ as judge. Bernard thinks that he will continue to defer to Percival, and what he might have thought: explaining that 'if I discover a new vein in myself I shall submit it to you privately. I shall ask, What is your verdict?' (W 122). Yet Bernard knows that this feeling will not last and that his memories of Percival will be overwritten by new experiences and influences.

There is no harrowing of hell in *The Waves*, but instead Woolf alludes to Dante's *The Inferno* to evoke hell on earth. Jinny, taking an escalator into the London underground, reflects that 'Millions descend those stairs in a terrible descent. Great wheels churn inexo-rably urging them downwards. Millions have died. Percival died'

(W 154). This recalls Dante's account of souls entering hell as 'an interminable train / of souls' and the reflection that 'I wondered / how death could have undone so great a number' (3, 55–7). Significantly, Woolf's allusions to Dante in *The Waves* are confined to *The Inferno*: there is no redemptive progression to Purgatory and Paradise, and no reunion with the beloved.

Thus, although the remaining friends' reunion at Hampton Court alludes to Holy Communion – the visit becomes a memorial journey, seemingly fulfilling an injunction to 'do this in remembrance of me' – the group struggle to become united and when they do, they are gathered around emptiness rather than a presence, for the seven-sided flower they had been earlier is now six-sided. Bernard's re-telling of this episode in his summing-up makes this point even more clearly: '[w]e saw for a moment laid out among us the body of the complete human being whom we have failed to be'. The group has failed to achieve unity and become the 'one body' presupposed by Holy Communion (the life-giving, life-affirming communion of saints);[32] instead they gather around a body 'laid out' like a corpse. When they start to put aside the tensions that divide them, significantly by sharing a bottle of wine, they become even more aware of death and of the 'huge blackness of what is outside us, of what we are not' and, in an allusion to Andrew Marvell, '[t]he wind, the rush of wheels became the roar of time and . . . we were extinguished for a moment' (W 222).

The final section of *The Waves* alludes to the Apocalypse, the moment of universal death and destruction. The concentric timescales of the novel are significant here, for the death of an individual is overlaid with images of the destruction of the entire world. The whole section has overtones of the Final Judgment, highlighted when Bernard introduces the episode as a 'sum[ming]-up', before proceeding to give an account of his life and the collective life of his friends. Echoing the Book of Revelation, where St John is shown pictures from a sealed book opened by the Lamb of God, Bernard is shown a picture-book by a nursemaid, who suddenly points to 'the truth': an image that again feminises the divine (W 230). When Bernard experiences a collapse (leaning against a gate like a 'dead man'), he describes it as an eclipse: combining an omen from Revelation that presages the end of the world ('the sun became as black as sackcloth of hair' (Revelation 6:12)), with an event that Woolf had witnessed herself in June 1927. This is the end of the world for Bernard: 'the rhythm stopped', 'Life has destroyed me', 'A man without a self, I said. A heavy body leaning on a gate. A dead man' (W 227–8). He plummets into decline, tottering and falling and lying on the floor like rubbish, like his beloved notebook of memorable phrases, which is going to be swept away by a cleaner. When he finally faces death, it comes like an enemy on horseback: a rider of the Apocalypse.

Having contemplated widespread destruction, however, the novel ends on a note of defiance: 'Against you I will fling myself, unvanquished and unyielding, O Death!' The final pages go beyond apocalypse and destruction to images of dawn and renewal: 'the eternal renewal, the incessant rise and fall and fall and rise again', alluding to the 'new heaven and new earth' that appear at the end of the Book of Revelation (W 238; Revelation 21:1). The ending of the novel therefore speaks of a life outside the individual and of a place outside time: indeed, Woolf's interest in this can be seen in her edition of the Greek Bible, where she had particularly noted Revelation 10:6 'there should be time no longer'. In layering timescales, then – the biblical narrative, the life of the world, the life of a group, and the life of an individual – Woolf points to a dimension outside time. The novel offers hope for renewal, but this is on a cosmic scale of the creation of a new world, rather than hope for the specific individual. It is found in the realisation of the idea she noted in her diary entry on beginning the novel: 'it is not ourselves but something in the universe we are left with' (D3 113).

Although Woolf's rendering of the biblical narrative appears to be bleaker and more sceptical in *The Waves* than in her other two novels, her diary shows that she found completing the novel both spiritually enriching and cathartic (D4 10). Fifteen minutes after completing the manuscript, she recorded a revelatory moment in which she was driven by something that seemed to come from outside herself: she has 'reeled across the last ten pages with some moments of such intensity & intoxication that I seemed only to stumble after my own voice, or almost, after some sort of speaker (as when I was mad).' It also brought her some comfort for the death of Thoby nearly 25 years earlier: 'I have been sitting these 15 minutes in a state of glory, & calm, & some tears thinking of Thoby & if I could write Julian Thoby Stephen 1881–1906 on the first page. I suppose not.' She also has a sense of completion: 'its done; & as I certainly felt at the end, not merely finished, but rounded off, completed, the thing stated.' The completion meant having 'netted that fin' that she had seen from her window in Rodmell. In doing so, Woolf expressed a vision that she had had in a space that, as

we have seen, she associated with withdrawal, mystic contemplation and spiritual renewal, all of which were to be found especially
when looking out of a window onto the natural world. Throughout
her Passion Trilogy Woolf fishes for images as she takes and tests
Christian images and uses them differently, like the images that her
'imagination picked up used and tossed aside' while finishing *The
Waves*. Her satisfaction on completing *The Waves* was both spiritual and aesthetic: she had absorbed Christian images into her art
but also changed them in her imagination, embedding them in literature, which was for her an immortal medium: a firm riposte to
Clapham's discourses of salvation and damnation.

Notes

1. Vance, *Bible and Novel*; Wright, *D. H. Lawrence and the Bible*.
2. 'On the Interpretation of Scripture', n.p.
3. *The Holy Bible* (Cambridge: J. Hayes, 1683).
4. *The Holy Bible* (Oxford: Oxford University Press, 1900). 'VW –
   presentee. Violet Dickinson – inscriber' (Pullman catalogue notes).
5. Buckridge, 'Books as Gifts', p. 68.
6. *The Holy Bible* (Oxford; New York: The University Press, 1893). 'LW
   – presentee, annotator. Marie Woolf – inscriber' (Pullman catalogue
   notes).
7. *The Holy Bible* (London: The British and Foreign Bible Society, 1909).
   'VW – presentee. LW – inscriber' (Pullman catalogue notes).
8. Vicchio, *Job in the Modern World*, p. 170.
9. *The Book of Job: According to the Authorized Version* (London: G. Bell,
   1900). 'LW – presentee. Lytton Strachey – inscriber' (Pullman catalogue
   notes). Stella Benson, *Tobit Transplanted. With Reprint of apocryphal
   Book of Tobit appended* (London: Macmillan, 1931). 'VW – presentee.
   The Author – inscriber' (Pullman catalogue notes).
10. *The New Testament: The Authorized English Version; with introduc-
    tion, and various readings from the three most celebrated manuscripts
    of the original Greek text*. By Constantine Tischendorf. Tauchnitz
    Edition, vol. 1000 (Leipzig: Bernhard Tauchnitz, 1869).
11. Latour, 'The Berlin Key', p. 10.
12. *The Holy Bible, an Exact Reprint Page for Page of the Authorized
    Version Published in the Year MDCXI* (Oxford: Oxford University
    Press, 1833). 'LW – signer' (Pullman catalogue notes).
13. *The Apocrypha: Translated out of the Greek and Latin Tongues, Being
    the Version Set Forth A. D. 1611 Compared with the Most Ancient
    Authorities and Revised A. D. 1894* (London: H. Milford; Oxford:
    Oxford University Press, 1926). *The Apocrypha: The Revised Version*

with the Revised Marginal References (London and New York: Milford; Oxford: Oxford University Press, 1927).

14. *The Holy Bible: Containing the Old and New Testaments: Translated out of the Original Tongues into Tamil, and with Former Translations Diligently Compared and Revised* (Madras: Madras Auxillary to the British and Foreign Bible Society, 1901). *Ha-Berit ha-hadashah: Ha 'atakah hadashah mi-leshon Yayan li-leshon 'Ivrit.=The New Testament in Hebrew and English)*, trans. Isaac Edward Salkinson (London: Trinitarian Bible Society, c. 1940). *The New English Bible: New Testament* (London: Oxford University Press, 1961).

15. *He Kaine Diatheke = The Greek New Testament: With the Readings Adopted by the Revisers of the Authorized Version* (Oxford: Clarendon Press, 1888). 'VW? – annotations' (Pullman catalogue notes).

16. *He Kaine Diatheke: Consisting of the Text of Scholz with the Readings, Both Textual and Marginal, of Griesbach, and the Variations of the Editions of Stephens, 1550, Beza, 1598, the Elzevir, 1633.* Narrow edn (London: S. Bagster and Sons, 1861). 'LW – signer, annotations. VW – annotations' (Pullman catalogue notes).

17. *Biblia Sacra* (Amsterdam: Schipper, 1669).

18. *The Four Gospels and the Acts of the Apostles, in the Authorized Version.* World's Classics, 344. (London: Oxford University Press, 1929). 'VW – binder' (Pullman catalogue notes). *The Old Testament, A. D. 1885.* World's Classics, pp. 385–8 (London: Milford; Oxford: Oxford University Press, 1931), 4 vols. 'VW – binder' (Pullman catalogue notes).

19. Froula, 'St. Virginia's Epistle', p. 47.

20. C. E. Stephen, *Quaker Strongholds,* pp. 95–6, emphasis added.

21. As Snaith suggests, this was probably The National Committee on the Cause and Cure of War (1924–41) (editor's note, *3G* 280). The NCCCW was comprised of nine women's organisations, including religious ones such as the Council of Women for Home Missions, the National Woman's Christian Temperance Union and the National Council of Jewish Women. It held annual conferences debating specific propositions and, given its composition, the topic that 'war is unchristian' is not unlikely. See <https://www.swarthmore.edu/library/peace/CDGA.M-R/ncccw.html> (last accessed 13 December 2017).

22. Venn, *Complete Duty,* pp. 487, 490, 492. Stephen, *Hours in a Library,* 3, 139.

23. Andrew McNeillie notes that the Bishop's article has not been identified (*E4* 329), so this may be an invention. However, Woolf's point is that a busy bishop has dashed off a piece of journalism and not given the matter sufficient consideration. Compare this with her dismissive comment on Dean Inge's journalism (*3G* 153).

24. L. Woolf, *Downhill All the Way,* pp. 205–6.

25. Briggs, *Inner Life,* p. 156.

26. Lewis, *Religious Experience and the Modernist Novel*, p. 17.
27. Fernald, 'Woolf and Intertextuality', p. 55.
28. Hutcheon, *A Theory of Parody*, p. 7.
29. Griesinger, 'Religious Belief in a Secular Age', p. 455.
30. Barton and Muddiman, *Oxford Bible Commentary*, p. 920.
31. Ibid., p. 884.
32. The Prayer after Communion in *The Book of Common Prayer* states that 'we are very members incorporate in the mystical body of thy Son, which is the blessed company of all faithful people' (p. 258). 'One body' is a quotation from 1 Corinthians 12:12 and Romans 12:5.

Conclusion: A New Religion?

This study of Woolf's engagement with Christian culture has revealed a set of deeply ambivalent responses. Woolf was certainly sceptical of Christianity as an organised religion and she was aware of the role that its mores, clergy, architecture, art, traditions and scripture had played in supporting patriarchy. However, she saw this bias as a distortion of the faith rather than integral to it, for a key point within Woolf's argument with institutionalised Christianity is that the church, both historically and in her own time, was failing to live up to its ethical calling and indeed failing to live up to biblical principles, particularly in its treatment of women and its inability to prevent war. She was therefore frustrated by the way in which the hierarchical organisation of the church led to its apparent failure to meet spiritual needs.

In tension with this scepticism, Woolf had a sense of the sacred that *could* be accessed through Christian culture, if its artefacts were read differently. Thus, while robustly challenging the professional status of the clergyman, Woolf recognised the important roles that ministry should play in terms of pastoral care, nurturing spirituality, teaching and administering the sacraments. Woolf also recognised the importance of church buildings for culture and a sense of belonging. She saw cathedrals as spaces where people could find spiritual refreshment and the home as a space that could facilitate contemplation and creativity. While critiquing representations of the Virgin Mary for their role in reifying impossible expectations of women, Woolf also recognised the sacred character of womanhood and family relationships, and the important function of the Madonna in expressing this. While dismissing patriarchal ideals of sexual purity, Woolf also valued chastity as a means of sexual liberation from men. The crux of Woolf's reaction to Christian culture is her view of the

Bible: having dismissed it as scripture, she was able to read it critically but also imaginatively as literature, to probe more deeply into
questions about the value of life.

We are now in a position to provide a nuanced account of Woolf's
views and how they sit with Christian ideas. It is inaccurate to describe
Woolf as atheist: she speculates far too often about the existence and
nature of God for us to say that she had a thoroughgoing and consistent conviction that God did not exist. It is inaccurate to describe her
as irreligious: she shows far too much empathy with believers and
far too much curiosity about religion for this. It is also inaccurate
to describe her as consistently anti-religious, although she certainly
voiced anti-religious sentiments at times. Equally, it would be dis-
ingenuous to suggest that Woolf had leanings towards Christianity:
for all the fascination she shows towards its cultural expressions, her
responses are always tempered with resistance and a sense of dissatisfaction with its answers on matters of key importance. Woolf's
verdict on conventional literature that 'the current answers don't
do' (D1 259) applies equally to her views on conventional belief. It
would also be too simplistic a distinction to see Woolf as rejecting
Christianity as an organised religion while embracing a spirituality
that could be found outside the confines of faith (a position described
by sociologists of religion such as Linda Woodhead as 'spiritual but
not religious')[1] for this would not do justice to the extent to which
she used Christian ideas and culture as a point of reference for thinking about spiritual matters.

A useful way of understanding Woolf's complex response to Christianity is to see it as a form of feminist theology: just as she is widely
recognised for having paved the way for the concerns and arguments
of the second wave of feminism, so she also anticipated more radical
approaches to religion. Feminist theology is not an apologetic for
Christianity that makes the religion palatable to feminists. Rather, the
discipline encompasses a whole range of critiques of religious texts,
doctrines and principles from a feminist perspective, often coming to
quite radical conclusions. Natalie K. Watson describes it as the 'critical, contextual, constructive, and creative re-reading and re-writing
of Christian theology'.[2] As Nicola Slee's definition shows, it has an
important place in the wider project of feminism: 'Feminist theology,
or more properly, *theologies*, has emerged in modern times as a challenge to the male bias in religion and society as a whole.'[3] As we have
seen, Woolf makes critiques of this kind and her arguments offered
ways of rewriting the patriarchal, imperial scripts that had been so

influential on society, as a way of changing society and its ideologies. Woolf had female antecedents in this quest, notably Caroline Emelia Stephen, who offered ways of reconfiguring the ideas and images of Evangelical Christianity, and Jane Harrison, who challenged Christianity by revealing its antecedents in alternative religious systems and by critiquing the construction of the notion of a 'god'.

Woolf's clearest statement of her feminist theology is found in a key passage in *Three Guineas*, which sums up important ideas expressed throughout her work:

> By reading the New Testament in the first place and next those divines and historians whose works are all easily accessible to the daughters of educated men, they would make it their business to have some knowledge of the Christian religion and its history. Further they would inform themselves of the practice of that religion by attending Church services, by analysing the spiritual and intellectual value of sermons; by criticizing the opinions of men whose profession is religion as freely as they would criticize the opinions of any other body of men. Thus they would be creative in their activities, not merely critical. By criticizing education they would help to create a civilized society which protects culture and intellectual liberty. By criticizing religion they would attempt to free the religious spirit from its present servitude and would help, if need be, to create a new religion based it might well be upon the New Testament, but, it might well be, very different from the religion now erected upon that basis. (*3G* 189)

The first sentence in this passage shows Woolf's awareness of how church tradition had evolved in ways that reinforced patriarchy and its values, including the way in which the Bible had been interpreted to support the status quo. It was therefore important to test the works of 'divines and historians' against the Bible to see the bias of their interpretation. Importantly, Woolf saw such works as 'easily accessible to the daughters of educated men': in her case, this involved the family legacy of the Clapham Sect, including the vast library she had inherited. As we have seen, Woolf was repeatedly concerned with making a riposte to Clapham and its values, including critiquing their views of God and the Bible; she began this critique in conjunction with Caroline Emelia Stephen, who was herself closely involved in freeing herself from the constraints that her Evangelical upbringing had placed upon her.

Woolf also notes that women should inform themselves of the practice of that religion by attending Church services, by analysing sermons, both for their spiritual and their intellectual content. Woolf did this, as we have seen in her descriptions of chapel services in *The Voyage Out*, *Jacob's Room*, and *The Waves* and the funeral in *The Years*. The church remained important both in politics and in society throughout Woolf's lifetime, and the exclusively male clergy remained integral to middle-class life. In this key statement, Woolf advocates rejecting any claims the clergy may have had to special treatment, instead insisting that they should be criticised along with any other professional group. The clergymen in Woolf's novels are mostly ineffectual, opinionated and ignorant; the only sacramental figure is Mrs Ramsay presiding over her dinner party: a prototype woman priest.

Woolf also stresses in this passage that women need to be creative and not merely critical. Women must *criticise* education in order to *create* a 'civilized society'; in 'criticizing religion' they would perform the creative task of liberating the religious spirit to '*create* a new religion'. This reflects the project of '*critical*' and '*creative* re-reading and re-writing of Christian theology' that Watson sees as key to feminist theology. Woolf's statement here also suggests that the new religion need not be entirely different: it could be created 'if need be', and 'it might well be' based on the New Testament, though equally 'it might well be' different from the Christian religion as it stands. By emphasising creativity, Woolf shows that analysing religion is not merely about eradicating what has gone before, but about opening up new creative possibilities. Creativity goes hand in hand with critique.

Critical creativity is particularly pertinent to Woolf's use of the Bible and here we need to acknowledge the importance of her allusive techniques. Anne Fernald has described Woolf's allusiveness as operating on every level,[4] and Woolf savours fragmentary verses such as the phrase from the funeral service ('I am the resurrection and the life') that bursts out 'like music' (Y 76), as well as using biblical stories in her Passion Trilogy to enact what Linda Hutcheon has described as 'extended repetition with critical difference.'[5] Woolf's creative use of the Bible liberates it from Evangelical understandings of scripture: it is not fixed and does not express everlasting and unalterable truths, but it is instead open for revision and reinterpretation for the present time.

The aspect of Christian theology that Woolf subjected to the most intense scrutiny was the idea of Heaven and the afterlife. Woolf revises the Evangelical understanding that eternal life is the reward for living according to the social mores that had enshrined

separate spheres and female submission. Instead, she reinterprets
and reappropriates biblical images in her work to explore the value
of human beings, including women, and their relationships in the
present (a view set out by F. D. Maurice in the nineteenth century,
but which came to be held more widely as the First World War challenged popular piety).

Woolf consistently subjected Christian consolations to trenchant
criticism by showing that they cannot mitigate the realities of death
and loss. Writing was Woolf's way of preserving her loved ones in literary works and this partly involved rescuing their legacy from other
people's narratives, in particular, seeking to reclaim Julia Stephen
from Leslie's hagiography. Conversely, Woolf was haunted by her
dead loved ones: the problem for her was often not a case that they
were dead, but that they could not be forgotten. In writing about
them repeatedly (in her novels, and as late as 'A Sketch of the Past'),
Woolf sought to deal with the trauma of her bereavements. And so,
in rejecting Christian ideas of an afterlife, Woolf also explored the
idea, in *The Waves* that while death brought an individual life to an
end, human beings and humanity itself are part of a greater reality. It
is significant therefore that Woolf considered dedicating *The Waves*
to Thoby but that the dedication did not make it any further than her
diary. Woolf revived Thoby in Percival but she also tried to let him
go, recognising the incorporation of the individual within the cosmic
scheme of things.

Another aspect of Woolf's explorations that can be related to
feminist theology is her lifelong speculation about the existence and
nature of God. Woolf thought about the concept of 'God' in a complex and sophisticated way, and she had different responses to the
different aspects of the Trinitarian God. She anticipates Mary Daly's
argument from *Beyond God the Father*, by criticising the patriarchal conceptions of God that were used to reify male power. Woolf
therefore denounces the way in which patriarchy has constructed its
own notion of God, arguing that unwritten laws of behaviour that
had been thought of as 'natural' or 'God-given', can be seen to be
produced and reproduced by those in power: 'it is beginning to be
agreed that they were not laid down by "God", who is now very
generally held to be a conception, of patriarchal origin, valid only for
certain races, at certain stages and times' (*3G* 250, n42).

Woolf was also critical of the idea of a benevolent or omnipotent creator, because there is so much suffering, illness, death in the
world. Unlike Leslie Stephen who had argued that the presence of
evil in the world called the existence of God into doubt,[6] Woolf

often entertained the idea that there might be a vindictive force that could be spiteful, wrathful and rebuking (*D1* 166; *L2* 548; *D1* 123), or 'those ruffians, the Gods' that Clarissa Dalloway so resented (*MD* 70). However, in contrast to this, Woolf frequently envisaged a female creator figure, as in the opening scene of *The Waves,* and persistent female presences on the peripheries of vision in that novel, such as the lady writing or the nursemaid who shows the picture-book; or when she attributes divine or supernatural qualities to Violet Dickinson, Vita Sackville-West, Ethel Smyth and even, by way of Mrs Ramsay, to Julia Stephen. While Woolf could not conceive of a loving creator-god, she could recognise divinity in women and in the love between women.

Woolf was intrigued by the story of God the Son, whom she consistently referred to by the word 'Christ' and whom she invoked as a moral arbiter. As we have seen, Woolf reflects different aspects of Christ's story within her work, from sacrificial victim through to judge, and she refracts these onto both male and female characters, echoing a feminist theological view that, in Slee's words, 'both maleness and femaleness in their full humanity can image and symbolise God.'[7] Christ represents a human character, whose story took place in time: a human life and death that can be replicated in the stories of others. But in retelling his story, fragmented over many characters, Woolf denies the significance of the sacrifice 'once for all' (Hebrews 10:10). Finally, Woolf also conceived of the divine as spirit: from the 'life or spirit, truth or reality' that she wanted to capture in 'Modern Fiction' through to the 'religious spirit' she urged women to set free in *Three Guineas.*

Woolf also anticipates feminist theologians on the concept of redemption. Feminist theologians such as Rosemary Radford Ruether have challenged ideas of the atonement (the once for all sacrifice of Christ for the sins of the world), seeing redemption in other ways, such as justice and peace for all humanity, including all women. This is seen in Woolf's inclusive vision in *Three Guineas* that 'as a woman my country is the whole world', and that even if a love of country intervenes, it should 'serve her to give to England first what she desires of peace and freedom for the whole world' (*3G* 185). Woolf saw that such peace and freedom would begin with liberation from patriarchal interpretations of Christianity. Woolf's arguments therefore offered ways of rewriting the scripts that had been so influential on society, as a way of changing society and its ideologies. In critiquing, changing and adapting Christian concepts, then, she worked towards a committed literature that valued all humanity.

Feminist theologians often emphasise working towards goals in the here and now, and not waiting until the hereafter. However, for Woolf this was not only a social or political vision, but it involved the possibility of spiritual experience in the present moment and so she frequently wrote of making connections with eternity within the present time, seen in moments such as Clarissa Dalloway's reaction to the death of Septimus, Mrs Ramsay's meditation before the lighthouse and sacramental dinner party, Woolf's mystical experiences at Rodmell, particularly in the run-up to writing *The Waves,* and Delia Pargiter's brief moment of understanding at her mother's funeral.

Woolf built on these insights in 'A Sketch of the Past' when she articulated the concept of 'moments of being'. Although this is the passage that leads her to her emphatic statement that 'there is no God', as we have seen this does not deny divinity, but relocates it in this world: 'we are the thing itself.' The key importance of this passage, however, is that it affirms her beliefs about writing. Woolf frequently described writing as a worthwhile activity, as in *A Room of One's Own,* where she presents it as something that gives purpose to life; she saw it as a way of preserving her loved ones and, as Leonard Woolf suggested, of gaining immortality for herself. However, in her diary entry on finishing *The Waves,* and then in 'A Sketch of the Past', she presents her fullest conception of how she saw her own writing practice as an activity that involved denying her own agency to express something greater than herself. Writing was Woolf's vocation. It was a spiritual activity in and of itself.

Notes

1. See, for example, Heelas and Woodhead, *The Spiritual Revolution.*
2. Watson, *Feminist Theology,* pp. 2–3.
3. Slee, *Faith and Feminism*, p. 1.
4. Fernald, 'Woolf and Intertextuality', p. 55.
5. Hutcheon, *A Theory of Parody,* p. 7.
6. Stephen, *History of English Thought,* 1, 328.
7. Slee, *Faith and Feminism*, p. 30.

Bibliography

Primary Sources: Works by Virginia Woolf (in order of publication)

Woolf, Virginia. *The Voyage Out* [1915]. Ed. and intro. Lorna Sage. Oxford: Oxford University Press, 1992.

—. *Night and Day* [1919]. Ed. and intro. Suzanne Raitt. Oxford: Oxford University Press, 1992.

—. *Jacob's Room* [1922]. Ed. and intro. Kate Flint. Oxford: Oxford University Press, 1992.

—. *Mrs Dalloway* [1925]. Ed. and intro. Anne E. Fernald. Cambridge: Cambridge University Press, 2015.

—. *To the Lighthouse* [1927]. Ed. and intro. Margaret Drabble. Oxford: Oxford University Press, 1992.

—. *Orlando* [1928]. Ed. and intro. Rachel Bowlby. Oxford: Oxford University Press, 1992.

—. *A Room of One's Own and Three Guineas* [1929, 1938]. Ed. and intro. Anna Snaith. Oxford: Oxford University Press, 2015.

—. *The Waves* [1931]. Ed. and intro. Michael Herbert and Susan Sellers. Cambridge: Cambridge University Press, 2011.

—. *The Years* [1937]. Ed. and intro. Anna Snaith. Cambridge: Cambridge University Press, 2012.

—. *Between the Acts* [1941]. Ed. and intro. Mark Hussey. Cambridge: Cambridge University Press, 2011.

—. *Collected Essays*. 4 vols. London: Hogarth Press, 1966–7.

—. *Letters*. Ed. Nigel Nicolson, asst ed. Joanne Trautmann Banks, 6 vols. London: Hogarth Press, 1975–80.

—. *Diary*. Ed. Anne Olivier Bell, asst ed. Andrew McNeillie, 5 vols. London: Hogarth Press, 1977–84.

—. *Friendship's Gallery*. Ed. Ellen Hawkes. *Twentieth Century Literature*. 25 (1979): 270–302.

—. *Moments of Being: Unpublished Autobiographical Writings*. Ed. and intro. Jeanne Schulkind. 2nd edn. London: Hogarth Press, 1985.

—. *Essays*. Ed. Andrew McNeillie and Stuart Clarke, 6 vols. London: Hogarth Press, 1986–2011.

—. *The Complete Shorter Fiction*. Ed. Susan Dick. London: Grafton, 1987.

—. *The London Scene*. London: Snowbooks, 2004.

—. *A Passionate Apprentice: The Early Journals 1897–1909*. Ed. M. A. Leaska, pref. Hermione Lee, intro. David Bradshaw. London: Pimlico, 2004.

Other Primary Sources

Addleshaw, G. W. O. and Etchells, F. *The Architectural Setting of Anglican Worship*. London: Faber, 1948.

Alighieri, Dante. *The Inferno*. Trans. Mark Musa. Harmondsworth: Penguin, 1971.

Arnold, Matthew. 'Culture and Anarchy (1869)'. In *Selected Prose*, ed. P. J. Keating. Harmondsworth: Penguin, 1970, pp. 202–300.

Auden, W. H. 'A Consciousness of Reality'. Review of *A Writer's Diary*, *New York Review of Books*, 6 March 1954.

Austen, Jane. *Pride and Prejudice* [1813]. Ed. Tony Tanner. Harmondsworth: Penguin, 1972.

Boswell, James. *Boswell's Life of Johnson* [1791]. London: Oxford University Press, 1953.

Braithwaite, R. B. *The State of Religious Belief: An Inquiry Based on the 'Nation and Athanaeum' Questionnaire*. London: Hogarth Press, 1927.

Brontë, Anne. *Agnes Grey* [1847]. Ed. and intro. Angeline Goreau. Harmondsworth: Penguin, 1988.

Brontë, Charlotte. *Shirley* [1849]. Ed. Andrew and Judith Hook. Harmondsworth: Penguin, 1974.

Bumpus, T. Francis. *London Churches Ancient and Modern*, First and Second Series. London: T. Werner Laurie, 1908.

Church of England. *The Book of Common Prayer*. Cambridge: Cambridge University Press, 2004.

Dearmer, Percy (ed.). *Christianity and the Crisis*. London: Victor Gollancz, 1933.

Ditchfield, P. H., illus. Herbert Railton, J. A. Symington, H. M. James, H. Crickman, etc. *The Cathedrals of Great Britain: Their History and Architecture*. London: Dent, 1932.

Eliot, T. S. *The Idea of a Christian Society*. London: Faber, 1939.

Ellis, Sarah Stickney. *The Women of England: Their Social Duties, and Domestic Habits* (n.d. [1843?]). Extract in Josephine M. Guy (ed.), *The Victorian Age: An Anthology of Sources and Documents*. London and New York: Routledge, 1998, pp. 495–504.

Forster, E. M. *What I Believe*. Hogarth Sixpenny Pamphlets No. 1. London: Hogarth Press, 1939.

Fry, Roger. *Cézanne: A Study of His Development.* 2nd edn. London: Hogarth Press, 1952.

Hare, Augustus. *Walks in London.* 6th edition, 2 vols. n.p., 1894.

Harrison, Jane. *Epilegomena to the Study of the Greek Religion.* Cambridge: Cambridge University Press, 1921.

Holy Bible: King James Version. Reference Edition. Nashville, TX: Thomas Nelson, 1989.

Hügel, Baron Friedrich von. *The Reality of God and Religion and Agnosticism.* Trans. Edmund G. Gardner. London and Toronto: J. M. Dent, 1931.

Jones, Rufus M. *The Latter Periods of Quakerism,* vol. 2. London: Macmillan, 1921.

Maitland, Frederic W. *The Life and Letters of Leslie Stephen.* London: Duckworth, 1906.

Marvell, Andrew. *The Complete Poems.* Ed. Elizabeth Story Donno. Harmondsworth: Penguin, 1972.

Masterman, C. F. G. *The Condition of England.* 4th edn. London: Methuen, 1910.

Milton, John. *Paradise Lost.* Ed. Alastair Fowler. Harlow: Longman, 1968.

Murry, John Middleton. *Heaven – and Earth.* London: Jonathan Cape, 1938.

Muthesius, Hermann. *The English House,* 1904–5, 2nd edn, 1908. Ed. and intro. Dennis Sharp, pref. Julius Posener, trans. Janet Seligman. Oxford: BSP Professional Books, 1987.

Ruskin, John. *Sesame and Lilies: I: Of Kings' Treasures; II: Of Queens' Gardens* [1864]. Ed. A. E. Roberts. London: Macmillan, 1910.

—. *The Seven Lamps of Architecture,* with illustrations by the author. London: Routledge, 1907.

Sackville-West, V. *The Letters of Vita Sackville-West to Virginia Woolf,* ed. Louise De Salvo and Mitchell A. Leaska. London: Hutchinson, 1984.

Smyth, Ethel. *Impressions that Remained* [1919]. New York: Alfred A. Knopf, 1946.

Stephen, C. E. *Quaker Strongholds.* London: Kegan Paul, Trench Trübner, 1890.

— (ed.). *The First Sir James Stephen: Letters with Biographical Notes.* Private publication, 1906.

—. *Light Arising.* Cambridge: Heffer, 1908.

—. *The Vision of Faith and Other Essays.* Cambridge: Heffer, 1911.

Stephen, James. *The Slavery of the British West India Colonies Delineated.* London: Butterworth, 1824.

—. *England Enslaved by her Own Slave Colonies: An Address to the Electors and People of the United Kingdom.* Pamphlet. London: Hatchard and Arch, 1826.

—. *The Memoirs of James Stephen: Written by Himself for the Use of his Children.* Ed. and intro. Merle M. Bevington. Foreword Canon Charles Smith. London: Hogarth Press, 1954.

Stephen, Sir James. *Essays in Ecclesiastical Biography*. 5th edn. London: Longman, Green, Reader and Dyer, 1869.

Stephen, James Fitzjames. *Liberty, Equality, Fraternity*. London: Smith, Elder, 1873.

—. *A History of the English Criminal Law*. 3 vols. London: Macmillan, 1883.

Stephen, Julia. *Julia Duckworth Stephen: Stories for Children, Essays for Adults*. Ed. Diane F. Gillespie and Elizabeth Steele. New York: Syracuse University Press, 1987.

Stephen, Leslie. *History of English Thought in the Eighteenth Century*. 2 vols. London: Smith & Elder, 1876.

—. 'An Agnostic's Apology'. In *An Agnostic's Apology and Other Essays*. London: Smith & Elder, 1893.

—. *The Life of Sir James Fitzjames Stephen*. London: Smith, Elder, 1895.

—. *Social Rights and Duties: Addresses to Ethical Societies*. 2 vols. London: Swan Sonnenschein, 1896.

—. *Sir Leslie Stephen's Mausoleum Book*. Intro. Alan Bell. Oxford: Clarendon Press, 1977.

—. *Hours in a Library*. 3 vols. London: Smith & Elder, 1874–9.

Stephen, Sarah. *Passages from a Life of a Daughter at Home*. 1846, n.p.

Stephen, Thoby. *Compulsory Chapel: An Appeal to Undergraduates on Behalf of Religious Liberty and Intellectual Independence*. n.d., n.p.

Venn, Henry. *The Complete Duty of Man*. London: Newbery, 1763.

Warton, Rev. T., Bentham, Rev. J., Grose, Captain and Milner, Rev. J. *Essays on Gothic Architecture*. London: Architectural Library, 1800.

Weber, Max. *The Protestant Ethic and the Spirit of Capitalism*. London: Routledge Classics, 2001.

Woolf, Leonard. *Beginning Again: An Autobiography of the Years 1911–1918*. London: Hogarth Press, 1964.

—. *Downhill All the Way: An Autobiography of the Years 1919–1939*. London: Hogarth Press, 1967.

Secondary Sources

Andrews, Charles. 'Under the Volute: *Jacob's Room*, Pacifism, and the Church of England'. In Diana Royer and Madelyn Detloff (eds), *Selected Papers of the Seventeenth Annual Conference on Virginia Woolf*. Clemson, SC: Clemson Digital Press, 2010, pp. 64–9.

Annan, Noel. *Leslie Stephen: The Godless Victorian*. New York: Random House, 1984.

Ansari, Humayun. *The Infidel Within: Muslims in Britain Since 1800*. London: Hurst, 2004.

Barrett, Eileen. 'Matriarchal Myth on a Patriarchal Stage: Virginia Woolf's *Between the Acts*'. *Twentieth-Century Literature*, 33:1 (1987): 18–37.

Barton, J. and Muddiman, J. *The Oxford Bible Commentary*. Oxford: Oxford University Press, 2001.

Bell, Quentin. *Virginia Woolf: A Biography*, 2 vols. London: Hogarth Press, 1972.

Birch, Dinah. *Our Victorian Education*. Oxford: Blackwell, 2008.

Blair, Emily. *Virginia Woolf and the Nineteenth-Century Domestic Novel*. New York: State University of New York Press, 2007.

Bradley, Ian. *The Call to Seriousness: The Evangelical Impact on the Victorians*. London: Jonathan Cape, 1976.

Bradshaw, David, 'Beneath *The Waves*: Diffusionism and Cultural Pessimism', *Essays in Criticism*, 63:3 (2013): 317–43.

Briggs, Julia. *Virginia Woolf: An Inner Life*. Orlando: Harcourt, 2005.

—. *Reading Virginia Woolf*. Edinburgh: Edinburgh University Press, 2006.

Buckridge, Patrick. 'Books as Gifts: The Meaning and Function of a Personal Library.' *Australian Literary Studies* 27 (2012): 59–73.

Carr, Wesley. *The Priestlike Task*. London: SPCK, 1985.

Chambers, R. L. *The Novels of Virginia Woolf*. Edinburgh and London: Oliver and Boyd, 1947.

Clements, Elicia, 'Reconfigured Terrain: Aural Architecture in *Jacob's Room* and *The Years*'. In Elizabeth F. Evans and Sarah E. Cornish (eds), *Woolf and the City: Selected Papers of the Nineteenth Annual Conference on Virginia Woolf*. Clemson, SC: Clemson Digital Press, 2010, pp. 71–6.

Colaiaco, James A. *James Fitzjames Stephen and the Crisis of Victorian Thought*. London: Macmillan, 1983.

Curtis, V. *Virginia Woolf's Women*. Stroud: Sutton, 2003.

Daly, Mary. *Beyond God the Father: Towards a Philosophy of Women's Liberation* [1973]. London: The Women's Press, 1986.

de Gay, Jane. 'Behind the Purple Triangle: Art and Iconography in *To the Lighthouse*'. *Woolf Studies Annual 5*. New York: Pace University Press, 1999, pp. 1–23.

—. *Virginia Woolf and the Clergy*, Virginia Woolf Birthday Lecture. Southport: Virginia Woolf Society of Great Britain, 2009.

Delgarno, Emily. *Virginia Woolf and the Visible World*. Cambridge: Cambridge University Press, 2007.

Dell, Marion. *Virginia Woolf's Influential Forebears*. Basingstoke: Palgrave, 2015.

Edwards, David L. *Christian England*. 3 vols. Vol. 3: *From the Eighteenth Century to the First World War*. London: Collins, 1984.

Faber, Alyda. '"The Shock of Love" and the Visibility of "Indecent" Pain: Reading the Woolf–Raverat Correspondence'. In Anna Burrells, Steve Ellis, Deborah Parsons and Kathryn Simpson (eds), *Woolfian Boundaries, Selected Papers from the 16th Annual Conference on Virginia Woolf*. Clemson, SC: Clemson University Digital Press, 2007, pp. 58–64.

Fernald, Anne. 'Woolf and Intertextuality'. In B. Randall and J. Goldman (eds), *Virginia Woolf in Context*. Cambridge: Cambridge University Press, 2012, pp. 52–64.

Flint, Kate. 'Drawing the Line: Lily, Painting and *To the Lighthouse*'. *English Review* 4:1 (1993): 38–41.

Froula, Christine. 'St. Virginia's Epistle to an English Gentleman; Or, Sex, Violence, and the Public Sphere in Woolf's *Three Guineas*.' *Tulsa Studies in Women's Literature* 13:1 (1994): 27–56.

—. 'Mrs. Dalloway's Postwar Elegy: Women, War and the Art of Mourning,' *Modernism/Modernity* 9:1 (2002): 125–63.

Gill, Sean. *Women and the Church of England: From the Eighteenth Century to the Present*. London: SPCK, 1994.

Gilliat-Ray, S. *Muslims in Britain: An Introduction*. Cambridge: Cambridge University Press, 2010.

Gordon, L. *Virginia Woolf: A Writer's Life*. Oxford: Oxford University Press, 1984.

Gough, V. '"That Razor Edge of Balance": Virginia Woolf and Mysticism', *Woolf Studies Annual 5* (1999): 57–77.

Griesinger, Emily. 'Religious Belief in a Secular Age: Literary modernism and Virginia Woolf's *Mrs. Dalloway*.' *Christianity and Literature* 64 (2015): 438–64.

Groover, Kristina. 'Enacting the Sacred in *Mrs Dalloway*'. *Virginia Woolf Miscellany* 80 (2011): 11–13.

Harris, Alexandra. *Virginia Woolf*. London: Thames and Hudson, 2011.

Hastings, Adrian. *A History of English Christianity 1920–1990*. London: SCM Press, 1991.

Heelas, Paul and Woodhead, Linda. *The Spiritual Revolution: Why Religion is Giving Way to Spirituality*. Oxford: Wiley-Blackwell, 2004.

Heininge, Kathleen, 'The Search for God: Virginia Woolf and Caroline Emelia Stephen', *Virginia Woolf Miscellany* 80 (2011): 20–21.

—. *Reflections: Virginia Woolf and Her Quaker Aunt, Caroline Stephen*. New York: Peter Lang, 2016.

Hills, Helen. 'Architecture as Metaphor for the Body: The Case of Female Convents in Early Modern Italy'. In Louise Durning and Richard Wrigley (eds), *Gender and Architecture*. Chichester: Wiley, 2000, pp. 67–112.

Hindrichs, Cheryl. 'Feminist Optics and Avant-Garde Cinema: Germaine Dulac's "The Smiling Madame Beudet" and Virginia Woolf's "Street Haunting"'. *Feminist Studies* 35 (2009): 294–322.

Howard, Douglas L. 'Virginia Woolf'. In Rebecca Lemon, Emma Mason, Jonathan Roberts and Christopher Rowland (eds), *The Blackwell Companion to the Bible in English Literature*. Chichester: Wiley-Blackwell, 2009, pp. 629–41.

Humm, Maggie. 'Woolf and the Visual'. In Jessica Berman (ed.), *A Companion to Virginia Woolf*. Chichester: Wiley Blackwell, 2016, pp. 291–304.

Hussey, Mark. *The Singing of the Real World: The Philosophy of Virginia Woolf's Fiction*. Columbus: Ohio State University Press, 1986.

Hutcheon, Linda. *A Theory of Parody: The Teachings of Twentieth-Century Art Forms*. New York and London: Methuen, 1985.

Hylson-Smith, Kenneth. *The Churches in England from Elizabeth I to Elizabeth II*. 3 vols. Vol. 3: 1833–1998. London: SCM Press 1998.

Irigaray, Luce. *An Ethics of Sexual Difference*. Trans. C. Burke and G. C. Gill. London: Continuum, 2004.

Kane, Julie. 'Varieties of Mystical Experience in the Writings of Virginia Woolf'. *Twentieth Century Literature*, 41:4, 1995, pp. 328–49.

Knight, Christopher J. 'The God of Love is Full of Tricks: Virginia Woolf's Vexed Relation to the Tradition of Christianity'. *Religion and Literature* 39:1 (2007): 27–46.

—. *Omissions Are not Accidents: Modern Apophaticism from Henry James to Jacques Derrida*. Toronto: University of Toronto Press, 2010.

Kristeva, Julia. 'Stabat Mater'. In T. Moi (ed.), *The Kristeva Reader*. Oxford: Blackwell, 1986, pp. 160–86.

Kupar, Adam. *Incest and Influence: The Private Life of Bourgeois England*. Cambridge, MA: Harvard University Press, 2009.

Lackey, Michael. Review of Keith Clements (ed.), *The Moot Papers: Faith, Freedom and Society 1938–1947*, *Modernism/Modernity* 17 (2010): 959–61.

—. *The Modernist God State: A Literary Study of the Nazis' Christian Reich*. New York: Bloomsbury, 2012.

Latour, Bruno. 'The Berlin Key or How to Do Words With Things'. In P. M. Graves-Brown (ed.), *Matter, Materiality and Modern Culture*. London: Routledge, 1991, pp. 10–21.

Lee, Hermione. *Virginia Woolf*. London: Chatto & Windus, 1996.

Lewis, Pericles. 'Churchgoing in the Modern Novel'. *Modernism/Modernity* 11:4 (2004): 669–94.

—. *Religious Experience and the Modernist Novel*. Cambridge: Cambridge University Press, 2010.

Lilienfeld, Jane. '"The Deceptiveness of Beauty": Mother Love and Mother Hate in *To the Lighthouse*'. *Twentieth-Century Literature* 23:3 (1977): 345–76.

Lipscomb, Patrick C., III. 'James Stephen', *Oxford Dictionary of National Biography*, <http://www.oxforddnb.com/view/article/26373> (last accessed 13 May 2013).

Lockhart, J. G. *Cosmo Gordon Lang*. Edinburgh: Hodder and Stoughton, 1949.

Love, Jean O. *Worlds in Consciousness: Mythopoetic Thought in the Novels of Virginia Woolf*. Berkeley: University of California Press, 1970.

MacCulloch, D. *A History of Christianity: The First Three Thousand Years*. London: Allen Lane, 2009.

Maidstone, R. J. *Hagia Sophia: Architecture, Structure and Liturgy of Justinian's Great Church*. London: Thames and Hudson, 1988.

Marcus, Jane. *Virginia Woolf and the Languages of Patriarchy*. Bloomington: Indiana University Press, 1987.

Marwick, Arthur. *The Deluge: British Society and the First World War*. New York: Norton, 1970.

Mavor, Carol. *Pleasures Taken: Performances of Sexuality and Loss in Victorian Photographs*. Durham, NC and London: Duke University Press, 1995.

McMahon, David. 'Mindfulness, Literature and the Affirmation of Ordinary Life'. In *The Making of Buddhist Modernism*. Oxford: Oxford University Press, 2008, pp. 215–40.

Metz, Christian. 'Photography and Fetish'. *October* 34 (1985): 81–90.

Mills, Jean. *Virginia Woolf, Jane Ellen Harrison, and the Spirit of Modernist Classicism*. Columbus: Ohio State University Press, 2014.

Murphy-O'Connor, J. 'House-Churches and the Eucharist'. In E. Adams and D. G. Horrell (eds), *Christianity at Corinth*. Louisville, KY: Westminster John Knox Press, 2004.

Oldfield, Sybil. *The Child of Two Atheists: Virginia Woolf's Humanism*. Southport: Virginia Woolf Society of Great Britain, 2006.

Park, Sowon S. 'Apostolic Minds and the Spinning House: Jane Ellen Harrison and Virginia Woolf's Discourse of Alterity'. *Women: A Cultural Review* 22:1 (2011): 69–78.

Paulsell, Stephanie. 'Writing and Mystical Experience in Marguerite D'Ouigh and Virginia Woolf'. *Comparative Literature* 44 (1992): 249–67.

Pickering, Mary. *Auguste Comte: An Intellectual Biography, Vol. 3*. Cambridge: Cambridge University Press, 2009.

Raby, Alister. *Virginia Woolf's Wise and Witty Quaker Aunt: A Biographical Sketch of Caroline Emelia Stephen*. London: Cecil Woolf, 2002.

Raitt, Suzanne. *Vita and Virginia: The Work and Friendship of V. Sackville-West and Virginia Woolf*. Oxford: Oxford University Press, 1993.

—. '"The Tide of Ethel": Femininity as Narrative in the Friendship of Ethel Smyth and Virginia Woolf'. *Critical Quarterly* 30:4 (1988): 3–21.

Recht, Roland. *Believing and Seeing: The Art of Gothic Cathedrals*, trans. Mary Whittall. Chicago: University of Chicago Press, 2008.

Reed, Christopher. *Bloomsbury Rooms: Modernism, Subculture and Domesticity*. New Haven, CT and London: Yale University Press, 2004.

Rendell, Jane, Penner, Barbara and Border, Iain. *Gender Space Architecture: An Interdisciplinary Introduction*. London: Routledge, 2000.

Rice, Charles. *The Emergence of the Interior: Architecture, Modernity, Domesticity*. London: Routledge, 2007.

Roberts, Kathleen. *Alterity and Narrative: Stories and the Negotiation of Western Identities*. New York: SUNY Press, 2007.

Roessel, D. 'The Significance of Constantinople in *Orlando*'. *Papers in Language and Literature* 28 (1992): 398–416.

Rosman, Doreen. *The Evolution of the English Churches 1500–2000*. Cambridge: Cambridge University Press, 2003.

Rosner, Victoria. *Modernism and the Architecture of Private Life*. New York: Columbia University Press, 2005.

Rubin, Miri. *Mother of God: A History of the Virgin Mary*. London: Allen Lane, 2009.

Ruether, Rosemary Radford. *Sexism and God-Talk*. London: SCM Press, 1983.

Sawyer, Deborah. *Women and Religion in the First Christian Centuries*. London: Routledge, 1996.

Schwarz, Hans. *Theology in a Global Context: The Last Two Hundred Years*. Grand Rapids, MI and Cambridge: Eerdmans, 2005.

Scott, Bonnie. 'Ecofeminism, Holism, and the Search for Natural Order in Woolf'. In K. Czarnecki and C. Rohman (eds), *Virginia Woolf and the Natural World*. Clemson, SC: Clemson University Digital Press, 2011, pp. 1–11.

Seeley, T. 'Flights of Fancy: Spatial Digression and Storytelling in *A Room of One's Own*'. In Anna Snaith and Michael H. Whitworth (eds), *Locating Woolf: The Politics of Space and Place*. New York and Basingstoke: Palgrave Macmillan, 2007, pp. 31–45.

Shaw, A. G. L. 'Sir James Stephen', *Oxford Dictionary of National Biography*,<http://www.oxforddnb.com/view/article/26374> (last accessed 30 January 2012).

Showalter, Elaine. *A Literature of Their Own: From Charlotte Brontë to Doris Lessing*. London: Virago, 1978.

Slee, Nicola. *Faith and Feminism: An Introduction to Christian Feminist Theology*. London: Darton, Longman and Todd, 2003.

Smith, K. J. M. 'Sir James Fitzjames Stephen'. *Oxford Dictionary of National Biography*, <http://www.oxforddnb.com/view/article/26375> (last accessed 30 January 2012).

Snaith, A. and Whitworth, Michael H. 'Introduction: Approaches to Space and Place in Woolf'. In Anna Snaith and Michael H. Whitworth (eds), *Locating Woolf: The Politics of Space and Place*. New York and Basingstoke: Palgrave Macmillan, 2007, pp. 1–28.

Snaith, A. *Virginia Woolf: Public and Private Negotiations*. Basingstoke: Macmillan, 2000.

—. 'Wide Circles: The *Three Guineas* Letters'. *Woolf Studies Annual* 6 (2000): 1–12.

— (transcribed and annotated). '*Three Guineas* Letters'. *Woolf Studies Annual* 6 (2000): 13–168.

Spalding, Frances. *Vanessa Bell*. London: Weidenfeld and Nicolson, 1983.

—. *Virginia Woolf: Art, Life and Vision*. London: National Gallery, 2014.

Spurr, Barry. *'Anglo-Catholic in Religion':* T. S. Eliot and Christianity. Cambridge: Lutterworth, 2010.

Stamp, Gavin and Goulancourt, André. *The English House 1860–1914: The Flowering of English Domestic Architecture.* London and Boston, MA: Faber, 1986.

Tickner, Lisa. 'Vanessa Bell: Studland Beach, Domesticity, and "Significant Form".' *Representations* 65 (1999): 63–92.

Tolley, Christopher. *Domestic Biography: The Legacy of Evangelicalism in Four Nineteenth-Century Families.* Oxford: Clarendon Press, 1997.

Tsang, Philip. 'Desecularizing Modernism: Review of Pericles Lewis's *Religious Experience and the Modernist Novel'. Journal of Modern Literature* 35:1 (2011): 193–95.

Vance, Norman. *Bible and Novel: Narrative Authority and the Death of God.* Oxford: Oxford University Press, 2013.

Vicchio, Stephen J. *Job in the Modern World.* Eugene, OR: Wipf and Stock Publishers, 2006.

Ware, Owen. 'Dialectic of the Past/Disjuncture of the Future: Derrida and Benjamin on the Concept of Messianism'. *Journal for Cultural and Religious Theory* 5:2 (2004): 99–114.

Warner, Marina. *Alone of All Her Sex: The Myth and Cult of the Virgin Mary* [1976]. London: Vintage, 2000.

Watson, Natalie K. *Feminist Theology,* Guides to Theology. Cambridge: Eerdmans, 2003.

Wilkinson, Alan. *The Church of England and the First World War.* London: SPCK, 1978.

Wilson, E. *The Sphinx in the City: Urban Life, the Control of Disorder, and Women.* London: Virago, 1991.

Wright, T. R. *D. H. Lawrence and the Bible.* Cambridge: Cambridge University Press, 2000.

Zwerdling, Alex. *Virginia Woolf and the Real World.* Berkeley: University of California Press, 1986.

Online Sources

East London Mosque. <http://www.eastlondonmosque.org.uk/content/history> (last accessed 3 July 2014).

Gillespie, Diane. 'Introduction', *The Library of Leonard and Virginia Woolf* (Pullman: Washington State University Press, 2003), <http://ntserver1.wsulibs.wsu.edu/masc/onlinebooks/woolflibrary/woolflibraryonline.htm> (last accessed 13 December 2017).

Jowett, Benjamin. 'On the Interpretation of Scripture', The Victorian Web, <http://www.victorianweb.org/religion/essays.html> (last accessed 13 December 2017).

King, Julia and Miletic-Vejzovic, Laila (eds). *The Library of Leonard and Virginia Woolf: A Short-Title Catalog* (Pullman: Washington State University Press), <http://www.wsulibs.wsu.edu/holland/masc/OnlineBooks/woolflibrary/woolflibraryonline.htm> (last accessed 30 October 2017).

Lewis, Alison M. 'Caroline Emelia Stephen (1834–1909) and Virginia Woolf (1882–1941): A Quaker Influence on Modern English Literature'. *Quaker Theology* 2:2 (2000), <http://quakertheology.org/issue3-3.html> (last accessed 18 December 2017).

McIntire, Gabrielle. 'Notes Toward Thinking the Sacred in Virginia Woolf's *To the Lighthouse*'. *Modern Horizons* Online Journal (June 2013): 1–11, <http://modernhorizonsjournal.ca/wp-content/uploads/Issues/201306/201306_McIntire.pdf> (last accessed 18 December 2017).

Quakers in Britain, 'Our Faith', <http://www.quaker.org.uk/about-quakers/ourfaith> (last accessed 4 June 2016).

Smith College, *Sir Leslie Stephen's Photograph Album*, <https://www.smith.edu/libraries/libs/rarebook/exhibitions/stephen> (last accessed 13 December 2017).

Swarthmore College Peace Collection <https://www.swarthmore.edu/library/peace/CDGA.M-R/ncccw.html> (last accessed 13 December 2017).

The Thomas Wall Centre: Our History, <http://www.thethomaswallcentre.co.uk/index3.html/index-3.html> (last accessed 21 June 2017).

Weber, Max. 'Science as a Vocation', <http://anthropos-lab.net/wp/wp-content/uploads/2011/12/Weber-Science-as-a-Vocation.pdf> (last accessed 13 June 2017).

Index

abbeys
  Romsey, 117, 141
  Westminster, 16, 58, 65, 114,
    117, 130–8, 140
agnosticism, 4, 56, 58, 61, 99
  and Positivism, 169
  on scripture, 187
  in Stephen family, 1, 3, 15,
    19–20, 23, 38–41, 46, 60,
    114, 166, 171, 188
Alighieri, Dante, 46, 57, 192
  in *The Waves*, 213–14
Andrews, Charles, 130–1
Anglo-Catholicism, 75–6, 77–8,
    80; *see also* Eliot, T. S.
Annan, Noel, 21
anti-slavery, 21, 25–31, 37
Apocalypse, 57, 74
  in *The Waves*, 47, 74, 212,
    214–15
Arnold, Matthew, 32
Arnold, Thomas, 94
atheism, 11, 15–16, 69, 71,
    83–5
Auden, W. H., 9
Austen, Jane, 89

Barrett, Elizabeth, 105
BBC, 69–70
Bell, Angelica, 168
Bell, Clive, 75, 81, 171, 174
Bell, Julian, 168
Bell, Quentin, 9
Bell, Vanessa, 11, 75, 118, 125,
    149–50, 171
  Berwick Church murals, 168
Bennett, Arnold, 196–8
bereavement, 13, 98, 167, 180,
    189, 223
Bible
  Acts, 191
  Apocrypha, 189, 190
  Corinthians, 36, 97, 103–5,
    111, 155, 206
  Ephesians, 33
  Exodus, 197
  Galatians, 103, 196–200
  Genesis, 181, 205, 212–13
  Hebrews, 209, 224
  Isaiah, 181
  Job, 189
  John, 96, 110, 206, 208,
    212

Bible (*cont.*)
  Luke, 213
  Mark, 206, 207
  Matthew, 90, 110, 154, 193, 203, 206, 208, 209
  Proverbs, 67
  Psalms, 96, 192
  Revelation, 212, 214–15
  Romans, 196–200, 201, 203
  Ruth, 188
  Timothy, 103
  Titus, 36, 103
  Tobit, 189–90
bibles, Woolf's collection of, 188–92
Birch, Dinah, 89
Blair, Emily, 146, 148–9, 150, 152
Bodichon, Barbara, 79
Book of Common Prayer, 24, 33, 68, 75, 96, 200
  Woolf's copies of, 112n, 113n
Bowdler, John, 34–5, 36
Bradley, Ian, 23, 24, 29
Braithwaite, R. B., and Leonard Woolf's questionnaire, 56
Briggs, Julia, 9, 118
Brontë, Anne, 89
Brontë, Charlotte, 89, 105
Brontë, Emily, 102–3, 112
Brontë, Rev. Patrick, 105–6
Browne, Sir Thomas, 193
Buckridge, Patrick, 188
Buddhism, 2, 5, 15, 55

Burne-Jones, Edward, *Annunciation*, 168–9
Byron, George Gordon, 91

Calvinism, 4, 20
Camden Society, 127
Cameron, Julia Margaret, 3, 167–8, 176
Carlyle, Thomas, 38
cathedrals, 8, 100, 114–42, 151, 157–61, 219
  Canterbury, 135
  Grenada, 118
  Hagia Sophia, 114, 118–26, 130, 132, 140–1
  Notre Dame, 114, 117
  St Paul's, 19, 68, 114, 117, 128, 130–8, 140, 157, 213
  Salisbury, 114, 117
  Seville, 114, 117
  Siena, 171
  Wells, 2–3, 114
  Westminster, 134, 136
Catholicism, 40, 53, 55, 66, 71, 76, 79, 117, 119, 134, 161, 171–2
  and Virgin Mary, 165–7, 169
  in *To the Lighthouse*, 99–102
Cecil, Nelly, 189
Cecil, Robert, 77
Chambers, R. L., 9
Chekhov, Anton, 53, 199
Chesterton, G. K., 53
Church Missionary Society, 25, 27

churches
  Berwick, 168
  Rodmell, 162
  St Margaret's Westminster,
    157, 200
  St Mary Abbots, 112n, 114
  St Mary Magdalene,
    Warboys, 117
Clapham Sect, 3, 4, 8, 19–51,
    62, 76, 81, 89, 90, 101,
    117, 145–50, 161, 163,
    194–6, 216, 221
Clements, Elicia, 157
Colaiaco, James A., 31
Cole, William, 88, 107–8
Coleridge, S. T., 155, 193,
    194
Collins, Charles, 178
colonialism, 23, 28–31
Comte, Auguste, 40–1, 169
Cowper, William, 39
  'The Castaway', 210
crucifixion, 42, 181; *see also*
    Passion, The
Cunningham, John William, 31

Daly, Mary, 223
damnation, 13, 20, 23, 32, 38,
    46, 197, 201, 216
Darwin, Charles, 1, 4, 19, 175
Davidson, Randall (Archbishop
    of Canterbury), 69–70, 76
Dearmer, Percy, 77, 80, 111
Dell, Marion, 43
Dickinson, Violet, 4, 6, 11,
    19–20, 22, 54, 59–64, 72–6,

    80, 82–3, 88, 117, 118–19,
    124, 125, 188–9, 200, 224
Ditchfield, P. H., 130, 132
Douglas, Leopold Campbell, 89
Duckworth, George, 19, 116–17
Duckworth, Herbert, 190
Duckworth, Stella, 13, 19, 58–9,
    60, 73, 112n, 194

Edgeworth, Richard, 88
Edwards, David, 54–5, 57, 64
Eliot, George, 187
Eliot, T. S., 5, 53, 94
  conversion to Anglo-
    Catholicism, 1, 6, 53,
    75–6, 82
  The Waste Land, 5, 202
Elliott, Henry Venn, 38–9
Ellis, Sarah Stickney, 145–6
Evangelicalism, 3, 4–5, 6, 17,
    19–51, 60, 77, 81, 161, 163,
    192, 194–204, 210, 221, 222

Faber, Alyda, 9, 12
Fernald, Anne, 202, 222
Feuerbach, 187
Forster, E. M., 6, 15–16, 52,
    53, 77, 83, 126
  A Passage to India, 209
  Howards End, 145
Frazer, James, 2
Froula, Christine, 7–8, 10, 103,
    105, 193
Fry, Roger, 4, 98, 165, 168, 174
funerals, 44, 89, 96–8, 117,
    183, 222, 225

Galsworthy, John, 196–8
General Strike, 69–70
Gillespie, Diane, 186
Gisborne, Thomas, 24, 30,
    35–6, 90
Gordon, Lyndall, 118
Gore, Charles (Bishop), 82, 106
Gough, Val, 15, 155
Grant, Duncan, 168
Greene, Graham, 53, 76
Grensted, L. W., 105–6
Griesinger, 9, 16, 204
Groover, Kristina, 16

Hare, Augustus, 128, 139
Harris, Alexandra, 16
Harrison, Jane, 2, 6, 53, 55–6,
    71, 79, 98, 167, 221
Hastings, Adrian, 4, 56, 68, 76
Hawkesforde, Rev. J. B., 88,
    109
Heininge, Kathleen, 15, 43,
    44, 93
Herbert, George, 82
Hills, Helen, 115
Hinduism, 2, 5
Holmes, Oliver Wendell, 19
Holy Communion (Eucharist,
    Mass), 99–102, 206,
    212–13, 214
Howard, Douglas, 9
Hügel, Baron Friedrich von, 55
Hume, David, 99
Humm, Maggie, 182
Hunt, Holman, 213
Hussey, Mark, 9, 11

Hutcheon, Linda, 202, 222
Hylson-Smith, Kenneth, 58, 68

Inge, Dean William, 68, 70,
    106
Irigaray, Luce, 64
Islam, 120–5

Jex-Blake, Sophia, 105
John, Gwen, 53
Johnson, Samuel, 95, 103
Jones, David, 53
Jowett, Benjamin, 187
Joyce, James, 4, 57, 75, 196,
    198–9, 202

Kane, Julie, 15
King's College Chapel, 94–6,
    129–30
Knight, Christopher, 14, 16
Kristeva, Julia, 'Stabat Mater',
    166–7, 170–1, 172, 178, 183

Lackey, Michael, 15–16, 76
Lang, Cosmo (Archbishop of
    Canterbury), 76–80, 89
Latour, Bruno, 190
Lawrence, D. H., 5, 202
Lee, Hermione, 162
Lewis, Alison, 60
Lewis, C. S., 5–6, 53, 76
Lewis, Pericles, 4–6, 10, 14, 16,
    68, 84, 201
Lilienfeld, Jane, 101
Love, Jean, 9
Luther, Martin, 208

MacCulloch, D., 119, 122
McIntire, Gabrielle, 19
McMahon, David, 57
Madonna *see* Virgin Mary
Maidstone, R. J., 119
Maitland, Frederic, 45, 156
Marcus, Jane, 42–3, 46, 155
Martyn, Henry, 36
Marvell, Andrew, 97, 214
Marwick, Arthur, 65
Masterman, C. F. G., 57, 69
Maurice, F. D., 38, 223
Mavor, Carol, 168
Messianic time, 57, 74
Metropolitan Society for
    Befriending Young
    Servants, 42
Metz, Christian, 177
Mills, Jean, 55–6
Milton, John, 131, 192
    *Ode on the Morning of
    Christ's Nativity*, 39–40
    'On His Blindness', 154
    Paradise Lost, 155, 212
motherhood, 73, 101, 149,
    165–85
Murphy-O'Connor, J., 101
Murry, John Middleton, 5–6,
    52–3, 71, 76
mysticism, 5, 9, 12, 14, 15, 56,
    67, 71, 130, 155, 158, 163,
    204, 216, 225
    and Caroline Emelia Stephen,
    43, 46–7, 155–6
    and Vita Sackville-West,
    73–5

Newton, John, 'Amazing
    Grace', 201–2
nuns, 42, 143, 156, 157–8, 178

Oldfield, Sybil, 13
ordination, 20, 40, 89, 113n
    of women, 102–7
Orthodox Church, 53, 119–23,
    165
Owen, Wilfred, 193
Oxford Movement, 127

Paganism, 63, 138, 140, 167,
    180
Park, Sowon, 129
Passion, The, 17, 192, 202–16
Paulsell, Stephanie, 15
Perugino, 182–3
Picasso, Pablo, 167, 181
Post-Impressionism, 174–5, 181
Protestant work ethic, 4–5, 22,
    24, 26, 30, 33, 147, 154
Proust, Marcel, 4, 57, 118

Quakerism, 3, 4, 39, 47,
    50n, 53, 59–60, 75, 134;
    see also Dickinson, Violet;
    Fry, Roger; Stephen,
    Caroline Emelia

Raitt, Suzanne, 62, 73, 80
Raphael, 173, 175
Raverat, Gwen, 70–1
Raverat, Jacques, 70–1, 75, 204
Recht, Roland, 127
Reed, Christopher, 144–5

Renan, Ernest, 191
Rice, Charles, 152
Roberts, Kathleen, 120
Roessel, David, 125
Rosner, Victoria, 144–5, 151–3
Rossetti, Christina, 1, 66
Rubin, Miri, 165–7
Ruether, Rosemary Radford, 224
Ruskin, John, 138, 146, 149, 151, 157, 160

Sackville-West, Vita, 6, 15, 53, 54, 64, 72–5, 82–3, 124, 224
St Augustine, 7, 26
St Paul, 35–6, 103–5, 155, 191, 194; *see also* Bible: Corinthians; Ephesians; Galatians; Hebrews; Romans; Timothy; Titus
salvation, 4, 13, 17, 20, 23–4, 32, 46, 58, 147, 154, 192, 195–216
Sawyer, Deborah, 101
Scott, Bonnie Kime, 139–40
secularisation, 1, 4, 5, 53
Seeley, Tracy, 115, 153
separate spheres, 7, 24, 36, 41, 79, 105, 144–55, 208, 223
Shakespeare, William, 84, 131, 196
Shelley, Percy Bysshe, 189, 194
Shove, Fredegond, 53, 71
Showalter, Elaine, 152

Skinner, John, 88, 107
Slee, Nicola, 220
Smyth, Ethel, 1, 6, 54, 59, 80–3, 150, 188, 189–90, 224
Snaith, Anna, 6, 96, 115, 152, 162
soul, 10, 20, 23, 61, 106, 154, 169, 186
  in *Mrs Dalloway*, 200–2
  Woolf's belief in, 11, 13, 80–1, 98
Spalding, Frances, 162, 168
Stanton, Elizabeth Cady, *The Women's Bible*, 187
Stephen, Adrian, 44, 58, 66, 114, 170
Stephen, Caroline Emelia, 3, 15, 30–1, 39, 41–8, 53, 59–60, 75, 93, 99, 101, 103, 147, 153–7, 160–1, 187–8, 193, 212, 221
Stephen, Dorothea, 3, 19, 20, 31, 81
Stephen, Herbert, 30, 39
Stephen, James, 25–9, 33, 35, 37
Stephen, James Fitzjames, 24, 30, 31–3, 37, 38, 39, 40, 46
Stephen, Sir James, 29–31, 33, 38–40, 42, 43, 45, 145
  Essays in Ecclesiastical Biography, 21, 30, 34–7, 90, 187
Stephen, Jane, 30, 39

Stephen, Julia, 41, 73, 124–5,
    145, 168–71, 175–9, 186,
    190, 223, 224
Stephen, Katharine, 42
Stephen, Leslie, 3, 19–20, 22,
    23, 24, 25, 30, 32, 34,
    38–41, 43, 45, 46, 60–1, 88,
    109, 114, 127, 153, 186–7,
    195, 210–11, 223
  'An Agnostic's Apology', 1
  *Dictionary of National
    Biography*, 90
  *History of English Thought in
    the Eighteenth Century*, 99,
    223–4
  Mausoleum Book, 145,
    169–70
  photograph album, 175–9
  Social Rights and Duties,
    145
Stephen, Rosamond, 19, 31
Stephen, Sarah, 42, 146–8,
    154, 156
Stephen, Thoby, 12, 13, 20,
    33, 58, 59, 125, 212–13,
    215, 223
Sterne, Laurence, 88, 199
Strachey, Lytton, 189
Strauss, David, 187

Temple, William, 68
Thomson, William (Archbishop
    of York), 88, 106
Thornton, Henry, 24, 30, 36
Titian, 173, 175, 181

Tolley, Christopher, 31, 45
Tolstoy, Leo, 5, 53

Venn, Emelia, 30–1
Venn, Henry (the Elder), 20–1,
    28, 29, 30, 38, 145
  The Complete Duty of Man,
    21, 23–5, 35, 37, 187,
    194–5
Venn, Henry (the Younger),
    21, 38
Venn, John, 20, 25
Vicchio, Stephen, 189
Virgin Mary, 41, 165–85,
    206, 219

Wall, Thomas, 71
Ware, Owen, 57–8
Warner, Marina, 166
Watson, Natalie K., 220, 222
Watts, Isaac, 37, 191
Waugh, Evelyn, 53, 76
Weaver, Harriet, 199
Webb, Beatrice, 72, 75
Weber, Max, 4–6, 22
Wells, H. G., 196–8
Weston, Jessie, 2, 202
Wilberforce, William, 26–7,
    29, 30
Williamson, Elizabeth, 81
Wilson, Elizabeth, 116
Women's Co-operative Guild,
    66–7
Woodforde, James, 88, 107
Woodhead, Linda, 220

Woolf, Leonard, 6, 55–6, 58,
    69–70, 71, 89, 109, 196, 225
  Jewishness of, 2, 59, 79, 81,
    189
  library, 186–92
Woolf, Marie, 189
Woolf, Virginia
  ESSAYS
  'Abbeys and Cathedrals',
    132–3, 137, 139
  'How Should One Read a
    Book?', 123, 194–5
  'Modern Fiction', 75, 116,
    123, 144–5, 196–9, 200,
    201, 209, 224
  'Mr Bennett and Mrs Brown',
    198
  'On Being Ill', 195–6
  'The Leaning Tower', 127
  'Lives of the Obscure', 88
  'The Pastons and Chaucer',
    194
  'On Not Knowing Greek',
    52, 82
  'Outlines', 106–7
  'Pictures', 181–2
  'Professions for Women', 24,
    48, 147–8, 149–50
  A Room of One's Own, 33,
    44, 48, 66, 68, 102, 115,
    123, 148, 152–6, 159, 160,
    161, 162–3, 225
  Three Guineas, 1, 6, 7–8,
    10, 17, 25, 27, 33–8, 44–5,
    47–8, 52–3, 55, 58, 65,
    68, 70, 76–80, 82, 83–4,

    89–90, 92, 95–6, 102–7,
    108, 111–12, 126–7,
    130–1, 136, 145, 191,
    192, 193–4, 221–5
  'Two Parsons', 107
  MEMOIRS
  'Old Bloomsbury', 59
  'A Sketch of the Past', 1, 7,
    12, 22, 41, 48, 82–5, 114,
    123, 137, 148–51, 170,
    178, 182–3, 190, 223, 225
  NOVELS
  Between the Acts, 14, 16, 53,
    88, 108–12, 137–8, 186
  Jacob's Room, 13, 58, 65, 88,
    90–1, 94–6, 97, 107, 129–30,
    134, 136–7, 186, 222
  Mrs Dalloway, 7, 10, 13–14,
    16–17, 24, 63–4, 68–9,
    71, 72–4, 83, 88, 91, 97,
    118–19, 131–2, 134–5,
    137, 139, 144, 157–9, 161,
    162–3, 180, 199–205, 211,
    224, 225
  Night and Day, 88, 131,
    148–9, 151
  Orlando, 36, 64, 74, 83, 88,
    119, 123, 125, 131–2, 143
  The Voyage Out, 13, 44,
    59, 88, 92–3, 94, 95, 148,
    151–2, 192–3, 222
  The Waves, 7, 11, 12, 13, 16,
    47, 48, 56, 58, 72–4, 80,
    83, 88, 89, 93–4, 96, 132,
    137, 143, 163, 180–3, 202,
    211–16, 222, 223, 224, 225

The Years, 13, 15, 47, 88, 96–8, 131, 135–6, 222

To the Lighthouse, 7, 11, 13–14, 16, 57, 69, 73–4, 83, 99–102, 119, 123–5, 134, 148, 149, 157, 159–62, 170, 172–9, 183, 202, 205–11, 222, 224, 225

SHORTER FICTION

Friendship's Gallery, 62–4, 74, 83

'Kew Gardens', 67

'The Mark on the Wall', 91

'Memoirs of a Novelist', 61–3

'Miss Pryme', 88

'An Unwritten Novel', 17

'The Widow and the Parrot', 88

Wordsworth, William, 39, 72, 194

Yeats, W. B., 119

Zwerdling, Alex, 9